PRAISE FOR *THE POWER OF PARTNERSHIP*

"So comprehensive and groundbreaking that it will probably prove to be one of the most important books of this century. If you want to improve your life and your world, read this book!"

— Barbara Marx Hubbard, author of *Conscious Evolution*

"This extraordinary book is a life's work in itself, and a gift to anyone exploring how we can do our lives better, do our relationships better, do our work experience better, do our schools better, do our world better."

— David Mallery, director of professional development of the National Association of Independent Schools

"In *The Power of Partnership,* Riane Eisler offers all of us a way to transform our business, our community, and ourselves. It is "must" reading for any business owner who is looking for more meaning than the bottom line."

— Barbara G. Stanbridge, past president of the National Association of Women Business Owners

"Nothing can vanquish anxiety like clarity, which is what Riane Eisler delivers abundantly. Read this book and you'll come away with a new understanding of how the world works (and why it so often works atrociously). Even more important, you'll feel better about it — because you'll feel less helpless about it. And in a world that seems to be going mad we can all use some of that!"

— Daniel Quinn, author of *Ishmael*

"All those who value relationships — and those who don't — will do well to read this book and help reduce anger and violence."

— Arun Gandhi, founder/director of the M. K. Gandhi Institute for Nonviolence

"A step-by-step approach to personal development. Eisler is a brilliant role model as a global citizen — and one of the preeminent minds of our time."

— Hazel Henderson, author of *Beyond Globalization*

"If the Osama bin Ladens of this world were required to read this book and absorb its message, the human race would surge onto the fast track toward love and creativity."

— Howard Bloom, author of *Global Brain*

"Brings compassion, intelligence, and practical advice to the essential work of personal and social transformation. This book will be a treasured resource for helping us move forward in the twenty-first century."

— Judith V. Jordan, co-director of the Jean Baker Miller Training Institute, Wellesley College

"If our planet is to survive, it will need the kind of wisdom that shines through this book. Riane Eisler is one of the most creative and visionary thinkers of our time."

— Rabbi Michael Lerner, editor of *TIKKUN Magazine* and author of *Spirit Matters*

"More relevant than ever in a post-September 11, 2001 world, *The Power of Partnership* details the steps to build sound and lasting relationships with the self, the intimate partner, the world, and life itself. It is essential reading for every person searching for ways to improve our lives and our world."

— George Gerbner, Ph.D., dean emeritus of
The Annenberg School for Communications, University of Pennsylvania,
and author of *Telling All the Stories*

"In a stroke, Riane Eisler's simple, powerful message makes all other self-help books irrelevant. How can we live fuller, richer and more loving lives without also making it possible for others to do the same? By replacing individuals within our world, she demands that we work on healing the world and healing ourselves — a model that can create the ripples from which tidal waves are made."

— Michael Kimmel, author of *Manhood in America*

"Here is a book for the turning of the times, for what is offered here are the essential ways to make the world work. The wise and prescient Riane Eisler guides us through the paths of partnership that lie beyond the wasteland of dominator psychology. This is a radical work of social evolution that should be taken very seriously. It is a gift to the present historical moment and an enterprise of enormous importance."

— Jean Houston, Ph.D., author of *A Mythic Life*

"The Power of Partnership provides a superb framework for this new age and innumerable answers to achieving it. Its eight chapters could be the headings of the Wisdom Age for humanity on this miraculous, magic, and precious Planet Earth."

— Robert Muller, P.h.D., co-founder of the U.N. University for Peace
and author of *4000 Ideas and Dreams for a Better World*

"How wonderful to encounter in one book not only an incisive and clear understanding of what causes so much suffering in the modern world, but a compelling vision of how both personally and as a society we can change. Riane Eisler gives us a wise and very practical recipe for hope."

— Susan Griffin, author of *A Chorus of Stones*

"Those of us who believe that peace begins, and can only be lastingly and reliably achieved, with peace in our hearts, know that this depends crucially on our relationships: to ourselves, to our family, community, nation, the community of all nations, and to nature. Riane Eisler offers the essential guidelines for creating and sustaining relationships that can give us — and hence the world — the peace we so desperately need."

— Ervin Laszlo, P.h.D., president of the Club of Budapest
and author of *Macroshift*

"With insight, passion, and persuasion, Riane Eisler reveals the many disturbing faces of today's dominator society. Happily, she also shows how each of us can help evoke a future that matures beyond force and fear. A 'must read' for anyone interested in a better world for all."

— Jeff Gates, author of *Democracy at Risk* and *The Ownership Solution*

"From intimacy, to politics, to service, to sustainability... this remarkable book touches every critical node of vital partnership.... Exercises, action check-lists, and a rich bibliography complement the work at every stage. *The Power of Partnership* offers a compelling argument for the reality of conscious evolution."

— Jim Kenney, global director of the
Council for a Parliament of the World's Religions

"The Power of Partnership is an extraordinary, thoughtful, and timely book. Riane Eisler speaks with wisdom and compassion about the central concerns of today, including war and terrorism, education, and child-rearing. Anyone who is concerned about the state of the world, as well as the state of one's own home and family, should read this book."

— Christine Sleeter, Ph.D., director of the Institute for Advanced Studies
in Education at California State University Monterey Bay

"The Power of Partnership is an exceptional resource guide for personal and social transformation. It offers practical tools for creating a global community and a path for collaboration in all aspects of our lives."

— Angeles Arrien, cultural anthropologist and author of *The Four-Fold Way*

"Riane Eisler is one of the innovative thinkers of our time and the wisest woman I know. Here is her clear-minded, warm-hearted, practical guide through the daunting challenges of today's world. *The Power of Partnership* will help you make your own wise choices about how to act with empathy and caring whether the issue is global economics, the environment, terrorism, or your own most intimate relationships."

— Gina Ogden, P.h.D., author of *Women Who Love Sex*

"Now more than ever, we must switch from a dominator model to a partnership model if we are to survive. With her customary wisdom, clarity, and compassion, Riane shows us the way."

— Jean Kilbourne, author of *Can't Buy My Love*

"Riane Eisler's brilliant work should be read carefully by leaders in all fields across our cultures and by all people who wish to participate in the creative transformation of the human condition at this critical turning point in cultural evolution."

— Ashok Gangadean, co-founder/co-director of the
Global Dialogue Institute and cop-convenor of the World
Commission on Global Consciousness and Spirituality

"Marvelous! A treasure house of relational wisdom by which to be healthy and whole."

— Raffi, singer, author, and founder of the
Troubadour Institute for Child Honoring

"The great depth, awareness, and reflection of *The Power of Partnership* stems from Riane Eisler's personal and social experience. Her action steps show us how to create a future that we can embrace and wish for for our children and grandchildren."

— Eleonora Barbieri Masini, author of *Why Future Studies?*
and past president of the World Futures Studies Federation

BY RIANE EISLER

BOOKS

Tomorrow's Children:
A Blueprint for Partnership Education in the 21st Century

Sacred Pleasure:
Sex, Myth, and the Politics of the Body

The Chalice and the Blade:
Our History, Our Future

The Equal Rights Handbook

Dissolution:
Marriage, Divorce, and the Future of Women

The Gate

The Partnership Way:
New Tools for Living and Learning
(with David Loye)

Women, Men, and the Global Quality of Life
(with David Loye and Kari Norgaard)

AUDIO

The Chalice and the Blade:
Our History, Our Future

VIDEO

Tomorrow's Children:
Partnership Education in Action

SEVEN RELATIONSHIPS THAT
WILL CHANGE YOUR LIFE

THE POWER OF PARTNERSHIP

RIANE EISLER

NEW WORLD LIBRARY
NOVATO, CALIFORNIA

New World Library
14 Pamaron Way
Novato, California 94949

Edited by Marc Allen
Cover design by Mary Beth Salmon
Text design and typography by Tona Pearce Myers

Library of Congress Cataloging-in-Publication Data

Eisler, Riane Tennenhaus.
 The power of partnership : seven relationships that will change your life
/ Riane Eisler.
    p.   cm.
Includes bibliographical references and index.
 ISBN 1-57731-408-5 (paperback : alk. paper)
1. Interpersonal relations. 2. Respect for persons. 3. Social
psychology. 4. Conduct of life. I. Title.
 HM1106 .E357 2002
 302—dc21   2001005892
                                                                        CIP

First printing, February 2002
First paperback printing, April 2003
ISBN 978-1-57731-408-0
Printed in Canada on acid-free, partially recycled paper
Distributed to the trade by Publishers Group West

10 9 8 7 6 5 4 3

*To my children
and grandchildren*

CONTENTS

The Adventure
of Change

TWENTY-FIVE YEARS AGO, I STOOD AT A TURNING POINT. I had to rethink everything about my life. I was the single mother of two children, working as a family attorney, doing research, writing, lecturing, looking for the life companion I yearned for, grieving over the death of both my parents, not getting enough sleep, not paying attention to what I ate, pushing myself until I nearly collapsed. I became so ill that at times I thought I might die. When I walked, my heart pounded and my breath got so short I had to stop. I hurt everywhere, so much that I sometimes cried. I finally realized I couldn't go on this way — I had to make major changes in my life.

I began with simple things. I stopped taking all the drugs my doctors prescribed and instead radically changed my diet. I stopped eating the rich foods and pastries of my Viennese childhood: no more apple strudel and Sacher torte, more vegetables and fruits. I realized that I carried a great deal of pain that I had to process if I was going to heal. I began to meditate. I found a wonderful therapist. I became more accepting of myself and found new joy in my relations with others, particularly those closest to me.

I also began to think seriously about what I wanted to do with the rest of my life. I gave up my law practice and devoted myself to what I really wanted to do. For ten years, I researched a book I called *The Chalice and the Blade: Our History, Our Future,* which was published in 1987. It was a rereading of Western history going back over thirty thousand years. It showed that what we think of as natural and inevitable — destructive personal and social patterns such as domestic violence, chronic warfare, racial and religious prejudice, the domination of women by men — are not natural or inevitable at all.

Writing this book changed me and changed my life. *The Chalice and the Blade* became a best-seller translated into seventeen languages, but more significant for me was that I now saw clearly that the problems in my life were part of a much larger problem. As it turned out, thousands of readers felt the same. Letters poured in, and continue to pour in. I had hoped, naturally, to touch people. But I was astonished by the powerful response to *The Chalice and the Blade* — especially how women and men worldwide said it was empowering them to transform their lives. The knowledge that I was able to make this kind of contribution gave a whole new meaning and purpose to my life.

So while I didn't know it at the time, the turning point I faced twenty-five years ago — and the changes I then began to make — eventually led to the fulfillment of dreams I hadn't even let myself dream and of potentials I would not otherwise have realized.

You too may have been at such a turning point at some time in your life. You may be at one now. Perhaps, as I did, you suspect there must be a better way to live, that your life can be filled with more passion, joy, satisfaction, and love. You may also suspect something even more fundamental: that today we all stand at a turning point when changes in how we view our world and how we live in it are more important than they have ever been before.

WHY THIS BOOK

I WROTE MOST OF THIS BOOK before the terrorist attacks that have so radically altered all our lives. Unfortunately, these attacks make this book even more timely.

I originally wrote *The Power of Partnership* for four reasons. I wrote it because it can help people who — like me at my turning point — need and want effective ways to heal and change. I wrote it for my children and grandchildren, because I passionately want a good future for them. I wrote it because so many people have asked for practical applications of the ideas introduced in *The Chalice and the Blade.* And I wrote it to provide a new perspective and practical strategies for people and organizations concerned about the dangers we face in our country and the world — dangers that the terrorism on our own shores has brought home to us with deadly force.

The Power of Partnership is above all a practical book: a book to help us help ourselves, particularly at this time when so many of us feel helpless. It is a self-help book. But it is a self-help book that goes much deeper and further than the typical self-help book.

As the new reality of our lives demonstrates, the self can't be helped in isolation. All of us are always in relationship — and not just with the people in our immediate circle, in our families and at work. We are affected by a much wider web of relationships swirling around us and impacting every aspect of our lives.

If we don't pay attention to these less immediate relationships, then just trying to fix ourselves alone is like trying to go up on a down elevator. No matter what we do, we're trapped and headed in the wrong direction. Many people are beginning to realize this, as they go from self-help book to self-help book and workshop to workshop. Certainly working on ourselves is essential. But it is not enough.

We all want to be healthy, safe, and happy. We want this for ourselves, and we especially want it for our children. We work hard so we can send them to college and leave them well-provided financially. But, in our time when so much is happening we wish we didn't have to think about, many of us are beginning to realize that much more is needed.

The Power of Partnership offers a new approach to transformative change. It deals with personal change *and* the larger changes needed if we and our children are to have the good life we all want. It shows the connections between our personal problems and the global problems piling up around us, and how a happier self and a better world are interconnected. It provides a wealth of practical steps that will help you find more love, get along better with your loved ones, make your work more satisfying and meaningful, and help you feel more safe and live your life more fully. On the larger scale, it provides practical steps to move us toward a more secure, sustainable, and satisfying future.

THE POWER OF PARTNERSHIP DEALS WITH the seven key relationships that make up our lives. First, our relationship with ourselves. Second, our intimate relationships. Third, our workplace and community relations. Fourth, our relationship with our national community. Fifth, international and multicultural relationships. Sixth, our relationship with nature and the living environment. And seventh, our spiritual relations.

In the next seven chapters, you will see that there are two fundamentally different models for all these relationships: the *partnership* model and the *domination* model. You will see how these two underlying models mold all our relationships — from relationships between parents and children and between women and men to the relations between governments and citizens and between us and nature. As you learn to recognize these two models, you will see how both individually and collectively we can influence what happens to us and around us. As you learn to move relationships toward the partnership model, you will begin to make positive changes in your day-today life and our world.

While the terms domination model and partnership model may not be familiar to you, you've probably already noticed the difference between these two ways of relating — but lacked names for your insight. When we lack language for an insight, it's hard to hold on to it, much less use it. Before Newton identified gravity, apples fell off trees all the time but people had no name or explanation for what was happening. The partnership and domination models not only give us names for different ways of relating but also an explanation for what lies behind these differences.

In the domination model, somebody has to be on top and somebody has to be on the bottom. Those on top control those below them. People learn, starting in early childhood, to obey orders without question. They learn to carry a harsh voice in their heads telling them they're no good, they don't deserve love, they need to be punished. Families and societies are based on control that is explicitly or implicitly backed up by guilt, fear, and force. The world is divided into in-groups and out-groups, with those who are different seen as enemies to be conquered or destroyed.

In contrast, the partnership model supports mutually respectful and caring relations. Because there is no need to maintain rigid rankings of control, there is also no built-in need for abuse or violence. Partnership relations free our innate capacity to feel joy, to play. They enable us to grow mentally, emotionally, and spiritually. This is true for individuals, families, and whole societies. Conflict is an opportunity to learn and to be creative, and power is exercised in ways that empower rather than disempower others.

REMEMBER HOW THE FATHER TREATED HIS CHILDREN in the movie *The Sound of Music*? When Baron von Trapp (Christopher Plummer) blows his police whistle and his children line up in front of him, stiff as boards, you see the domination model in action. When the new nanny (Julie Andrews) comes into the picture and the children relax, enjoy themselves, and learn to trust themselves and each other, you see the partnership model in action. When von Trapp becomes much happier and closer to his children, you see what happens as we begin to shift from domination to partnership.

You may have worked for a boss who watches every little thing you do, who's afraid that if you don't follow orders to the letter everything will fall apart, who has to be in full control all the time. This is how the domination model manifests itself in management. If you work for someone who inspires you and facilitates your work, who gives you both guidelines and leeway, and encourages you to use your own judgment and creativity, you've experienced what happens when organizations begin to move away from the domination model toward the partnership model.

If your spouse abuses you emotionally or physically, you're in a dominator marriage. If you're in a relationship that gives you and your partner the freedom to be fully authentic and at the same time mutually supportive, you're experiencing partnership at home.

The famous "horse whisperer" Monty Roberts applies the partnership model to how he relates to horses. When Roberts "gentles" rather than "breaks" a young horse, he is using the partnership model. He does not force horses to obey using violence and inflicting pain (the domination model). Instead, he partners with them in learning — and these horses regularly win races all over the world. They are also a pleasure to ride, because they are your trusted and trusting friends rather than your fearful and hostile adversaries.[1]

If you look at the difference between people's lives in Norway and Saudi Arabia, you see how the partnership and domination models play out on the national level. In Saudi Arabia, where dominator habit patterns and the social structures that support them are still very strong, women don't even have the right to drive a car much less vote or hold office, and there is a huge economic gap between those on top and those on the bottom. By contrast, in the much more partnership-oriented Norway, a woman can be, and recently was, head of state, about 40 percent of the parliament is female, and there is a generally high living standard for all.

You can dramatically see how these two models play out on the international level when you compare Gandhi's successful nonviolent tactics in dealing with the British in India with the terrorist tactics of Muslim fundamentalists against the United States.

I will have much more to say about the differences between the partnership and dominator ways of life, about the family and social systems that support each, and about how transformation from one to the other can happen and has happened. Here I just wanted to give you a glimpse of these two models in action. No organization, family, or country orients completely to the partnership model or the domination model: it is always a continuum, a mix more or less one way or the other. But the degree to which these two models for feeling, thinking, and acting influence us in one or the other directions affects everything in our lives — from our workplaces and communities to our schools and universities, from our entertainment and health care system to our governments and our economic systems, from our intimate relations to our international relations.

OUR HIDDEN HISTORICAL BAGGAGE

THE DOMINATION MODEL is unpleasant, painful, and counterproductive. Yet, we live with it and its consequences every day.

Why would anybody want to live like this? I don't think anybody really does, not even those on top if they stop to consider the huge price they're paying. But what happens is that when people relate to each other as "superiors" and "inferiors," they develop beliefs justifying these kinds of relations. They build social structures that mold relationships to fit this top-down pattern. And as time rolls on, every-body gets trapped in them, as these ways of relating are passed on from generation to generation.

Sometimes people blame their parents for their problems. But our parents didn't invent their habits. They learned them from their parents, who in turn learned them from earlier generations, going way back in our cultural history.

If we look at this history, we see that many of our habits — whether in intimate or international relations — come from earlier times when everybody had to learn to obey their "superiors" unquestioningly. In those times, despotic kings, feudal lords, and chieftains had life and death powers over their "subjects," as they still do in many parts of our world today. Think of how only a few hundred years ago, if you balked or back-talked, your life was in danger. Think of the Inquisition, the witch burnings, and all the ways people were terrorized in the Middle Ages to instill habits of absolute obedience. Think of how kings were in the habit of chopping people's heads off, even those of their wives, as the English king Henry the Eighth did. Think of how slavery and child labor under the most brutal conditions were legal, and of how male heads of household also had despotic powers.[2] Think of commands like "spare the rod and spoil the child" justifying child-beating, of laws that not so long ago gave husbands the right to beat their wives, of how husbands until very recent times were given legal ownership of not only their wives' bodies but also of any property they had or any money they earned.

You might say that was then, and it's different now. Certainly in the United States we are fortunate to live in a country where despots no longer rule and the human rights of children, women, and people of color are gradually being recognized. But even here, the hidden baggage from earlier times still lives on. Over and over, habits we inherited get in the way of more fulfilling lives and a better world.

ONCE WE BECOME AWARE of what we carry unconsciously, we can change. Change involves two things: awareness and action. As we become more aware of what is really behind our problems, we can begin changing what we do and how we do it. But this is a two-way street.

Awareness and action are always in a dance together that takes us farther and farther from where we started. It's like when we stop eating junk food because we become aware that, despite all the ads about how good it is, it's bad for us. When we change this habit, we discover how much healthier we feel, less nervous and jumpy from all the sugar, stronger, more energetic. This new awareness in turn leads to other changes, perhaps avoiding foods high in fat, eating more balanced meals, and getting more exercise.

So new awareness and changed habits go together. As our personal relationships move toward partnership, the beliefs that guide our behavior change. As our beliefs start to support partnership rather than dominator relations, we begin to change the rules for relationships. This in turn helps us build more partnership-oriented families, workplaces, and communities. We then begin to change the rules for the wider web of relationships, including economic and political relations as well as our relationship with our Mother Earth. These rules, in their turn, support partnership relations all across the board, so that the upward spiral is given yet another boost.

One of the striking things about history is how many great visionaries, thinkers, and writers have pointed to exactly what we're looking at here. From Jesus and Buddha to Elizabeth Cady Stanton and Martin Luther King, Jr., they all recognized that just working on ourselves is not enough. They point to the road from the self to society and back again — that we also have to change the cultural beliefs and social structures that imprison us in a life we don't want. In essence, they point us to a partnership spiritual path.

THE TURNING POINT

MARTIN LUTHER KING, JR., historical baggage, social structures, international relations — these may seem a long way from my life crisis twenty-five years ago. But they are all related and interrelated.

I know from my own experience that personal change is possible. I know from my research for *The Chalice and the Blade* and subsequent books that, in our age of biological and nuclear technologies, the old dominator ways can lead to disaster, even to the extinction of our species. I know from my research that the turmoil of our time, as upsetting and confusing as it is, also offers an opportunity to make fundamental changes.[3]

As a mother and grandmother, I feel a great urgency to do what I can to help bring about these changes. The good news is that we don't have to start from square one. We've already left many dominator beliefs and structures behind and started to replace them with partnership ones. If we hadn't, I couldn't have written this book. Nor could you be reading it. This book would have been burned, and you and I would have been condemned for heresy.

Partnership is already on the move all over the world. In fact, the movement to shift from domination to partnership in all aspects of our lives — from the personal to the political — is the fastest-growing and most powerful movement in the world today.[4]

Millions of people are going to workshops and seminars to learn how to have better personal, business, and community relationships. Hundreds of thousands of grassroots organizations — from environmental and peace groups to human rights and economic equity organizations — are working to create the conditions that support our deepest strivings for love, safety, sustainability, and meaning. One of the most important aspects of the partnership movement is the search for young people for their voice. Indeed, young people are today often in the forefront of the partnership movement, intuitively manifesting partnership in their individual and collective actions, in innovations that are sparks for systems transformations.

Worldwide, the movement toward partnership is at the heart of innumerable causes with widely differing names, transcending conventional categories such as capitalism versus communism and religious versus secular. However, we don't read about this movement in the media because it is not centralized and coordinated — and because it has lacked a single unifying name. Without a name, it's almost as if it didn't exist, despite all the progress around us.

At the same time, there is also powerful resistance to this forward partnership movement. And there are regressive forces pushing us back toward the kinds of relationships we have been trying to leave behind. Our future hinges on the outcome of this still largely invisible struggle.

There are those who would reimpose patterns of domination. Some are terrorists from faraway lands. Others are in our own nation. And most of us carry inside us dominator habits that get in the way of the good life we yearn for.

Gandhi said we should not mistake what is habitual for what is natural. Indeed, changing what is habitual is one of the goals of self-help.

The Power of Partnership is about changing dominator habits — both personal and social. It's about small habits and huge habits. It's about the underlying causes of painful and dysfunctional habits. It's about what you and I can do to make partnership a reality.

This doesn't mean that every one of us has to do everything. But wherever we are and whenever we can, every one of us can do something to move us from domination to partnership.

I know from the joy, imagination, and creativity that are my grandchildren's natural gifts — as, given half a chance, they are every child's — that the human spirit can soar into as yet unimagined realms of possibility. We have been endowed by nature with an amazing brain, an enormous capacity for love, a remarkable creativity, and a unique ability to learn, change, grow, and plan ahead. We were not born with the unhealthy habits we carry. We had to learn them. So we can unlearn them, and help others do the same.

We can all learn partnership ways of living. I invite you to join me in the adventure of creating a way of life where the wonder and beauty latent in every child can be realized, where the human spirit is liberated, where love can freely do its magic.

Your Relationship with Yourself

BODY, MIND, AND SPIRIT

None of us can change everything. But we can all change something. A good place to start is with ourselves.

In this chapter, you will discover a new way of looking at who you are and how you became that person. Broadening your awareness will help you break free of limiting assumptions and stressful habits, enabling you to discover new ways of relating to yourself that are more satisfying and fulfilling.

COMMON SENSE WOULD SAY that your relationship with yourself should be one of partnership. Unfortunately, it probably is not.

Many of us treat ourselves less as a partner than as someone to bully and manipulate. We push our bodies around whether they are tired or not. We get mad at ourselves. We criticize ourselves unmercifully. And most of the time we aren't even aware that this kind of treatment is something we learned and don't have to put up with.

Do you find yourself going over things you did, focusing on what an inner voice says you've done wrong? Do you have a secret inner tyrant who keeps saying you're not good enough? Do you carry a load of floating anxiety so that you shift from fear of one calamity to another, stifling your creative and spontaneous juices?

Maybe you don't have these particular habits. But chances are you have some dominator habits that you aren't even aware you use against yourself. Like many of us, you may carry resentments that leech energy you could channel into constructive actions. And like most of us, you were probably taught to suppress important aspects of yourself.

Some of us focus on our minds, on our intellectual achievements, and ignore the wisdom of our hearts. Some of us dedicate ourselves to exercise and beauty programs, and devote far more time to the physical body than to the heart, soul, and spirit. Many of us are trapped in stereotyped gender roles that deny and distort our full humanity. If you take a moment to look, it becomes clear that we often let one part of ourselves dominate the other parts, instead of letting all parts function fully.

Health and happiness are a question of balance, and this is exactly what the partnership model leads to. By respecting all aspects of our being, we express our full range of needs and possibilities. We become aware that what we label body, mind, and spirit are interconnected parts of a multifaceted, miraculous whole. We are healthier, wiser, and happier, and have more energy to be co-creators of our personal and collective lives.

SETTING THE STAGE

I HAVE ALREADY TALKED about how I made changes in my life that enabled me to become a much better partner with myself. Now I want to tell you how my discovery of the partnership and domination models made it possible for me to untangle what happened in my early life, and beyond this, to begin to untangle what makes it so hard for many of us to move forward.

On November 10, 1938, a gang of Austrian Nazis came for my father. It was "Crystal Night": the streets of Vienna were bright with the fires of burning synagogues and littered with broken glass from

Jewish stores and homes. The Nazis banged on our front door yelling, "Gestapo!" We knew they would take my father away, so he was hiding in the attic. My mother had no choice but to answer or they would have kicked the door down. The men burst in and began to loot. They found my father, dragged him from his hiding place, and shoved him down the stairs. My mother left me with a neighbor and followed them to Gestapo headquarters. By some miracle, she got my father back.

The next weeks were a time of terror — but we eventually managed to escape. My parents and I were on one of the last refugee ships admitted to Cuba before the *St. Louis* was turned back and the 936 Jewish women, men, and children on board were forced to return to Europe, where most died in concentration camps.[1]

I was seven years old when this happened. So at a very young age, I began to ask questions you too may have asked — questions that haunted me for decades. Is all the cruelty, violence, and suffering in our world inevitable? Is there an alternative? What is it? And what can we do to get there?

As I grew up, I looked for answers to these questions in books. I tried to find them in universities during my undergraduate and graduate studies. But I couldn't find any that were satisfactory. One problem was that I was still a captive of the conventional one-subject-at-a-time approach. When I studied sociology, psychology, anthropology, biology, law, and other disciplines, they were taught as if they had nothing to do with each other — and often, as if they had nothing to do with real life.

Then I took a job as a social scientist at the Systems Development Corporation, an offshoot of the Rand Corporation. That was my first introduction to systems science, an approach that analyzes how different parts of a system relate to each other and to the larger whole. I soon found out that the focus at the Systems Development Corporation was on weapons systems, and what interested me was totally different. Nonetheless, it was an invaluable experience. I didn't know it then, but it was my first step on the road that eventually led to the findings on which this book and my other works would be based.

That was in the 1950s, and many things happened in my life before I returned to the fundamental questions I had never answered. By the time I did, I had developed an approach that is very different from most studies of human society.

Instead of studying one period at a time, I looked at the whole of our history — including the long period before written records that we call prehistory. Unlike conventional studies often aptly called "the study of man," I took into account the whole of humanity — both its female and male halves. Rather than focusing mainly on politics and economics, I looked at the whole of our lives — including our family and other intimate relations.

We all know that when we look at only part of a picture, we can't see the whole, and we certainly can't see patterns — relationships between different parts of the picture. If you pick up a newspaper and look very closely at a little segment of a photo, all you see are tiny dots. In order to see the whole picture, you need to connect the dots. The same is true when studying human societies.

As I examined this larger picture, I began to see connections between different parts of the picture: patterns that kept repeating themselves. Some of what I saw I recognized from earlier studies such as the work of psychologist Else Frankel-Brunswick, who saw a relationship between the family backgrounds of "authoritarian" versus "democratic" personalities and religious and racial prejudice. But what I was discovering were even larger patterns that hadn't been identified within the scope of modern science — patterns that began to answer my questions about viable alternatives to chronic violence, insensitivity, and suffering.

I realized that I had identified two contrasting blueprints or models for molding and organizing relationships. Since there were no names for them, I called them the partnership model and the dominator or domination model. Later, I also began to call them the respect model and the control model, because these two words describe their essential qualities.

These models take us beyond familiar categories such as capitalist or communist, religious or secular, Eastern or Western, technologically advanced or primitive. For example, as I looked at some of the most brutally violent and repressive societies of the twentieth century — Hitler's Germany (a rightist society), Stalin's USSR (a leftist society), Khomeini's Iran (a religious society), and Idi Amin's Uganda (a tribalist society) — I saw that, despite obvious differences, they all share the same dominator blueprint.

One core element of this dominator blueprint is authoritarianism — strong-man rule in both the family and the state or tribe. A second is rigid male dominance — the ranking of one half of humanity over the other half. A third is socially accepted violence, from child and wife beating to chronic warfare. A fourth core element is a set of teachings and beliefs that dominator relations are inevitable, even moral — that it's honorable and moral to kill and enslave neighboring nations or tribes, stone women to death, stand by while "inferior" races are put in ovens and gassed, or beat children to impose one's will.

As you move to the other end of this continuum — from domination to partnership — you find a very different type of culture. In the partnership model, you find a democratic and egalitarian social structure, equal partnership between women and men, and less socially accepted violence in all relations — from intimate to international — because violence is not needed to maintain rigid rankings of domination. You also find beliefs about human nature that support empathic and mutually respectful relations. And you see that qualities denigrated as "feminine" in the domination model, such as caring and nonviolence, are valued in men *and* women, and guide social policy. (For a summary of the core elements of these two contrasting blueprints, see "The Partnership/Domination Continuum" charts in "More Partnership Tools" at the end of this book.)

Societies modeled on the partnership blueprint can be very different from each other. For example, this configuration — a democratic and egalitarian social structure, partnership between women and men, and less social acceptance of violence — is found today in some tribal societies and in the industrialized, technologically advanced Scandinavian nations. You can find this same pattern in many Western and Eastern prehistoric societies, as described in my work and in the work of scholars at the Chinese Academy of Social Sciences.[2] And if you look around, you can see movement everywhere toward family and social structures that are closer to the partnership than domination blueprint.

In short, as I began to see the world through the lenses of the partnership and domination models, blinders I had not even known were there began to fall from my eyes. I now understood that I was born into a time of massive dominator regression — the rise of the Nazis in Europe. I also realized that much of what I was struggling against was not unique to me but the result of traditions of domination. And I saw how profoundly all our relations have been influenced by the degree to which a society, family, or other organization orients to the partnership model or the domination model.

DOMINATION FROM BIRTH

IF YOU TAKE A LOOK AT YOURSELF, you will probably find ways that your own relationship with yourself has been affected by the domination blueprint we've inherited. When societies orient mainly to the domination model, families instill in children habits of domination and submission from birth. Most of us were taught some of these habits. And, unfortunately, all over the world today children are still being raised under this model, which not only causes enormous pain and suffering but also perpetuates the system that continues to cause pain and suffering across the globe.

A basic lesson children learn in dominator settings is strict conformity to orders. One of the ways this is taught is by demanding rote, mechanical obedience.

Of course, we all learn physical skills through repetition — whether it's to use a fork and spoon, play the piano, or perform surgery. But *how* we learn these skills is markedly different in a partnership or dominator context.

If as children we are forced to strictly conform to orders when we practice new skills, we have little leeway for finding our own way. We become accustomed to directing our attention outside ourselves, to focus on what authorities tell us to do, and to become disconnected from our own experiences. When this training is severe, the naturally experimental infant is slowly turned into someone who will docilely obey "superiors."[3]

A SECOND LESSON CHILDREN ARE TAUGHT in dominator settings is never to express anger or frustration against the adults who cause them pain — out of fear of even more pain. So what happens? Since we can't directly express these negative feelings, we turn them against ourselves or against those we are taught to perceive as weaker, inferior, or immoral. Frustration and anger inevitably build up, and we learn to habitually feel bad — afraid, angry, depressed, guilty, unhappy.

Feeling bad goes against human nature, which seeks pleasure rather than pain. But since relations of domination are backed up by fear and force, in a family or society that orients primarily to the domination model, pain becomes part of the fabric of our lives. We get caught in a vicious cycle that perpetuates emotional habits and behaviors that reinforce tense and painful feelings. And when we chronically feel pain, we also learn to deaden our senses.

None of this has to happen. In the absence of a physical impairment, we're born with the capacity to be attuned to our bodies, to move and develop freely and joyfully. If you look at babies, you see they have this natural capacity. As Steven Shafarman writes in his book *Awareness Heals,* "Babies learn by playfully exploring and imitating, motivated mostly by innate curiosity and guided always by exquisite awareness of comfort."[4] But although we humans are born with this natural capacity, we are robbed of much of it in the course of dominator childrearing and education.

We also know that babies and children are innately motivated to learn, practically from the moment they're born. This too is a wonderful human trait. But it too gets distorted in dominator environments. Trying to feel good becomes trying to avoid pain, either by rote conformity or by shutting down. So our great capacity to learn often backfires, because what we learn is how to adapt to an inherently painful and constrictive dominator environment.

MORE DOMINATOR LESSONS

AS MOST OF US KNOW, how we relate to ourselves is largely shaped during childhood. But this does not mean we can't change. Within each of us is a human spirit that yearns for the more pleasurable and fulfilling partnership way. We have an amazing capacity to overcome childhood conditioning and continue to learn throughout our lives.

An important step toward change is to recognize that our parents didn't intentionally raise us in dominator ways. They were simply copying how they were raised, which was a legacy of generations before them. Understanding this allows us to break free from suppressed anger that restricts our emotional and personal growth. It allows us to reexamine our childhood and to prevent destructive hidden patterns from being perpetuated in future generations.

You can start by observing how you hold your body. As children we learn from our caretakers not only their verbal language but also their body language. If that body language models shallow breathing, holding the body stiffly, and other tense postures characteristic of adults who carry a heavy dominator load, we are likely to do the same. As a result, many of us have learned to carry fear and tension in our bodies without even knowing what it is that makes us feel anxious and unhappy.

Children imitate parents far more than we realize. Even physical problems thought to be inherited, including chronic ailments, can be transmitted in dominator families through imitation. "Most people, including scientists," Shafarman writes, "presume some genetic cause whenever children and parents or siblings develop similar diseases or difficulties. As we have all observed, however, as children grow they imitate their parents' postures, gestures, attitudes, and dietary preferences, usually without knowing they are doing so. Asthma, arthritis, and other conditions may involve genetic predispositions, yet organic learning affects how, when, or if problems develop."[5]

But the basic problem is that dominator childrearing inevitably produces fear and tension. Fear-based childrearing brings chronic tensing up, stiffening, holding our breaths, and other ways of dealing with fear and pain. And precisely because living with constant fear is too much for us to cope with, the tense bodily states we learn in order to avoid getting in touch with painful emotions become habitual. So we often carry these bodily habits all our lives — unless we become aware of them and learn other ways of being.

ANOTHER LESSON CHILDREN LEARN in dominator families is to suppress parts of themselves to conform to externally imposed ideas of what men and women should be like. This lesson not only molds girls' and boys' minds and bodies to fit rigid gender stereotypes; it also teaches them that men should dominate and women should be dominated. Once again, this lesson teaches children to accept the dictates of external authority, even in something as basic as how they should move or hold their bodies.

As Don Hanlon Johnson writes, boys are taught "the swaggers and shrugs appropriate for men, including the nonverbal vocabulary that signals their socially assigned superiority to women." By contrast, girls are taught "the facial movements, ways of holding their hands, and posture that manifest their roles as adjuncts to men."[6]

Girls also learn another key lesson. No matter how much pain it entails, the very shape of their bodies must conform to what pleases men. Conformity can mean footbinding, sexual mutilation, stiletto high heels that cripple the spine, or starvation diets that lead to bulimia and anorexia. The connection between advertising and the eating disorders many girls suffer from has been extensively documented. But the susceptibility of girls and women to these ads goes much deeper, to their earliest lessons that, regardless of pain or discomfort, the most important thing in their lives is to please others.[7]

Of course, there's nothing wrong with pleasing others. In fact, acting in ways that make others feel good rather than bad is basic to partnership relations. But there needs to be balance — and the domination/control model makes it extremely hard to find a balance between meeting our own needs and meeting the needs of others.

DECIDING WHAT REALLY MATTERS

A FOUNDATION OF PARTNERSHIP LIVING is to be a good partner with yourself. This means taking the golden rule and looking at its flip side — do unto yourself as you would do unto others — and applying this to your life.

At first blush you may think that being a good partner to yourself is selfishness, but it isn't. Selfishness is being insensitive to others. Partnership with yourself means being sensitive to both yourself and others.

I struggled a great deal in my own life with not wanting to be selfish because I was taught that "good women" neglect themselves for the sake of everyone around them. When I tried to fit into this feminine stereotype, I suffered, and so did those around me. A routine of self-sacrifice doesn't work for anyone, as we see in relationships in which one person is always serving the other and ends up playing the part of martyr or victim.

Ultimately, partnership means balancing personal needs with the ability to give to others. The question is how to do this.

The first step is deciding what really matters. A good example is the saying "The dust will wait, but your baby won't."

It took me a long time to be able to decide what really mattered in my life. And even after I did, I had to keep reminding myself.

One thing you may want to do is to jot down the first three things that come to your mind in response to this question: What is important to me?

Another thing you could do, which I found extraordinarily effective, is to make notes on how you would like to see yourself in five years. I call this "imaging a better future." Be as specific as you can. Write down where you'll be living, the kinds of people you want to be sharing your life with, the kind of work you'd like to be doing, how you would like to be feeling. Then simply put that essay aside and let it live in your unconscious.

After I did this bit of writing, amazingly, most of what I wrote actually came to pass — from finding David, my wonderful life-partner, to devoting myself to research and writing.

There were differences in the details. I ended up living with a writer rather than with a painter. And the stream I envisioned didn't run through the woods around my house, but right under the house: the basement kept flooding until we put in a better drainage system. On the whole, however, imaging this better future for myself really worked. It empowered me to think in a focused, positive way, and it unleashed my unconscious to help me fulfill my dreams.

If my image of a better future had been constricted by the domination model, my dreams would have been much more limited. I shudder to think what kind of future I would have visualized for myself during the 1950s, before many of the old dominator assumptions were challenged in mainstream culture. At that time, I couldn't have imagined myself as independent, creative, and living with a man who saw me not just as a wife who supports his ambitions and talents, but as someone with ambitions and talents of her own that he also supports.

DEPROGRAMMING OLD INNER TAPES

THIS TAKES US TO THE SECOND STEP toward a better relationship with ourselves: deprogramming the old dominator tapes we carry in our heads. Most of us know these tapes all too well, those inner voices saying "You never do things right," "You should be more like so-and-so," "You're always messing up," and so on. Many of us internalized these negative messages, even though they limit and distort our full humanity.

If we're African Americans, Jews, Latinos, or members of other minority groups, chances are we also carry tapes echoing prejudices against us. I know this from my own experience as a little girl. When the Nazis came to power in Vienna in 1938, the simmering old anti-Semitism was fanned into a flame of raging hate. My child's mind was seared not only by terrible fear, but also by a burning sense that there must be something horribly wrong with me and others like me to be so abhorred and persecuted. Even later, when I was able to look back and understand what really lay behind the Nazi propaganda vilifying Jews, those tapes, and the pain and fear that came with them, continued to take their psychic toll.

But as difficult as it was for me to deal with these tapes, I gradually became aware that there were other tapes in my head that played even louder. These were the tapes flooding me with messages about what women and men should be like. While I never fully believed the anti-Semitic messages, it never occurred to me to question the messages about gender stereotypes. I had been taught that these roles were the way things ought to be — they defined what I should be like but couldn't measure up to. It wasn't until I got involved in the women's movement in the 1960s that I saw how these messages force women and men into emotional straitjackets that do incredible damage — to ourselves and others around us.

Expressing anger, even expressing anger violently, is considered normal for boys and men in the dominator scheme of things. Think of all the movies, TV shows, books, and songs where the male hero is violent. This constant modeling of "masculine" violence clearly has some connection with the kind of violence in our society: more than 90 percent of violent crimes are committed by men.

Girls and women, on the other hand, are generally forbidden from expressing anger, particularly against men. Anger can be used to control others, and men, not women, are supposed to be in control. Small wonder that both men and women are uncomfortable with "angry women" — a term often used to condemn feminists and other women who step out of their assigned gender roles.

But one thing we know from psychology is that when anger is repressed it inevitably finds a way to express itself. What happens with women's suppressed anger?

Some women direct their suppressed anger against men they feel are weak or vulnerable — their sons, for example. The psychologist David Winter found that women living in countries or periods of extreme male dominance tend to be very controlling of their sons, who are the only males it is safe for them to vent against. Women in these circumstances are often subtly, or not so subtly, abusive of their sons. I remember the stories of a psychiatrist who worked for a while in Saudi Arabia. She told of old women sexually abusing boy babies under the guise of pleasuring them. And how some Saudi boys were egged on by their own mothers to drive at breakneck speeds to demonstrate their daredevil manhood — sometimes with fatal consequences.

Many women turn their suppressed anger against other women. For example, if a man they love has an affair, the brunt of their rage is often directed against the woman. This casting of "the other woman" as the villain is dramatized in the film *Fatal Attraction,* a fascinating dominator morality tale. Here the other woman (played by Glenn Close) turns into a homicidal maniac against whom the husband must protect his wife and child — so in the end the philandering husband becomes the hero!

But probably the most common way women who've learned stereotypical feminine roles deal with suppressed anger is self-blame. This ingrained habit of self-blame in women has been extensively documented. In a poll conducted by *Glamour* magazine in June 1998, for example, women were asked to keep a daily log of how often they say "I'm sorry." Some women reported that they apologized more than twenty times in a day. "I'll apologize to my boyfriend if anything goes wrong," one woman said. If he then said, "There's no need to apologize," she would apologize for apologizing! Other women apologized to their assistants for asking them to file something (which was their job), to their boyfriends for complaining about their day, and even to their male mail carriers for not wearing makeup. Since *Glamour* is directed at a readership of women in their late teens, twenties, and thirties, this poll shows how difficult it is even for today's young women to shed their "feminine" socialization.[8]

CHANGING GENDER STEREOTYPES

TURNING ANGER INTO SELF-BLAME is one of the mainsprings for women's famous lack of self-esteem. Millions of women suffer from this, often putting up with degrading and abusive treatment.

But changes in stereotypical gender behaviors, including harmful emotional patterns, are possible. They're happening all around us. Women are becoming more assertive, increasingly taking on the "masculine" roles of managers and leaders. Men are becoming more nurturing, increasingly taking on the "feminine" role of providing babies and children the kind of intimate care not so long ago only associated with mothering.

Gender roles aren't cast in stone. This knowledge helps you take the third step on the path to a more integrated, healthier sense of self. After becoming watchful of your inner programming, and after taking a close look at what makes sense and what doesn't, the next step is to make the appropriate changes.

We hear a lot in New Age circles about "essential" masculinity and femininity: traits and behaviors that are supposed to be inherently male or female according to Jungian archetypes. This may sound fresh because of its New Age packaging, but when we look closer, we find a replay of old dominator gender stereotypes. For example, in "Iron John" and other tales popular in the New Age movement, the hero must kill before he gets to mate.

Men are not innately violent. This is obvious if we look around at all the men who are gentle — despite the constant linking of masculinity and violence in stories, toys, movies, and TV. Contrary to Jungian masculine and feminine archetypes gaining renewed popularity, when a woman is assertive and logical, she is not accessing her masculine side; she is simply expressing qualities that are her own. In the same way, when a man is gentle and caring, he is not accessing his feminine side; he is expressing a part of his own inherent nature that's been stifled by dominator culture.

By acknowledging that your good qualities — whether they're thought of as masculine or feminine — are fine for you, you begin to enhance your sense of self-worth. You stop berating yourself, and access your full humanity because you're in touch with yourself as a full human being.

I can personally attest that changing ingrained notions of masculinity and femininity is a healing experience — healing in the real sense of the word, of reclaiming your own inner balance and accepting yourself for who you are. Once I freed myself from the straitjacket of gender stereotypes, I began to accept myself more completely. I was able to move forward in my personal development. And, as you will see in the next chapter, it was only after I became a better partner with myself that I was able to draw a true life partner into my life.

Many women and men are having similar experiences. It isn't easy to change, to adopt traits and behaviors we were forbidden because of our sex. But precisely because it's not easy, when we begin to make these changes we learn a vital lesson. We learn that changes that once seemed unimaginable are actually possible, and deeply rewarding.

LEARNING TO FEEL GOOD

AS WE MOVE TOWARD PARTNERSHIP with ourselves, we become more attuned to our bodies. I am still struggling with this, as I tend to drive myself hard. But being more in touch with my body has increased both my capacity for pleasure and my sensitivity to messages I need to heed to stay healthy.

When I was growing up, if someone had said, "I'm out of touch with my body," they would have been asked, "What kind of nut are you?" People just didn't talk about their bodies that way. Today it's increasingly part of everyday speech.

Emotional problems too are increasingly talked about. And more and more of us are learning new (actually in some cases very old) techniques for preventing illness and promoting bodily well-being.

We get more exercise. We try to eat more wholesome foods and get more fresh air. Some of us run or practice yoga or meditation to quiet our chatting minds and get in touch with our deeper selves. When needed, we get professional help for both physical and emotional ills. We begin to let go of old pain as we experience what we really feel in our bodies, and we access new pleasure. We begin to distinguish between sex as just a release of tension and real sexual pleasure. And as our sense of self-worth and well-being improve, we are better able to reach beyond ourselves, which in turn also makes us feel better.

The first step, as psychologists have long told us, is to let ourselves become aware of what we actually feel. Only then can we consciously analyze the events that triggered our painful feelings in the first place. We can then reevaluate these events in perspective — not by constantly dwelling on them, which reinforces them, but by working to change our emotional and physical habits.

Psychotherapy, psychological counseling, drug treatment programs, hypnosis, and other ways of accessing negative feelings have helped people better deal with painful memories, and reverse, or at least lessen, the damage. These approaches are also helpful for healing chronic depression and other severe problems.

In recent years there's been an upsurge of the self-help groups that first surfaced in the 1960s. Here people share their experiences, offer one another emotional support, and work together to feel better. The best-known examples are the many twelve-step groups based on the approach pioneered by Alcoholics Anonymous. There are also groups using books such as *The Partnership Way* that I wrote with my partner David Loye, which includes experiential exercises, discussion topics, and action suggestions.[9]

Because we unconsciously carry many of our negative feelings and experiences in our bodies, new body/mind healing techniques can be particularly helpful. For example, the Feldenkrais, Alexander, and Rosen methods can help people become more aware of the pain they carry in their bodies and learn ways of relaxing and changing bodily habits. There are also books that offer suggestions for body and emotional healing, such as *The Touch of Healing, Creative Visualization,* and *Present Moment, Wonderful Moment: Mindfulness Verses for Daily Living.*[10]

Positive affirmations that contradict painful internal voices that tell us we're bad and deserve to be punished can help refocus our attention on aspects of ourselves we feel good about. We can also help ourselves feel better through practices such as yoga and meditation, which calm our thoughts and emotions, and often bring a sense of quiet contentment.

But as important as these activities are, unless we go further we will still only be dealing with symptoms rather than underlying causes of pain. As long as the old dominator patterns in our culture remain in place, our efforts will be countered at every step.

BROADENING OUR PERSPECTIVE

AS YOU HAVE SEEN, dominator/dominated childhood relations tend to drive us into denial and numbness to escape our own pain or the pain we cause others, keeping us trapped in dysfunctional and painful habits. And much of our mainstream culture does the same.

Alcohol, noisy bars, frantic TV ads, and violent "action" entertainment are all desensitizing. This too makes it hard for us to be in touch with our feelings.

More and more people are working harder and longer. Only a short time ago, the pace of work, and life, made it possible for some of us to take an occasional breather. Today the pace is so fast that we're chronically behind and chronically out of time.

Even the way many of our technologies are being used contributes to this problem. Certainly technologies such as washing machines and computers have helped us escape backbreaking and mind-numbing labor. But the speed and omnipresence of today's communication technologies — from the Internet to cell phones to fax machines to e-mail to voicemail — is out of sync with the natural rhythms of our bodies. We can't keep up with the pace of it all. This makes it hard for us to reflect on our lives and our world, much less to find time to do things that bring about positive change.

Shrinking distances and compressing time in spectacular ways can be amazing and wonderful. At the same time, as many people are finding, the space in our lives for deep feeling and thought is also shrinking. We're being pushed into an ever more frantic pace that is still further alienating us from consciousness of ourselves and the world around us. Increasingly we find ourselves controlled by the very technologies that are supposed to free us.

Of course, the problem is not the technologies but an economic system we inherited that was not designed to take human needs into account. We don't have an economic system that uses advanced technologies in ways that take the rhythms of our bodies into account — just as we don't have an economic system that uses technologies in ways that take the rhythms of nature into account. All this adversely impacts our health.

If your employer doesn't provide health insurance — and many low-income jobs don't — you end up doing without proper health care. If you're in the lower rungs of the dominator hierarchy, you can't afford pesticide-free food, and organically grown produce may not even be available in your neighborhood.

High-stakes testing are making children tense and fearful of failure. High-stakes jobs are making executives drop dead from sudden heart attacks.

When you have to work two jobs to make ends meet, you don't get enough rest. Even if you're affluent, chances are you're working long hours. Millions of people in the U.S. are sleep-deprived. A major reason is that U.S. workers today have the longest work week in the industrialized world, even longer than Japan's.

So if we are to access our natural capacity for being attuned to our bodies, for feeling good, and for living in ways that are conducive to physical, emotional, and spiritual health, we also have to pay attention to the environmental, economic, and social conditions that cause many of our problems in the first place — and do what we can to change them.

IT'S IRONIC THAT WHILE MILLIONS of people are trying to change their lifestyle — to slow down and live in healthier ways — billions of dollars are being made from an economic system that drives us toward sickness rather than health. Billions are being made from the sale of cigarettes, hard liquor, legal and illegal addictive drugs, junk food, high sugar and caffeine sodas, and other harmful products. Billions are being made from pesticides, petrochemicals, and other products that are environmentally polluting and damaging to our health. Billions more are being made by an entertainment industry peddling mind-polluting, empathy-deadening movies, television shows, and video games, many of them aimed at young people in particular.

Albums that gross millions describe the "fun" of raping your own mother or organizing the gang rape of your little sister. They have lyrics like those recorded by Ice Cube in the song "It's a Man's World": "Women they're good for nothing no maybe one thing, To serve needs of my ding-a-ling." Highly publicized video games produce phenomenal profits by teaching players how to disembowel and dismember "opponents" in gruesome ways that further cut off feelings of empathy and caring.

How thoroughly these commercial products deaden empathy is illustrated by a young reviewer's sardonic assessment of the video game *Mortal Kombat.* "Personally," he writes, "I find the amount of flying body parts a little disturbing," but then he quickly adds, "not because of the general gore — I like gratuitous violence as much as the next reviewer. No, my gripe is that when you off an opponent there seems to be a disproportionately large and anatomically incorrect number of body parts on the screen....I suspect that one or more of the programming team may have skived biology class at high school — educational standards aren't what they used to be."[11]

Of course, there are excellent nonviolent video games, but these are a small percentage of the industry. There are song lyrics with incisive social critiques, and some popular music is sophisticated and beautiful. But it's often so loud that it not only numbs us but, as we're now learning, damages our hearing. Even the constant flicker of the television screen itself, besides shortening our attention span, has a somewhat anesthetic effect.

Constant noise and motion are built into other aspects of our high-tech age. Ads in particular bombard us with high-speed messages telling us that if we want to feel good, all we have to do is buy, buy, and buy some more, so we can live up to what they tell us our bodies, homes, clothes, children, and lives should be like.

While many women today may feel more liberated, society now demands that they be superwomen — that they find the inner resources as well as time and energy to do everything perfectly. And this pressure is not just on women who have paying jobs or professions, but on homemakers as well.

Thousands of homemakers try to keep up with the likes of Martha Stewart, the multimedia lifestyle guru marketed as a paragon of domestic perfection. The jokes about the Martha Stewart complex — like when Martha forges her own pan to make her own super-omelette from her own free-range chicken's eggs — are examples of how pervasive Stewart's influence is. No wonder there are Martha therapy groups for women who feel they're failures because they can't keep up with a role model who is actually a multinational conglomerate supported by a huge staff.

Martha Stewart's mass marketing is just one example of the enormous commercial pressure on us to conform to outside messages about what we should be like. All this still further disconnects us not only from our own experiences but from our own bodies.

This disconnection is unhealthy. It is also disempowering. If we don't even know what is happening in our own bodies — how we really feel, what we really need — we can't hope to find what makes for real physical, mental, and emotional health. If we become accustomed to respond to outside messages — even about something as basic as the shape of our bodies — we also become conditioned to accept controls in other areas of our lives.[12]

HEALING OURSELVES

IT'S EASY TO SAY that people should just ignore all these social, economic, and cultural pressures and live healthier lives. But it is very hard to do.

Still, because so much in our environment is unhealthy, we hear a great deal today about healing. Good health is certainly a key element of a good relationship with ourselves. So part of partnership with ourselves is taking care of our health. But here too we have to pay attention to the invasive beliefs and institutions that work against us.

Consider how many of our ailments are a result of dominator institutions and lifestyles. Millions of adults and children suffer from chronic conditions that have been linked to harmful commercial products and processes. Heart disease is linked to the high-fat, high-sugar fast-food diet that is mass-marketed to the American public. Children in poor families often lack adequate nutrition, making them more susceptible to illness. Poor people, and particularly poor African Americans, have shorter lifespans due to the stress of poverty and lack of adequate healthcare. Petrochemicals in plastics and other commercial products and processes, as well as pesticides in crops, have been implicated in rising rates of cancer in children as well as rising rates of learning disabilities.

At the same time, a thriving high-tech medical and pharmaceutical industry makes billions of dollars from treating all these ailments. And unfortunately, contemporary medical practice is still largely in the dominator mode.

Physicians, for instance, have long known that many illnesses are related to stress. But the conventional medical approach to treat stress is to prescribe tranquilizers and other pharmaceuticals. Prescription drugs certainly have their place. But we've become a society addicted to legal (as well as illegal) drugs to escape from the pain and trauma inherent in dominator lifestyles and relations. And stress-related illness is being diagnosed in ever younger children.

Today more than one million American children are prescribed the powerful pharmaceutical Ritalin. It is given for all kinds of symptoms, including hyperactivity, even though Ritalin is classified by the Drug Enforcement Agency in the same category as amphetamines and cocaine because of its potential for addiction. Ritalin may help children with severe conditions, and it may make some hyperactive children calmer, and thus easier to control at home and in school. But it can also have very damaging side effects — not just habituation to taking drugs, but extreme lethargy, facial tics, and, in some cases, even suicidal tendencies.

By contrast, the partnership approach for helping hyperactive children is a combination of enhanced nutritional support, including avoidance of junk foods, a more nurturing atmosphere at home, and a more responsive partnership-oriented learning environment at school. This approach avoids harmful side effects, and can do much more than make hyperactive children "more manageable." As John Robbins writes in his book *Reclaiming Our Health,* it can make it easier for children themselves to learn "to manage the challenges and opportunities life brings them."[13]

What is needed, as Robbins points out, is a partnership medicine — an approach that doesn't discard conventional medicine where it can be most effective but focuses more on disease prevention and less on quick-fix intervention after the fact. We need to be taught the fundamentals of good health. We need to learn to prevent illness in the first place by noticing the messages from our bodies, rather than just relying on outside counsel.

This more holistic approach is beginning to gain currency. Dr. Andrew Weil, for example, who recommends herbal remedies, breathing exercises, biofeedback, and other holistic techniques, was given the cover story in *Time* magazine (May 12, 1997), and Dr. Christiane Northrup's books, including *Women's Bodies, Women's Wisdom,* which emphasizes what Northrup calls "cultivating the wisdom of our bodies," have been on the best-seller lists.[14]

When we learn to be better partners with ourselves, the opportunities for better physical and emotional health are enormous. As we leave behind the old dominator mental and emotional baggage, we have far less stress in our lives. We have more energy to invest in constructive personal and social changes. Not only that, we begin to recognize the essential unity of what we call body, mind, and spirit — a partnership principle today increasingly validated by science.

PARTNERSHIP LIVING AND NATURAL HIGHS

PHYSICISTS RECOGNIZE THAT ON THE SUBATOMIC level the distinction between matter and energy is artificial. Scientific research shows that our emotional states are more than just ideas in our minds. Emotions have a very real existence in our brain chemistry. This is just beginning to be understood by experts like Candace Pert, former chief of brain biochemistry at the National Institute of Mental Health.

As Pert notes, scientists are still in the early stages of this type of biochemical research. But we already know that in this partnership between what we call body, mind, and spirit there are certain kinds of behaviors that make us feel good.

Actually, most of us know this from our own experiences. We know, for instance, that euphoric high of falling in love, or how happy we are around a little baby. But what we are now finding out is that there are bodily chemicals behind these good feelings — that we are built so that loving produces chemicals that make us feel good.

Scientists have found that our brains release chemicals that give us enormous pleasure both when we are loved and when we give love to others. This makes evolutionary sense, since caring behaviors are basic to the survival of human infants.[15] But we are also biologically programmed to feel good when we are caring to adults — including ourselves.

In his book, *The Chemistry of Love,* psychiatrist Michael Liebowitz writes that we all carry bodily chemicals (endorphins) that reward us for giving love.[16] The release of these chemicals explains the intense pleasure parents experience caring for babies. It also explains the euphoria of falling in love, and the fact that we humans can experience intense and prolonged sexual pleasure. These chemical rewards explain why people in loving relationships speak of a great sense of contentment, and why people with a deep, caring relationship often describe sexual pleasure in not only erotic but emotional and spiritual terms.

Indeed, as I note in my book *Sacred Pleasure*, it's not coincidental that the word *passion* is used to describe both mystical and sexual ecstasy. Both are natural highs that we can all experience as we move to partnership ways of thinking, feeling, and living.

Creativity also releases chemicals that make us feel good. But here again, we run into the domination model, which not only sets up roadblocks to loving relations but also to the expression of our creative capacity. In dominator settings, it is dangerous to step out of line, so people are conditioned to constrain any new or "different" thoughts and just go along with what they feel is safe.

Even music and dance can lead to natural highs. Many tribal people know this well. There are scenes of ritual circle dances in the more partnership-oriented prehistoric art I describe in my books *The Chalice and the Blade, Sacred Pleasure,* and *Tomorrow's Children.*

The mystical experiences we read of in books on spirituality are another example of natural highs. But in a partnership spirituality that no longer splits spirituality from the body, these natural highs are accessible without having to become a mystic — and without the terrible personal and social costs of drug and alcohol abuse.

Helping people learn to be better partners with themselves, and creating the social and economic conditions that make this possible, would be far more effective in solving the problem of drug abuse than the so-called war on drugs. Current drug policies have made the United States the nation with the largest prison population in the world — even larger than in the former Soviet Union, or in South Africa when mass arrests were made to prevent the end of racial apartheid. Billions of dollars have been spent to stop drug trafficking. Thousands of lives have been lost in the drug wars, both internationally and nationally, between gangs fighting for drug-dealing territory — not to mention the lost potential of the lives of the thousands now warehoused in our prisons for drug use. The "just say no" policy of the Reagan administration did not work either because escape to drug and alcohol addiction is a symptom of dominator personal and social conditions.

Sometimes people, particularly young people, use drugs because they yearn for intense experiences. They want to experiment, and then they get hooked because they find in drugs an escape from unpleasant feelings and realities. Here too partnership living brings change. It lessens the desire to escape. And it makes it possible for young people to realize that highs can be had without drugs — that there are natural highs in which, without the aid of artificial stimulants, our senses are heightened at the same time that our spirits are free to soar.

THE ISSUE IS what conditions will open up these opportunities. Natural highs only come when we are aware and alive. They can't come when we numb ourselves into insensitivity. And this is precisely what people tend to do to avoid the pain and other unpleasant feelings inherent in dominator living and the social and economic systems that support it.

If we live in a culture that pushes us to tune out rather than tune in to ourselves, it's difficult to be aware and fully alive. If different aspects of our being are chronically suppressed to fit into dominator families, workplaces, and other social and economic institutions, we not only learn to suppress these aspects but we also learn to disengage from our capacity for feeling — including our great capacity to feel joy and love.

In a society that supports and rewards partnership relations — with ourselves, our families, and in all areas of life — we can take full advantage of the natural high of love that is our evolutionary birthright. Here the natural chemicals in our bodies that make us feel good when we are cared for and care for others can flow freely.[17]

Peak experiences and altered states of consciousness *can* become part of our day-to-day lives. But this will only happen as we build a world where partnership rather than domination holds sway.

PUTTING PARTNERSHIP TO WORK

All of us to varying degrees carry dysfunctional and painful habits we learned in our childhoods. We can try to escape through alcohol and food addictions, through drugs, through compulsive sex, or other obsessions. Or we can break free of these habits and learn to be attuned to our bodies and to develop freely and joyfully.

On the following pages are some steps you can take right now. Choose one or two that speak to you, and use them to help you move toward the kind of relationship you want with yourself.

ACTION CHECKLIST

FIRST STEPS

❑ Observe the tension you carry, and bodily habits such as stiffening your shoulders or holding your breath. Just observe,
without being critical. Then take three deep breaths, breathing
out slowly, letting yourself feel the tension go out and the
calm and well-being come in. (Thich Nhat Hahn recommends
"breathe in calm, breathe out smile.")

❑ Try sitting still and watching your breathing for five minutes a
day, as a way to center yourself.

❑ Think about the ways you were taught to be embarrassed about
your body. Consider how teaching us to feel bad about our own
bodies is a form of domination.

❑ Think about how gender stereotypes affect how you feel about
yourself and how your body should look.

❑ Read John Robbin's *Reclaiming Our Health* on holistic healing
and healthy eating, *Sacred Pleasure* on the rejoining of spirituality and sexuality, and other works that can help you feel more
healthy and whole.

NEXT STEPS

❑ Consider how deafeningly loud music, the constant flickering
and frantic pace of television, noisy bars, violent action movies,
and other forms of popular entertainment get you to "tune out"
from your own experiences.

❑ Consider how the rush of adrenaline that comes from violent
action entertainment or horror films is a counterfeit substitute
for the natural highs of partnership living and loving.

❑ Observe the natural high you get from exploring new possibilities, from creating, and from helping those in need.

GOING FURTHER

❑ Familiarize yourself with the differences between the domination/control and partnership/respect models (see charts in "More Partnership Tools" at the end of this book).

❑ Consider the connections between your personal life and the degree to which your family, workplace, social group, and society orient to the partnership or domination model.

❑ Think of ways to help people, particularly children, become more aware of media messages that teach that domination and violence are normal, fun, and inevitable.

❑ Reach out to young people and engage them in learning about partnership relations.

❑ Use breathing, music, and/or dance to attain natural spiritual highs that produce no hangovers or addictive or other harmful effects.

❑ Form a discussion group to talk about the materials in this book, and how you can make constructive changes in your life.

Your Intimate
Relations

THE HEART OF THE MATTER

Next to your relationship with yourself come your intimate relations. Actually, the two are intertwined. We first learn how we relate to ourselves through our intimate relations with our parents and other caregivers. We then unconsciously carry some of these lessons into our romantic relations, and later into our own family relations, where we often raise our children the way we were raised.

In this chapter, you will discover dominator patterns for intimate relations that most of us carry. You will find that when you become more aware of this hidden programming, you can begin to leave it behind. You will find useful new information, myths about human nature that get in the way of change, and practical guidelines to help you move to the more satisfying intimate relations we all yearn for.

LOVE, WE ARE TOLD, makes the world go round. But love in a partnership context is very different from love in a dominator context.

Relations with your siblings, parents, spouse, children, and intimate friends can give you unique, indispensable pleasure. But these

relations can also cause you a great deal of pain. Using your new awareness of the partnership and domination models will help you have
better relationships with family members and others close to you.

Remember that no relationship conforms perfectly to the partnership model. As you practice new behaviors, give yourself some
slack. This will help you be a better partner to yourself and earn more
respect and affection from others. Remember not to blame, shame, or
punish yourself if you sometimes "lose it" and revert to dominator
ways of relating.

Keep in mind that change, whether personal or social, doesn't
happen without occasional setbacks. There is resistance, and there are
regressions. So it's important not to be too hard on yourself if you find
yourself backsliding a little. The main thing is to be aware and to keep
the faith.

Have you noticed that people who carry a lot of guilt and are
plagued by critical inner voices are often defensive? They refuse to
take responsibility for their hurtful behavior and blame others for
anything that goes wrong. If you're too critical of yourself, you may
also be too critical of others, which gets in the way of change.

When we give up bossing ourselves and others, when we stop
always criticizing ourselves and others, we are less tense and more
open and caring in our lives. As we change our relationships toward
the partnership/respect model, we create the conditions that will
make us and those around us feel good. At the same time, we also lay
the foundations for more caring families, communities, and a better,
less violent world.

GETTING STARTED

SINCE CHILDHOOD HAS SUCH A PROFOUND EFFECT on our intimate
relations, reflecting on our early life experiences is a good place to
start. As you reflect, you may want to keep some of the questions that
follow in mind and jot down your spontaneous answers for further

reflection. You could also keep a journal with these questions as a guide after you've started to make changes.

What do you remember of your first childhood relations? What did they teach you about love? About discipline? What were the taboos? What did you learn to be afraid of? What did you learn to feel guilty about?

What were you taught about being a girl or boy? What are your first memories of being male or female? How did you find out about sexual differences? Could you then and can you now imagine your parents making love? Did you learn about sex on the street? Or did your parents first tell you about sex in a simple, natural way? Did people hug or were they distant and contained? How was love expressed in your home?

Next you may want to think about how people in your family relate to each other today. Your answers to some of the following questions can be eye-opening.

Do members of your family generally look for things to praise or to criticize? Which do you do more: praise or criticize? Do your family members bottle up their feelings and pretend everything is fine even when they're seething inside? Or do they have ways of communicating and resolving conflicts that are not abusive to themselves or others? Which do you find yourself doing?

How are children treated in your family? Are they supposed to be "seen and not heard"? Are they given total free rein? Or are they taught to respect and honor both their own needs and those of others?

Are you and those around you trapped by gender stereotypes? Or does your family mix allow for variation, flexibility, and growth? Are all the caregiving and nurturing roles delegated to females, with the action, decision-making roles reserved for males? Or is there a healthy balance between these roles? Are there other restrictions based on cultural assumptions about gender, or is there freedom to be your true self?

WE'VE LEARNED SOME BASIC LESSONS about healthy relations during the last decades of therapeutic breakthroughs. We now know that healthy relations require trust, respect, and honesty with ourselves and others — the fundamentals of partnership relations. As we saw in the last chapter, we have to have balance between body, mind, and spirit. We know that what happens to us as children has a huge impact on the rest of our lives. There is a close connection between how you learned to treat yourself and your body and how you learned to connect with other people, particularly with "the opposite sex." The ability to freely play and experience joy in childhood is key to how we relate to ourselves and others. Without a sense of humor and a sense of growing, relations become static and stilted. Relations that have a spiritual dimension, where we experience the awe and beauty of love, are deep and lasting.

As you begin to use this chapter to move toward partnership ways of relating, remember that all of us have an innate capacity for love. Remember that the heart of the matter is putting love into action. Remember that once you become aware of the partnership/respect alternative, you can consciously change habits that get in the way of what you really want and need.

As you learn new relationship skills based on mutual respect, trust, nonviolence, and caring, not only in your family and other intimate relationships but in all your relationships, keep in mind that our first lessons about human relations are not learned in workplaces, businesses, or even schools, but in parent-child and other intimate relations. This is where we first learned to respect the rights of others — or where we first learned violence, cruelty, exploitation, oppression, and prejudice. This is where you and I every day practice either dominator or partnership relations.

Our intimate relations are heavily influenced by social, economic, and historical factors. We don't live in isolation in our families. The way we're treated in our communities and our nation influences how we relate to others.

But this isn't a one-way street. We have choices about how we relate to others, both inside and outside our families. We can change relationships so that they're more caring and empathic.

ARE WE WIRED FOR DOMINATOR RELATIONS?

PEOPLE WILL TELL YOU that talking about caring and empathic relations is all well and good, but totally unrealistic. Isn't evolution about the survival of the fittest — about ruthless competition and strife? Isn't this our evolutionary heritage from which there is no escape?

As you try to move toward partnership relations, you will often hear this argument. A simple response is that survival of the fittest does not mean survival of the meanest. That view has been poked full of holes. It's not even close to Darwin's own writings about what happens in evolution, particularly at the human level.[1] But there is a more interesting response, based on a largely ignored side of evolution: the evolution of love, empathy, and caring.

Most of what we've been taught about human nature deals with only part of the evolutionary picture. Think of all the books and nature documentaries on TV where the focus is on animal predation and aggression. Who beats up or eats who, and in what horrible ways? This, we're told, determines whether a species survives or dies out.

In reality, empathy and caring also play a crucial role in determining survival or extinction for many species. And for us humans, the balance tips heavily toward empathy and caring. Indeed, the emergence of caring on the evolutionary stage is one of the most dramatic turning points in the history of life on our planet. It is an evolutionary milestone. With humans, we see another evolutionary milestone — the emergence of love.[2]

Unlike most insects, fish, and reptiles, all mammals and birds need some parental care for their young to survive. So the evolutionary movement from reptiles to mammals and birds is also an evolutionary movement toward caring. Some reptiles, such as crocodiles, already show parental caring. But most reptiles — lizards, for example — lay their eggs and leave them to hatch on their own. Even worse, the young of species such as the rainbow lizard must be preprogrammed to scurry off immediately after hatching so their own parents won't eat them. By contrast, baby mammals, like baby birds, can't survive without being provided food, protection from predators, and parental guidance in learning survival skills.

Among some birds and mammals, fathers as well as mothers are the caregivers. For example, fathers are actively involved in baby and child-care among kiwi birds, marmosets, owl monkeys, and tamarin monkeys. Among wolves, dolphins, and many other mammals, other members of the herd join to provide empathic caring. Elephants, for example, make a protective circle around the young when danger threatens.

But this surge of empathy and caring is most fully developed in our own species.[3] It extends far beyond our immediate kin to include other humans and even other species. We humans will even risk our lives out of empathy and caring — like the people who risked, and sometimes lost, their lives and even the lives of their families, helping African Americans escape slavery or Jews in Nazi Europe escape the death camps.

So empathy and caring are not something we have to tack on to a brutal and callous "human nature." The capacity, and need, for empathy and caring are biologically built into our species as part of our evolutionary heritage. To survive, human babies require a much longer period of care and protection than any other species. At least some degree of empathy and caring are biological necessities for us.

Religious sages, psychologists, and philosophers tell us that what makes us truly human is not our capacity to inflict pain but our great capacity to love. There are even chemicals in our bodies that make us feel good, both when we receive love and when we give love.

We all know this from our own experiences. When we really give love — whether to a child, a lover, a friend, a pet, our sister and brother humans, or our Mother Earth — we receive biochemical rewards of pleasure.

So why then are some people so uncaring, so emotionally shut down? Here we again come to the effects of the domination and partnership models.

LOVE AND DOMINATION OR PARTNERSHIP

BABIES DON'T HAVE COMPLETELY DEVELOPED BRAINS when they're born. During the first years of life, the brain undergoes major changes. Starting shortly after birth, a baby's brain produces trillions of connections between neurons — many more than it can possibly use. But then, depending on a child's life experiences, the brain weakens those connections (or synapses) that are seldom or never used and strengthens those that are. The result is a mind whose patterns of emotion and thought are largely molded, for better or worse, during the early years of life.[4]

If babies are given empathic attention and stimulation — that is, partnership parenting — they thrive intellectually and emotionally. If they're treated insensitively, neglectfully, and abusively — the results of dominator parenting — they fail to develop their potentials.

How do we know this? Psychologists have long told us about the importance of our early life experiences. But now we also have evidence from neuroscience about the critical importance of early childhood.

Researchers such as Dr. Bruce Perry of the Baylor College of Medicine and Dr. Linda Mayes of the Yale Child Study Center found that regions of the brain's cortex and its limbic system, which is responsible for emotions, are 20 to 30 percent smaller in abused children than in normal children. The brain areas in abused children also have fewer synapses or neural connections. Dr. Megan Gunnar of the University of Minnesota found that children from high-stress early environments also have problems in attention regulation and self-control. This causes hyperactivity, anxiety, and difficulties with inhibiting destructive impulses.[5]

Empathic childcare that relies heavily on caring touch, encouragement, and affection has very different effects on the young brain. This kind of childcare releases the chemicals dopamine and serotonin into areas of the brain that play an important role in determining emotional states. These chemicals produce waves of good feelings that promote emotional stability and mental health. The release of these chemicals also strengthen the capacity to control aggressive impulses. In addition, it promotes the capacity for long-term planning.

These findings show that partnership parenting is much better for children — and for society. They show that loving childcare that does not rely on violence and threats is essential for partnership and respect. They also show that the partnership model is more in tune with evolution. It supports, rather than inhibits, the buildup over millions of years of the evolutionary movement toward caring, empathy, and love.

Empathy — or the capacity to feel what others feel — is built into human biology. Newborns seem to already have it. I have a photograph of two little premature twins showing the healthier and stronger baby putting his arm over the weaker, at-risk twin. It was sent me by the babies' parents, who said that his brother's embraces seem to have been a factor in saving the weaker baby's life.

All great religious traditions recognize the human capacity for empathy. The Golden Rule of "do unto others as you would have them do unto you" tells us to use this capacity. But how can partnership spiritual teachings such as this be applied in real life, to real relationships, if in childhood our innate capacity for empathy has already been dampened, fragmented, or suppressed, and if much in our culture inhibits rather than supports this capacity?[6]

DOMINATOR PARENTING

LIKE ALL HUMAN CAPACITIES, empathy has to be cultivated. But can empathy be cultivated if it must be blunted or suppressed to maintain relations based on rankings of domination?

Consider the stereotyped male upbringing we have inherited from more rigid dominator times. Doesn't it teach boys that they must be tough, that they must at all costs avoid being "soft" like women? But what really is "feminine sensitivity"? Isn't it simply the human capacity for love and empathy that is part of the biological equipment of *both* women and men? Boys and men must be taught systematically to suppress their basic humanity to make it possible for them to obey orders without question, even to kill. Small wonder that in traditional military training men are constantly taught to despise "being like a woman."

Of course, violence is also part of our biological repertoire. But the point is that our experiences, shaped by the culture that surrounds us, can inhibit or encourage either violence or nonviolence.

Teaching boys to equate "real masculinity" with domination and violence, as Rob Koegel writes in *Healing the Wounds of Masculinity*, has caused both men and women much suffering. We see this, for example, in the high rates of violent death among men and the high rates of domestic violence against women.[7] But it can be changed.

If you watch today's dads in public places, you see that millions of men are discovering that they are even more of a man by nurturing a baby, that fathering doesn't have to be all that different from mothering. Millions of men today are rejecting the association of masculinity with violence and domination.

But other men, and women, remain trapped in dominator stereotypes because people subjected to parenting based on fear and violence often find it difficult to change. People subjected to dominator parenting often think that in every situation there must be someone who dominates and someone who is dominated. For many of them, the only alternative to being dominated by those above them is to rebel, turn the tables, and themselves dominate. They can think only in either/or terms: either you dominate and give orders, or you are dominated and must obey. You can scapegoat those underneath you in the pecking order, beat your wife, kick the dog, show minorities who is boss, terrorize "morally inferior enemies," and so on. There is no partnership alternative for these people, because they have no experience of it.

Boys in dominator families are taught that they will one day grow up to dominate women. But they too are taught to accept domination and submission as the natural order of human relations. This lesson can be learned indirectly, as when they observe how "inferior" girls are subject to the will of others. Or the lesson can be learned directly through severe punishments.

Indeed, deliberately inflicting pain on boys is sometimes considered necessary to make them grow up to be "real men." I remember one day in a park hearing a child's wails followed by the sound of slaps and an angry male voice saying, "I am not going to stop hitting you until you stop crying. Little men don't cry."

CHILDREARING BASED ON FEAR AND VIOLENCE is a deeply entrenched cultural practice in both Eastern and Western cultures. Even in the nineteenth century, when the use of violence was beginning to be questioned by educators, some still advocated, as an alternative to beatings, that parents establish the "habit of obedience" by tying their child to a chair or lightly burning a child's fingers with hot tea.[8]

The domination/control model was even more firmly entrenched in the 1700s and early 1800s, when we find autobiographies reporting how routine violence in homes and schools sometimes resulted in lifelong damage, even death, with no prosecution.[9] One man wrote in his diary how his little brother died after being beaten by his father. A woman recalled how her nanny put her in a dark closet for hours when she was "bad," and how she twisted her arm to teach her "respect." Many wrote of being punished by their schoolmasters with knotted cords, metal bars, or horsewhips, and of even seeing children die from beatings.

These kinds of practices came from a time when not obeying the orders of authoritarian chieftains, feudal lords, or kings — or even talking back to those in authority — could bring the most terrible torture, even death. This upbringing was designed to produce people who would view relations of domination and submission as only normal and natural. It is, however, totally inappropriate for the more democratic, equitable, less violent way of living we all want.

THE FIRST STEP TOWARD CHANGE is becoming aware of the legacy of dominator childrearing we still carry in ourselves and in our culture. The problem is that people tend to replicate the kinds of relations they experienced in their early lives. They tend to follow the domination blueprint when they form their own families. They also replicate it in the schools, workplaces, governments, and other social institutions they create. And unfortunately "spare the rod and spoil the child" is still part of childrearing traditions passed down from generation to generation all over the world, in a vicious cycle that unconsciously perpetuates violence and abuse.

Even today, dominator (that is, abusive) parenting is still considered by some women and men as moral and right. Countering what they call permissive parenting, a slew of parenting books and workshops admonish parents not to "overindulge" their children. They tell them to follow "God's way" — which they claim means teaching "highchair manners" by forcing babies as young as eight months to sit with their hands on their trays or laps, and squelching any fussiness through threats and violence. These popular books irresponsibly misinform parents about what babies and children are capable of. They scare parents into not following their own loving impulses. They give unsound and dangerous advice that, as the American Academy of Pediatrics warned, may even "put babies at risk for poor weight gain and dehydration."[10]

Although they totally ignore what we today know about child development, these books are successfully marketed (one book alone has sold more than a quarter of a million copies)[11] because they confirm the domination model of our past. Another reason for their uncritical acceptance is that parenting education is still not incorporated into either our formal or informal education.

Ultimately, changing domination-based childrearing habits will require major changes in education, both in schools and through the mass media. It will require more partnership role models for both boys and girls. Beginning in our earliest grades, it will require teaching both boys and girls empathic caring and caregiving skills appropriate for partnership rather than dominator parenting. But there's a lot you can do right away.

PARTNERSHIP PARENTING

WE HAVE A LARGE BODY OF SCIENTIFIC KNOWLEDGE showing that dominator parenting stunts child development and that partnership parenting helps children grow up into emotionally stable, caring, and creative adults. This scientific knowledge about what is, and is not, sound parenting must become an integral part of education.

Every one of us, whether we have children or not, can work to change educational systems to make parenting and childcare literacy a required part of the school curriculum. We can talk about this to our friends and colleagues. We can notice what kinds of stories children bring home from school, and whether they're learning physical, emotional, and verbal violence. We can call teachers and find out what is happening on playgrounds.

We can bring bullying out into the open and work to introduce nonviolent conflict resolution. We can talk about how common violence against little girls still is — the poking, the mean, contemptuous remarks little boys learn from older boys, and later the sexual harassment. We can bring the racial slurs and putdowns of children who are "different" out into the open. We can use conferences with teachers and principals to insist these things be dealt with, and write letters to the editor about them. We can go to PTA meetings and discuss what helps children become caring and responsible adults.

All of us can learn to relate to children in caring and respectful ways — whether they are our own children or not. And every one of us who has or is planning to have children can learn to use partnership parenting principles.

Sometimes this change can be the most difficult, since it involves habits we unconsciously learned in our own childhoods. I know this from my own experience. My parents loved me and did the best they knew how. But there were things they did that I promised myself I would not do with my own children. Yet when my children came, I found myself following some of the same traditional methods my parents had learned from their parents, methods focusing on punishment and control.

I did make some changes, although all too often I simply rejected dominator methods without knowing quite what to do instead. Today, as I observe how my children and many others of their generation parent, I see that we're beginning to make real progress. For example, one of my daughters figured out that you can't simply tell little kids, "Okay, it's time to go," and expect them to jump into their car seats. As any of us would with adults, she gives her children ample notice of what's expected, and she's found that they respond well: when it's time to leave, they're usually prepared and ready to go. In other words, she treats her children with respect, as partners, rather than just ordering them around, as most of us were in our childhoods.

THERE ARE MANY WONDERFUL RESOURCES that didn't exist only a generation ago: excellent books such as Martha and William Sears's *The Baby Book,* Penelope Leach's *Your Baby and Child,* and Thomas Gordon's *Parent Effectiveness Training,* and easily available magazines such as *Child* and *Parenting.* For those who want more, there are parenting classes and parenting counselors. [12]

These resources often highlight the scientific evidence that traditional fear-and-violence-based childrearing is actually counterproductive, that when we use violence against children, we are teaching them that it's okay for those who are stronger to use violence to impose their will on those who are weaker.

Studies at the Family Research Laboratory at the University of New Hampshire show that spanked children are statistically, over a huge sample, more likely to become aggressive. This contradicts the idea that naughty children get spanked more because they're naughty. The reality seems to be the other way around. As the child psychologist Penelope Leach observes, "spanking comes first, and the extra naughtiness comes after." [13]

Dr. Irwin Hyman, a psychologist at Temple University and author of *The Case Against Spanking,* argues that the spank-or-not-to-spank debate misses the point. When parents ask why they shouldn't spank children, he believes the more appropriate question is why *should* they spank children. "Do you hit your spouse? Co-workers? Friends? Why is it okay to strike your child?" he asks. [14]

Many parents today are trying new approaches that still set limits, which children need, but also involve methods believed to spoil children not so long ago. Both mothers and fathers today are much more attuned and responsive to their babies and children. Instead of violence, many use positive reinforcements and teaching of consequences as alternatives to spanking.

In Scandinavian nations such as Norway and Sweden, spanking has been illegal since the 1980s. This is not coincidental. It is because the Scandinavian world is closer to the partnership model than most other world regions.

But does violence-free parenting work? "Don't kids need a slap once in a while so they'll behave?" a woman asked me after a lecture. Like many of us, this is what she was led to believe. In fact, nonviolent parenting not only works but works better, as other members of that audience were quick to point out from their own experiences as parents.

I too have seen how successful violence-free partnership parenting is in the respectful way my daughters and their husbands treat my little granddaughters and grandsons. The loving attention they get hasn't made them spoiled or self-centered. Because they're encouraged to assert their needs and wishes while learning limits and respect for others, they're by and large loving and empathic as well as secure in their valuing of themselves.

CONFLICTING MESSAGES

THERE IS AN URGENT WORLDWIDE NEED for education about partnership parenting. Although we've seen progress toward partnership parenting, entrenched patterns of violence and abuse erupt again in periods of social and economic stress such as ours. This is part of the global backlash to the movement toward partnership. As the human rights of women and children begin to be recognized, violence and abuse are also increasing to force them to "stay in their place."

This dominator backlash is evident in the mass media. Rather than offering news and entertainment that model caring and nonviolent relations, much in the mass media teaches us the opposite. Situation comedies on TV are full of sarcasm and humiliation — of "fun" at someone else's expense. "Heroic" and "fun" violence permeate not only prime-time shows but also children's cartoons. Angry popular music with violent lyrics is marketed to ever younger children. Many video games aimed at boys are not only violent, but brutal, teaching them how to be mean and cruel not just by example, but through practice in virtual reality — through what they routinely do for "entertainment."

All these media messages deaden empathy and provide schooling for uncaring, hurtful, and violent behaviors. Instead of teaching young people how to relate in partnership ways, they make domination and violence seem normal, manly, and — despite all the real-life suffering they cause — the best and the greatest kinds of fun.

As Lt. Col. Dave Grossman warns in his book *Stop Teaching Our Kids to Kill,* the supposedly harmless video games boys play with have serious real-life effects. He documents how the same kinds of simulations are used by the military to train soldiers to kill — with great success.[15]

ALTHOUGH MANY OF US MAY NOT THINK OF IT this way, the media modeling of uncaring and hurtful behaviors as "cool" sets a negative standard for all our relations — including romantic ones. When I watch music videos on TV, I think of the blatantly contradictory messages directed at young people — and all of us — about how women and men should relate. On the one hand, we hear a lot about equality, nonviolence, and caring. But on the street and in much of popular music and TV, we hear and see precisely the reverse. Here relations of domination, humiliation, inequality, and violence are made to seem sexy, glamorous, desirable — things the superstars who are young people's icons do and enjoy.

Again, the problem isn't just the mass media. We have deeply ingrained cultural scripts that insist on the dominance of men and the submission of women. According to these scripts, which are all around us and *in* us, women want to be dominated and humiliated, and think men who dominate them are sexy. These messages tell us that everyone in these unequal relations has a great time.

In reality, there is no scientific evidence that women have an innate desire to be dominated. Nor is there any evidence that men have an innate desire to dominate. Men and women have just been trained that way. Given half a chance, women want to be treated with respect, consideration, gentleness, and caring. And when men treat women in this way, they find greater self-respect and pleasure in their own lives.[16]

Then there are cultural scripts telling women to invest themselves primarily in their relations with men, but telling men to invest themselves primarily in their individual pursuits and careers rather than their relationships with women. These are obviously contradictory scripts, and they make for a lose-lose situation for both women and men. Women don't get the close intimate relations they are taught are primary. And men can't figure out why women are so dissatisfied, since men have been taught that their careers are the main thing in life — and the main thing women should do in their lives is to support men's goals.

All these scripts are variations of one basic dominator idea: men must always be in control. One outcome of this notion is violence against women. Another is a suspicion in men that women are trying to manipulate them. And people who are not supposed to exercise power often do manipulate: this is the only way they can get what they want. Small wonder that so many people are flocking to counselors, workshops, conferences, and retreats that promise them new relational skills.

But no matter how many new techniques we learn, or how skillful we become at them, as long as we remain within the trap of dominator relations, we're not going to get what we want. We won't satisfy our needs for trust and safety, for respect and consideration, for being recognized and loved for who we really are. Nor will books like *The Rules,* which advise women how to better manipulate men, do more than drive us further into the dead-end trap of traditional relations based on domination and submission.

CHANGING OLD LIFE SCRIPTS

DYSFUNCTIONAL OLD IDEAS about women and men are a major obstacle to change. I can speak to this from personal experience. I spent many unhappy years totally unaware of the impact on my life of stereotyped gender roles and relations. I thought our marital problems were unique to me and my former husband.

When I woke up to the connection between the culturally prescribed life scripts hammering at me and my personal problems, my

consciousness and my life were transformed. This was during
the 1960s. Women were coming together in the second wave of the
modern feminist movement — the women's liberation movement
that took up where the nineteenth-century movement for the vote
and education left off. For some of us, this awakening was gradual.
For me, it was dramatic and sudden.

Before then, I had already begun to make big changes in my life.
I had quit my job at a Beverly Hills entertainment law firm, my marriage, and smoking, all within three months. Clearly, I was ready for
a major change of direction.

One day, I found myself reading the want ads, not quite sure what
I was searching for. But when I saw this one ad, I knew instantly it
was what I had been looking for. It was an ad for a volunteer attorney
to help found the first Women's Center on the West Coast, the
second, after New York, in the United States.

I answered the ad, and that was the beginning of a whole new
career as an organizer, human rights advocate, and lecturer. I founded
the first legal program in the United States dealing with what was
then the novel concept of women and the law. I wrote a Friend of the
Court brief to the United States Supreme Court arguing what was
then also a novel concept: that women should be defined as "persons"
under the Equal Protection clause of the Fourteenth Amendment. I
marched in demonstrations, spoke on women's rights at universities
and other places, read everything I could find on women's history,
feminism, and the dynamics of social change, and taught the first
courses at UCLA in what was later known as Women's Studies.

Because I had very little external or internal support for my new-
found independence, and because I was still in the dominator mode
when it came to relations with myself, I pushed myself so hard I
became very ill. But that illness was the time of greatest transformation. It gave me the space and time to reassess the overall direction of
my life.

When I did, I came face to face with a tape in my head I hadn't even known was playing — a tape that kept telling me I was a horrible, selfish person because I was pursuing my own development and creativity. I also realized there was another tape telling me I was a bad person because I wasn't working to help others, as I had before, but to help those of my kind — girls and women. These tapes played so often and so loud that I had to keep telling myself almost daily that nothing terrible would happen if I got what I wanted.

This went on for a long time, until finally I began to do what I had always wanted to do: seriously devote myself to research and writing. While this shift in direction didn't stop the tapes, I found after a while that I could ignore them, and move on with my life.

It was an exciting time, a time of intense changes, changes that were vastly accelerated when, after writing two published books — one on women and no-fault divorce, the other on the proposed Equal Rights Amendment [17] — I embarked on the research that eventually led to publication of *The Chalice and the Blade* and many other books and articles.

In the process of changing so many old habits of thinking, feeling, and behaving, my relationships with men also radically changed. As I was no longer willing to play the conventional "feminine" role, the kinds of men I began to date were quite different from those I had known earlier, who were themselves still immersed in stereotyped gender roles.

Then I met David. And because I was able to leave behind much of my old gender programming, I now have — and have had for more than twenty years — a true partnership with a man who has also left much of his gender programming behind.

Of course we quarrel, of course there are times when we don't get along, times when we get angry and upset. Some issues we've never resolved, and probably never will. But most of the time we are exuberantly grateful that we found each other — and grateful that we live in a time when both women and men can be more completely realized as human beings, loving and nurturing, assertive and creative, fully human and fully alive.

Because neither of us expects the other to fit into a particular mold, David and I have grown a great deal together. We are able to support each other's personal and creative growth. Some of our creativity has been channeled into inventing new ways of relating, ways to help us keep an even keel when we're not getting along. (A box at the end of this chapter describes the "mini-session" — a technique we use when things look grim either for us individually or for our relationship.)

So I speak from experience when I say partnership works. Like a growing number of others who've struggled to leave their dominator psychic baggage behind, I've been blessed to find what I had almost despaired of finding: a true partner with whom to share my life and my love.

SEX, PLEASURE, AND LOVE

MORE THAN ANYTHING ELSE, we humans want meaningful connections. We want love and we want pleasure. When we don't have these, we become distressed, out of touch with ourselves and others, and all too often distorted — mean and mean-spirited, insensitive and cruel, angry, even violent. This then spills over from intimate relations to other relations — to insensitivity to the pain of others, to social and economic policies that perpetuate inequality and inequity, to crime, terrorism, and war. Dominator intimate relations are at the base of the entire dominator pyramid. To build a better world, shifting intimate relations away from the pain, fear, and rage inherent in the domination model is foundational.

Relations of domination and submission are not conducive to either real love or real pleasure. They even get in the way of the pleasure that comes through our unique human sexuality.

Although sexuality has been reviled as part of our "animal nature," human sexuality is very different from the sexuality of other species. In humans, sex can be purely for pleasure rather than just for procreation. Females can be sexually active throughout the year, rather than only during certain periods. Humans also have the capacity for much longer and more intense sexual pleasure. For us, sex can provide what Masters and Johnson called "the pleasure bond," a sense of well-being and togetherness.[18] But having sex that gives us this pleasure bond is not easy in relations where tension, mistrust, fear, contempt, guilt, and other negative emotions keep getting in the way.

When for men sex means sexual conquest, when it's associated with "scoring" and control, it becomes difficult for men to let go in the way that is most conducive to prolonged and deep orgasmic experiences. When men view women as sexual objects rather than full-fledged human beings, it's difficult for them to experience the caring connection that makes sex a wondrous experience rather than a mere release of tension.

When women's sexuality is under strict male control, you find practices ranging from the sexual mutilation of girls to the stoning to death of "immoral" women, all of which numb and terrorize women in ways that make it impossible for them to be in touch with their natural, joyful sexuality. And when women are deprived of reproductive choice, as they are in rigid dominator societies, sex can become bondage rather than bonding.

I believe that it is immoral to deprive people of family planning methods. I say this not only because of what it does to women, but because of what it does to children. I believe every child has a right to be born wanted. I also believe it is immoral to deprive people of knowledge about human sexuality. Of course, depriving people of knowledge is a way to maintain domination. So it shouldn't surprise us that wider knowledge about sexuality, including information about contraception, has gone hand in hand with the movement toward partnership.

When I was growing up, talking about sex was completely taboo, not just in polite company but even among close friends and family. My mother never explained anything about sex to me. She was simply too embarrassed and had no clue as to how to broach the subject. Even pregnancy was considered unfit for children to see or know anything about. We were told that the stork delivers babies — an absurd story that lingers on.

Because of the cultural movement toward partnership, much has changed. Today, many parents explain human sexuality to their children as soon as they ask about it. Childbirth is shown on the Internet, and children are often present when younger siblings are born. More and more of us are recognizing that there is nothing wrong with our bodies (we all get one), that sex is not dirty (everyone has sexual urges), that sex is not evil or sinful (though sexual violence and domination are), that women as well as men have sexual urges and a great capacity for sexual pleasure (including the capacity for multiple orgasms), that some people are homosexual or bisexual (and that this shouldn't be a reason for discrimination or persecution), that we're all entitled to education about sexuality (including education about family planning), and that there is a spiritual dimension to human sexuality.

This is all part of the movement toward the kind of sexuality that goes with a partnership rather than domination model. However, these healthy trends are only part of the story.

There is, at the same time, a great deal pulling us back toward the kind of sexuality appropriate for dominator relations. In the name of sexual liberalism, violence and domination are graphically sexualized in movies, CDs, and video games, so that a natural act designed to give us pleasure is linked with pain, humiliation, and violence. In the name of religion, there is a push to again deny women reproductive choice, to maintain rigid male control over women's sexuality, and to demonize homosexuality. There is also the constant association of sex with preadolescent dirty talk, of slang sexual insults and swear words, of sex as something we hold in contempt, something we're angry about.

Using the lenses of the partnership and domination models helps us sort these messages into the point-counterpoint of two very different views of our bodies and sexuality. But it does more than that: It helps us become aware of what makes for more fulfilling sexual lives, for more pleasure and less pain, and for the more meaningful and loving relationships we all want.

ONE OF THE MOST INTERESTING, though not widely known, facts about sexuality is that orgasmic states have some of the same characteristics as mystical experiences.[19] Both involve altered states of consciousness.

This linking of sexuality and spirituality actually goes back to ancient times. Religions from more partnership-oriented ancient societies celebrated the sacred marriage of a female divinity or Goddess with her divine lover.[20] In archeological findings, we see indications of a veneration of this act that gives us life and pleasure. For example, the explicitly sexual sculpture of the "Gumelnita lovers," excavated in Romania, dates back more than six thousand years.

Mystical literature, both Western and Eastern, has many clues to an earlier spiritual tradition in which woman's body, man's body, and sexuality were sacred. We read of spirituality in erotic terms — of passion, of intense feelings, and in some mystical writings such as Tantric yoga, of sexual union between woman and man as a path to the divine.

Can you imagine a spirituality in which sex and the human body are part of the sacred? Can you imagine a world where our most intimate bodily relations — sexual relations and birth-giving — are seen as part of the miracle of life and nature?

You and I can begin moving toward this world by liberating

ourselves from centuries of the wrong tapes. As we leave behind
dominator habits we've inherited, as we move toward a partnership
view of love, pleasure, and sex, we move closer to a world where our
deep human yearning for love, pleasure, and caring connection can
be fulfilled.

PUTTING PARTNERSHIP TO WORK

THE MINI-SESSION

Having partnership relations doesn't mean we only have positive feelings. So how do we deal with our negative feelings?

One way is a technique my husband, David Loye, and I developed: the mini-session. We adapted it from a method called "re-
evaluation co-counseling" developed by Harvey Jackins.[21]
Instead of going to a professional counselor, peers take turns
being client and counselor.

David and I use the mini-session when one of us is upset
about something in our relationship. We also use it when we're
depressed about something that has nothing to do with our
relationship. The mini-session is a way of processing feelings,
gaining insights, releasing pain — and feeling better.

Here's how it works:

When you're upset about something, you ask your partner for a
session. Your partner doesn't have to be a spouse or lover; they
can be friend, parent, anyone you're close to. You can also initiate a session when you see that your partner is upset. You can
offer her or him a session.

A session can be quite short (hence the name mini-session). But it can be long if both of you have the time.

To start your session, you have to share something that is "new and good." This can be difficult when you're upset. But it's essential because it shifts your consciousness to something positive. It can be as simple as saying, "What's new and good is that it's a nice day," or "What's new and good is that I had a nice dinner last night," or even "What's new and good is that I remembered to ask for a session."

The second step is to say something about yourself that you like. Again, this may be difficult. When we're depressed and upset, we tend not to like ourselves. But this step is also essential because it too shifts consciousness from negative to positive. What you say could be as simple as, "What I like about myself is that I am not a quitter," "What I like about myself is that I'm basically a good person," or even "What I like about myself is that I have good hair."

The third step is to say something you like about your partner. This can be easy if the subject of the session has nothing to do with him or her. But it can be hard if the session is about how your partner upset you. But that's precisely why saying something positive is important. It's a good reminder that, no matter how mad you are at your partner, she or he has good qualities. Again, this can be as simple as, "What I like about you is that you're a good listener," "What I like about you is that you're a good person," or even "What I like about you is you really know how to dance."

These preliminaries set the stage for the mini-session. Now you get the opportunity to express your disappointment, anger, hurt, fear, jealousy, or other painful feelings. Often, you realize as you start talking that what upset you re-stimulated an earlier painful experience. In other words, you find that the intensity of your current pain stems from a deeper wound from your past.

You could, for instance, be upset because your partner forgot an important occasion. This is irritating and upsetting in itself. But for some of us it's even more upsetting because of past experience with an insensitive parent or former partner. Talking about this earlier experience helps diffuse the intensity of the feeling, although old emotional tapes may never completely stop playing. It also helps your partner understand why something that may seem minor can cause so much pain.

The first rule: When you talk about how your partner upset you, stay focused on how you feel. Don't say, "You made me feel...," or, "When you do this, I always feel...." Try your best to say it in a way that doesn't sound like an accusation — like, "When such and such happened, I felt...."

The second rule (and this is vital): Your partner may not interrupt you during the session. Typical arguments involve people interrupting each other in a game of who can out-dominate the other — until neither hears anything the other says. You want to avoid this.

There are two exceptions to the "do not interrupt" rule. One is that the listening partner can delicately interrupt with validations if you are feeling so bad about yourself you can only think of what's wrong with you. The other exception is that, if you are in deep distress, the listening partner may gently ask, "When is the first time you remember feeling like this?" This can help you go deeper so you can better understand why your distress is so great, as it's often rooted in earlier painful experiences.

It's up to the person taking the session to end it, unless a time limit has been agreed upon in advance. There are also rules for how to end the session.

You end by telling your partner something you're looking forward to. This can be a particular event, like finishing a difficult task, seeing a friend, or going out to dinner. If you can't think of anything else, you could just say you look forward to feeling better. In any case, this closing is a way to refocus your consciousness on something positive rather than negative.

The mini-session is not a substitute for seeking counseling or other help. But it is a good tool for maintaining a sense of perspective and equilibrium. David and I have found that being partners for the mini-session helps us get over rough spots so that anger and hurt feelings don't fester and grow.

One big caution about the mini-session is that it's not a time to play psychologist and psychoanalyze your partner. The job of the listening partner is not to interpret, but to be there as a caring, supportive friend.

ACTION CHECKLIST

From the action steps below, choose the ones that speak to you. Don't try to do all of them at once. Even working on a few will help you move toward the kinds of relationships you want.

FIRST STEPS

❑ Think of the relationship in your life that most closely approximates the domination model. How does it make you feel to be in this relationship? Observe and write down how your shoulders, throat, and stomach feel when you think about this relationship.

❑ Now think of the relationship that in your own experience most closely approximates the partnership model. Again, observe and jot down what's happening to your muscles and your breathing.

- ❑ Observe and jot down how you relate to yourself and others so you can become more conscious of your emotional habits. Don't expect yourself to be perfect.
- ❑ Observe and jot down your childcare and parenting habits to become more aware of your attitudes and behaviors.
- ❑ Take an inventory of the toys, games, music, and videos your children have, and consider what they are learning from them about themselves and their relations to others.
- ❑ Write down some examples of your gender programming. Sort out what you want to keep and what you want to leave behind.
- ❑ Consider ways our language reflects cultural attitudes of embarrassment and disdain toward sexuality, and think of ways to talk about sex that honor our bodies and those of others.

Next Steps

- ❑ Use the mini-session described in this chapter to improve your intimate relations.
- ❑ Use positive parenting alternatives and avoid traditional discipline methods such as yelling, shaming, ridiculing, hitting, and spanking. Remember to be gentle with yourself when you're not perfect.
- ❑ Limit, and where possible avoid, television for your children and yourself.
- ❑ Buy toys, games, and videos that model creativity, resourcefulness, caregiving, flexible gender roles, respect for diversity, and nonviolent conflict resolution.
- ❑ If you don't have children, you can still model partnership relations with a child — a niece or nephew, or the child of a friend or neighbor. Just spending half an hour playing with a child in a

caring and respectful way can give her or him a sense of well-being, and relieve a stressed parent as well.

❑ Talk with friends about how gender roles and relations affect our lives, and how they differ in the domination and partnership model.

❑ Jot down what comes to mind about the "sexual revolution." Consider which aspects are part of the movement toward partnership and which reinforce dominator attitudes and relations. Discuss this with others.

❑ Find out more about our biological and cultural evolution (*Tomorrow's Children, The Chalice and the Blade,* and *Sacred Pleasure* are good resources).

GOING FURTHER

❑ Form a study group to explore the partnership and domination model in depth. (*The Partnership Way* is a good resource for discussion and experiential exercises.)

❑ Let children's book publishers, toy manufacturers, book and toy store owners, and CD publishers know what kinds of books, toys, and CDs you will or will not buy.

❑ Work to make parenting and childcare literacy a required part of the school curriculum by going to PTA meetings and talking with your school board and other policymakers about the kind of education you want for your children.

❑ Teach your children that sexuality is a sacred and natural part of life, and work to support sex education in your schools.

❑ Organize a public forum to raise awareness about the implications of the first years of life not only for individual children but for the kind of world we live in.

❑ Support, join, and become active in organizations working for cultural change and the social structures needed for healthy psyches and relationships. (The Center for Partnership Studies, [www.partnershipway.org], founded to support partnership research and education after the publication of *The Chalice and the Blade*, is a good place to start.)

Your Work and Community Relationships

THE WIDENING CIRCLE OF CARING

Next to your intimate relations, your most immediate relationships are at work and in your community. Whether you have an outside job or work full-time at home cleaning, cooking, doing the laundry, taking care of your children or elderly relatives, chances are you spend more time working than doing anything else. So how you feel at work and how others treat you at work is a big part of your life. Then there are your relationships with your neighbors, local businesses, government agencies, and others in your surrounding community. The quality of these relations also directly affects how you feel as you go about your day-to-day life.

In this chapter, you will see how the partnership and domination models impact your work and community relationships — and how shifting to partnership relationships will greatly improve how you and those around you feel.

ONE OF THE FIRST QUESTIONS people ask when they meet is, "What do you do?" — meaning, "What kind of work do you do?" This is because many of us define ourselves and others by our work.

When I stayed home with my children and people asked what I did, I remember how unimpressed they were when I said, "I'm a housewife." Their reaction made it crystal clear that this work was not valued.

Is your work valued? Is it meaningful, useful, satisfying? Does it use your potentials?

How do you feel when you work? If you have a job outside the home, does it leave you enough time for your family? How are you treated and how do you treat others? Are the pay and benefits adequate? Are working conditions safe? Are your company's products and industrial processes harmful to you, others, or your natural environment? Do you feel respected and cared about, or are your ideas and feelings discounted?

Moving from work to community, here are some more questions you may want to ask. As you ask them, think about what you would like the answers to be, and what they actually are.

What is the tenor of relationships in your community? Do you worry about harm to you and your loved ones on the street, or even at home? How do you feel when you talk with your neighbors, or when you visit local businesses, offices, or government agencies? Do you live in a community where people help and support each other? Or are only those who are part of the "in-group" helped and supported, whereas those who are "different" are invisible, or worse, humiliated, even persecuted? Is there prejudice against racial and other minorities? Are schools in poor districts underfunded? Or is there a spirit of caring for all children and all those in need?

Do the people in power look out for your health and safety? What do they do about racial profiling? Are there times when it seems their decisions are made with an eye to what's best for themselves and their friends? Or are their decisions made for the common good? Do people who want to impose their religious beliefs on others control policies in schools, hospitals, or the media? Or do your community's policies promote respect and caring for all?

Your answers to all these questions about work and community will depend on the degree that relationships are shaped by the domination/control or partnership/respect model. This will be true regardless of whether your community is rural, suburban, or urban, or whether you work in the retail, manufacturing, or service sector. Your answers will also tell you a great deal about what kind of lives you and your children have — whether you feel good or bad, and even about how long you're likely to live.

Yet not so very long ago, asking any questions that could anger those in positions of authority — at work or in your community — was a very risky business. Think of the Middle Ages, when saying the "wrong" thing could get you burned alive. Think of the "robber baron" days of capitalism, when worker safety or, for that matter, any worker rights, were subversive ideas that would immediately get you fired, or even shot, as happened to some labor organizers.

That we can ask probing questions about our workplaces and our communities shows that there's been movement away from the domination/control mode of relations. This is the good news.

The bad news is that much in our workplaces and communities is still far from the partnership/respect mode. What each of us does about moving toward partnership relationships in our workplaces and communities will make a huge difference in our lives and the lives of our loved ones.

FEELING GOOD IS GOOD FOR YOU — AND FOR BUSINESS

IF YOU WORK IN A PLACE where everyone's talents are valued and utilized, you feel good. If you work in a start-up company, you may feel good simply because you're excited to be part of a new venture. If you work in a place where managers are encouraged and rewarded for treating people well, with respect, consideration, and caring, that too makes you feel good.

Many people aren't so fortunate. They don't feel good at work.

You probably know people who feel this way. You may be one of these people.

For centuries, workers couldn't question their working conditions. Can you imagine a slave or serf questioning the idea that people work best when they're whipped? Can you imagine a nine-year-old working sixteen hours in a coal mine or sweatshop asking their boss to help them feel good rather than bad at work?

Even now, people will tell you that feeling good has nothing to do with working. They believe that feeling good is an indulgence that gets in the way of doing the work that has to be done. Many of us were taught to believe this. But as it turns out, it is not true.

Scientific studies show that when we feel good we do much better work. In a series of experiments, the psychologist Alice Isen and her colleagues found that feeling good enhances our ability to think clearly.[1] It leads to greater creativity in problem-solving and negotiation. It improves efficiency and thoroughness in decision-making.[2] When people feel happy, they come up with more ideas, see more associations among ideas, and see more similarities or differences among things, than people in a neutral feeling state.[3] Other experiments also indicate that feeling good promotes innovation, the ability to put ideas together in new, useful ways.[4]

These scientific findings have important implications. Knowing that when we feel good we learn and work more effectively, it makes sense, if only for economic reasons, to shift to the partnership model.

In the early days of industrialization, workers were viewed as just cogs in the industrial machine. The typical company was organized like a pyramid, with rigid top-down hierarchies of control.

Men occupied almost all the ownership and management positions, and their orders had to be obeyed to the letter. Not only women but so-called feminine values such as caring and compassion were excluded from shaping the company culture, which was largely one of control, fear, and sometimes outright violence against union organizers and others agitating for more humane working conditions. That's not to say there were no women workers. In the early days of the Industrial Revolution, women and children were among the first to be hired to work in unhealthy, unsanitary, and unsafe workplaces. A grim case in point is the Triangle Shirt Waist Company fire in which 146 women lost their lives because the doors were locked to prevent them from taking breaks. But women were excluded from governance — along with "feminine" values such as sensitivity and caring, which are considered inappropriate for men in the dominator mindset.

The human costs to both men and women of this model of business were enormous. But it was generally believed that this uncaring, fear-based way of producing goods was necessary for economic productivity.

Today, business experience shows that these once standard attitudes are actually roadblocks to productivity and creativity. In *When Giants Learn to Dance,* Harvard Business School professor Rosabeth Moss Kanter pointed out that the traditional large, hierarchic corporation "is not innovative or responsive enough; it becomes set in its ways, riddled with pecking-order politics, and closed to new ideas or outside influences."[5] In *The Search for Excellence,* management consultants Tom Peters and Bob Waterman reported that "excellent companies" are abandoning rigid top-down hierarchies of control, emphasizing teamwork and worker participation in decision-making rather than chains of vertical command.[6] John Naisbitt and Patricia Aburdene noted in *Reinventing the Corporation* that the growing numbers of women entering the workplace — and with this, the growing acceptance by both men and women of more stereotypically feminine values in business — has contributed to "the humanization of the workplace."[7]

What is gradually emerging is a more partnership-oriented view of the workplace. As Clement Russo writes in "Productivity Overview: Recognizing the Human Dimension," this is a workplace where we can "transform the 'daily humiliations' of work into an activity that gives meaning, direction, and self-fulfillment" to our lives. It is a workplace that can provide "the opportunity to cooperate with others in a common enterprise that stimulates respect, creativity, and commitment that will ultimately benefit everyone."[8]

MOVING TOWARD A PARTNERSHIP WORKPLACE

WHAT CAN YOU DO TO HELP make your workplace a more partnership-oriented environment, where you feel less tense, are more at ease with yourself, and have better relationships with your co-workers and bosses?

The studies by Alice Isen can help you convince your company's decision-makers and your co-workers that partnership relations get better results. Real-life case histories of successful organizations that are moving toward the partnership model will probably be even more helpful.

As early as the 1960s at a Volvo plant in Sweden, workers' teams met together to decide how they wanted to divide their jobs, when to stop and start the assembly lines, and even what hours to work. The result was both higher productivity and a lower number of defective cars.[9] In an article in *Fortune,* "Creating a New Company Culture," Brian Dumaine tells how a DuPont plant in Towanda, Pennsylvania, was "organized in self-directed work teams where employees find their solutions to problems, set their own schedules, and even have a say in hiring." Productivity increased by 35 percent.[10]

In many companies, management is proving that partnership makes better business sense. The Saturn car company, for example, gives every employee — from mechanics to office staff — a voice in company policies and decisions. The managers in these more partnership-oriented companies treat people with respect. They trust them to make decisions rather than controlling their every move. These policies have led to innovations and greater productivity.

Other successful companies are discovering alternatives to the old top-down organizational structure. For example, Dee Hock put together the highly successful VISA credit card network. He linked thousands of owner/members together in a new structure he calls "chaordic," which is not a top-down organization but one in which all members both cooperate and compete.[11]

Paying attention to employees' needs — thinking of them as whole persons with responsibilities to care for others outside of work — is one of the best ways to make a company more successful. For instance, the Marriott International and Hyatt hotel chains, Aetna Insurance, and the Target chains recently got together to see how to better help employees meet both job and family responsibilities. They recognized that a top concern for American workers today is balancing their caregiving responsibilities with their responsibilities at work.

One innovative business owner sent buses to pick up employees and drop their children off at school on the way, installed washing machines where employees could do their laundry at work, and offered childcare subsidies and parenting classes. In just one year, business profits jumped 80 percent, employee turnover dropped to almost zero, and absenteeism became almost nil. Needless to say, employee loyalty skyrocketed, as did productivity. Why? Because this company recognized that the best investment is in happy employees — employees who feel truly cared for.

If you're the CEO of a company, the manager of a division, or the boss in your own business, you can obviously do a lot to implement more caring, and effective, partnership policies. For example, Harry M. Jansen Kramer, president and CEO of Baxter International, sees to it that the employees of his highly successful corporation get to take time off to be with their children, not only when they're sick but for important occasions like a basketball game or a ballet performance. Since many of the workers at Baxter International have children, this helps them feel good.

Kramer himself sets an example from the top that makes others feel comfortable doing this. He'll announce at a meeting that he has to leave by a certain time so he can go to his son's baseball game. In these ways, he incorporates partnership values into both his company's employment policies and his own life.

You don't have to be a manager, of course, to model partnership. You can apply partnership principles to your communication with the people you work with. For instance, you will get better results if you don't put people on the defensive, if you don't blame and shame them. When you validate people for what they do well, you reinforce behaviors you want. When you become a good listener, you not only learn more but also foster good relationships with your clients, co-workers, employees, and managers. If you're more caring of others, chances are that they will be more caring in return.

This matter of caring is a key to success in the partnership workplace. When Bill Brandt, CEO of American Woodmark, brought the partnership model into his business, he took an unprecedented step: he included a unit on caring in his management training program. This program seemed strange at first to many people in the company. But as the new attitude took hold, both job satisfaction and sales shot up.

To help companies implement the insight that caring for employees leads to better work, new organizations such as the Work-Life Alliance and newsletters such as *Work & Family Life* have sprung up. They provide professional assistance and useful information for business owners, managers, and employees. Another new group, the Child Care Action Campaign, lobbies for government and business policies that support workers in meeting caregiving responsibilities.

The companies that fully integrate the partnership model into their organizational structure are still exceptions. But there is movement in bits and pieces toward partnership structure. We can all help accelerate this movement.

WHAT IS A PARTNERSHIP ORGANIZATION?

IT IS SIGNIFICANT that the mission statements of companies often use the term *partnership*. They speak of accountability not only to shareholders and customers but also of a widening responsibility to employees, communities, and the planet. They talk about caring for the needs of their employees, rather than treating them as if they had no life outside of work. All these signal changes in consciousness.

Profit sharing, corporate boards that include union representatives, and employee stock ownership are even more concrete partnership trends.[12] When people get a share of the benefits from their labor, they work better and harder. This also benefits employers and the economy.

The same is true when workers have a greater voice in the decisions made in their companies. They work harder, are more creative, and deliver better results.

But teamwork and greater worker participation in decision-making are not only good for business, they are also good for the nation's health. A study of civil servants working in rigid dominator hierarchies found that those lower in the hierarchy, with little control over their work, have a higher risk of death from coronary heart disease, strokes, cancer, gastrointestinal disease, accidents, and suicides. The risk of dying of a heart attack for workers in the bottom tier was more than 2.5 times greater than for those in the top tier.[13]

The movement toward a partnership organizational structure can help us get beyond these kinds of statistics and the human suffering they reflect. It can help employees enjoy better health and even live longer, because a sense of achievement, self-esteem, and control over one's work and life have tremendous benefits for health and well-being.

BUT AS WE MOVE AWAY from the old domination model, we must be careful not to confuse a partnership structure with a completely flat organization or one where everything is run by consensus. Neither a completely flat organization nor mandatory consensus makes for a partnership organization. This is important to keep in mind, since when these extreme ideas don't work out in practice — as they usually don't — some will say this failure proves rigid controls from the top must be reinstated.

Although there's a great deal of consultation among all workers in a partnership organization and some group decisions are made by consensus, this doesn't mean that all decisions in a partnership culture must be agreed to by everyone. In fact, requiring that all decisions be approved by each and every person can lead to a new kind of domination. When consensus is mandated, one person can make it impossible for anything to get done.

While linking rather than ranking is a key partnership principle, to be effective all organizations need some hierarchies or lines of responsibility. But these hierarchies are very different in a partnership context. They are what I call *hierarchies of actualization* rather than *hierarchies of domination.* In hierarchies of actualization, group leaders empower rather than disempower others. Managers don't function as cops or controllers, but as mentors and helpful facilitators.

Some people fear that change from the control model of management will undermine leadership. In fact, a partnership organization naturally facilitates the emergence of more leaders with real leadership ability. With more flexibility and better communication, larger numbers of employees are able to use their knowledge and abilities to meet new business challenges.

But leadership in hierarchies of actualization differs widely from leadership in hierarchies of domination. The management style is a more stereotypically feminine one of helping others be the best they can be, like what is traditionally expected from a good mother. Not coincidentally, companies with more partnership-oriented management styles are often companies with more women in management positions.

This isn't to say that only women can function in partnership ways. Despite women's upbringing to be empathic, caring, and supportive to others, there are women who pride themselves on being "tough as nails." Many men are empathic, caring, and supportive of others. It's a peculiarly dominator way of thinking that labels empathy, caring, and support as feminine traits. Both men and women have these abilities, and in a partnership organization men are more apt to feel comfortable expressing them.

But because women are not socialized to function in the "man's world," women often bring effective skills for a partnership-oriented organization. Women tend to have a management style that is more encouraging and empowering of colleagues. Studies also show that because women are taught to focus on relationships, they're often better negotiators.

The problem, however, is that if women find themselves in dominator organizations, they attain positions of authority only if they take on stereotypically masculine or "hard" ways of operating. You see this in the famous case of the tough policies and management style of former British prime minister Margaret Thatcher, sometimes referred to as "the best man in England."

In sharp contrast are the innovations used by successful women managers to fundamentally alter the workplace, as described in Sally Helgesen's book *The Female Advantage: Women's Ways of Leadership*. Organizations run by these women, Helgesen writes, are more like "webs of inclusion" than hierarchies of exclusion. These more partnership-oriented companies are successful because they permit greater flow of information, with more points of contact than organizations where the information flow is strictly up or down along prescribed channels.[14] And they're much more pleasant to work for.

TOWARD A MORE CARING AND INCLUSIVE WORKPLACE CULTURE

THE ENTRY OF WOMEN — and with them more stereotypically feminine values — into management has been a major driving force behind corporate innovations such as flextime, daycare programs, parental leave, and other policies that treat employees as human beings with lives and responsibilities outside of work. But both men and women need to join together to create a more humane, inclusive, and caring — and thus ultimately more productive and creative — company structure and culture.

Laws enacted during the second half of the twentieth century prohibiting employment and workplace discrimination on the basis of gender, race, and age were important steps toward partnership. Unfortunately, the typical U.S. workplace is still largely stratified along racial and gender lines, with the preponderance of African Americans, Latinos, and women in the lower-income and lower-status jobs.

The exclusion of minorities and women from top management positions is also still the norm. It's taken at least fifty years for American professions to accept, respect, or even promote women and minorities as equal and competent.

In my first year of law school in the mid-1950s, I was one of only five women in a class of almost four hundred. Our reception by the all-male faculty and the other students was a mix of curious stares, patronizing remarks, snickers, and whistles. To say we were treated as outsiders is an understatement. We were trespassers, and we were reminded of this every day. Professors would walk into a classroom and say, "Gentlemen, today we will..." — sometimes pointedly looking at one of us. The male students excluded us from their seminars to prepare for tests. When we spoke in class, we knew we wouldn't be taken seriously, even when, as it turned out, some of us got the highest grades on tests. In fact, when we did, we met outright hostility.

In my second year of studying law, which was ten years later, during the 1960s, things were somewhat better. There were a few more women in my class, and as the good-looking "older woman" (I was in my early thirties) I elicited quite a bit of interest among the men. I was invited to seminar for one of my classes by a group of the top male students. But when I earned the highest grade in that class, I was again shut out.

When I graduated, I was in the top 10 percent of my class. This meant that I had to be automatically interviewed by the most prestigious law firms. But neither I nor two other women with stellar grades were invited to join any of them.

Today, there are more women and minorities in law schools and medical schools.[15] There are more women and minorities in prestigious firms and management positions. But there's still a great loss of talent and diversity of approaches in a workplace that is far from integrated.

There are, however, positive signs. One of these is the growing movement away from a tough or stereotypically "masculine" corporate culture. I want to emphasize again that we are talking here about gender stereotypes, and not individual men and women. I also want to re-emphasize that a more partnership-oriented culture doesn't mean a laissez-faire, everyone-do-what-they-want style in a totally horizontal workplace. On the contrary, it involves clear expectations, standards, and guidelines — but without the fear and rigidity inherent in the old "hard," stereotypically masculine approaches.

As our society moves toward partnership, more and more men, including CEOs of corporations, are rejecting old dominator values. But if men find it possible to shift toward more supportive or stereotypically feminine values and behaviors, it's largely because of the rising status of women and, with it, the higher valuation of "feminine" values and behaviors.

I still remember with embarrassment an exchange I had with the senior partner of a Beverly Hills law firm I joined in the mid-1960s. I had been very happy to get that job. I was even happier the day I was invited into the senior partner's plush office because he wanted to praise my work.

"You don't think like a woman," he told me, smiling — and I smiled back.

Today I wonder how I could have been so unaware of what a put-down that was, of the contempt for women reflected in his "praise." I wish I could say that was then, and it's all different now. But unfortunately that's not the case. Many people still believe that men are better thinkers and workers than women.

This, of course, is an unfounded belief. Both women and men vary greatly in their abilities, and there is absolutely no evidence that men as a group are better workers than women. In fact, women often have to do better work than men to "prove" themselves and overcome the prejudices against them.

Both women and men are also increasingly concerned about similar issues. As Susan G. Butruille writes, the trends we see today in the workplace go along with important trends in people's personal and family lives — particularly the trend toward the sharing of roles by women and men both at work and at home. Butruille reports how men are increasingly interested in such "women's issues" as good childcare and elder care, flextime, and parental leave.[16]

As work and family relations shift more to partnership, we see a blurring of stereotypical gender-linked attitudes and roles. As more women enter management positions, and the status of women rises, men no longer find it a threatening loss in status to shift to stereotypically feminine values and behaviors — be it in the workplace or other spheres of life.

In short, the shift toward a more humane — and thus more effective — workplace culture is part of a larger social and economic shift. The movement toward partnership in work, family, racial, and gender relationships is linked to the movement toward caring and equality in our communities. Underlying all this is the reexamination of a fundamental question we will return to many times in this book: What do we really value in our lives — at work, at home, and in our communities?

WHAT DO WE REALLY VALUE?

LIKE MANY WOMEN AND MEN TODAY, if you are married or live with a "significant other," both of you probably do some of the housework, shopping, and cooking. This is very different from how it was even a few decades ago, when most families were like my first marriage, where as the wife I was expected to care for the children and the household on my own. By contrast, my second husband and I share household responsibilities. Both of us are researchers and writers, so we both have professional as well as family roles.

With over 60 percent of U.S. mothers now in the labor force, chances are good that if you're a woman with children you also have a job or profession. So one of your main problems is probably how to manage your time so you can do justice to both roles.

If you're the father of young children, unlike your father, you probably also take care of your little ones on a day-to-day basis. So you too are trying to juggle your work and family roles.

While there's some movement by progressive companies to more family-friendly policies, the underlying problem goes much deeper. It is that neither you nor your spouse get any income or other financial support for all the time and effort you spend on this foundational work of caregiving.

So no matter what happens in the workplace to make it a little easier for you, the time, skill, and energy you put into this essential work of caregiving is not rewarded in any way that helps us put food on the table or a roof over our heads. This work of caregiving is not even included in measures of economic productivity such as Gross Domestic Product (GDP), which instead counts work such as building and using weapons, making and selling cigarettes, and other activities that destroy rather than nurture life.[17]

Even when caregiving work is done for pay, the pay is much less than for work in other professions. Often childcare workers, the people to whom you entrust your child, get lower wages than parking lot attendants, the people to whom you entrust your car. This makes absolutely no sense.

Why is the work of caregiving given so little economic value? We would all be dead if it weren't for the work of caring for children, the elderly, and the sick. We would be in very bad shape if our day-to-day needs for food, clean clothes, and a habitable place to live weren't cared for. There wouldn't even be a labor force to go to their jobs or businesses if it weren't for the work of caregiving. So clearly the reason this essential work is given little or no value has nothing to do with logic.

To understand the devaluation of caring work, we have to look beyond logic to what has, and has not, been considered valuable in rigid dominator societies. Here we come back to the enormous impact of cultural beliefs and economic rules that we've inherited from more rigid dominator days.

AS YOU SAW EARLIER, a mainstay for the domination model of relations is the ranking of the male half of humanity over the female half. This led to the devaluing of anything stereotypically associated with women, including the "women's work" of caring and caregiving. In other words, with the subordination of women to men, anything associated with the gender stereotype of men and masculinity was given higher value than anything stereotypically associated with women and the feminine. The results were economic systems — tribal, feudal, capitalist, communist — that give little or no value to the work of caring and caregiving.

Obviously both men and women are able to give care. Some men do so better than some women. But according to the belief system we've inherited, this work is unfit for "real men." In rigid dominator societies, caregiving is supposed to be done by women for free in male-controlled households. It's simply taken for granted as men's due, like the air they breathe, so it has no visibility.

Caregiving work, particularly mothering, is sometimes idealized in rhetoric, as in the American mantra "motherhood and apple pie."

But in reality, mothering is not valued. For example, in programs to aid families with dependent children, no economic value whatsoever is given to the work of caregiving. And even when this work is paid, it is paid less than work associated with men. Professions that involve caregiving such as childcare and elementary school teaching, where women predominate, are typically lower paid than those where caring and caregiving are not integral to the work, such as plumbing and engineering, jobs in which men predominate. Workers in childcare centers often still work for minimum wages, with no benefits.

As is characteristic of dominator mindsets, current economic rules and practices are heavily based on denial. They are based on the systematic denial that caregiving has tangible economic value, that it is in fact the most indispensably valuable human activity. These rules are also based on another characteristic dominator bias: stereotypically masculine activities are given greater attention in education and economics than stereotypically feminine ones.

So we have been taught that it is natural to have government-funded training for the "men's work" of wars and weapons, including pensions for soldiers. But we have been taught to think it strange to have government-funded training and pensions for those who perform the "women's work" of caring for children and the sick. And we're still taught this — even though high-quality caregiving is essential for children's welfare and development, and that without this work we would all be dead.

Of course, this is illogical. It's also inhuman. It prevents us from imbuing our lives and our communities with what we all want — more caring.

BUILDING CARING HOMES, WORKPLACES, AND COMMUNITIES

THINK OF ALL THE STORIES you read in the newspaper every day about relationships where there's lack of caring: reports of shootings, knifings, and other brutalities. Of old people bilked out of their life savings by trusted neighbors or friends. Of women beaten by husbands or lovers. Of girls raped or sexually mauled for "fun." Of children killed by other children and even by their own parents. Of corporate executives who put profits over human welfare and even life. Of the homeless freezing to death on our streets. Of mayhem, murder, and cruelty.

Politicians give us catchy slogans like "a more gentle, caring world" and "compassionate conservatism." But when it comes to caring for children, for the sick, the elderly, and the homeless, their policies are far from caring.

And why would these policies be caring when the devaluation of the "women's work" of caring and caregiving is deeply embedded not only in our unconscious minds but in the economic rules and models most politicians unconsciously accept? How realistic is it to talk about a more equitable economic system as long as the indispensable, life-sustaining caring work is given a lot of lip service but few if any economic incentives or rewards? Indeed, how can we seriously talk of more caring communities, when we continue to go along with these old dominator rules?

Learning to value or devalue caring is a basic lesson for life. Learning or not learning skills for giving care is another basic life lesson. Which of these two very different lessons people are taught at home, at work, and in our communities profoundly affects all of our relationships.

Take a moment to consider all the pain you would have been spared if everyone around you had learned to truly value caring. Think of all the pleasure you would have had if everyone learned the skills for caring and caregiving. Think of what kind of communities, and what kind of world, we would have if we really gave value in our education and our economics to caring and caregiving.

Think of all the talk we hear today of how the emerging post-industrial information economy requires "high-quality human capital"

— people who have the ability to relate to one another easily, to be flexible, productive, and creative. And think of what we are learning from neuroscience about how the quality of childhood caregiving profoundly affects our ability to relate, be flexible, productive, and creative.

THE KIND OF NEURAL AND BIOCHEMICAL PATHWAYS laid during childhood affect whether we're venturesome and creative, able to resolve conflicts nonviolently, and whether we can work with peers or only take orders from above. As you saw in chapter 2, the kind of neural pathways that are laid largely depends on the kind of child-care and early education children receive. Developing the high-quality workforce needed for the post-industrial economy largely depends on caring childcare and stimulating early childhood education.[18]

But can we seriously talk about providing better care for children as long as childcare is paid so little in the labor market, and caregiving at home is not given any economic value at all? Is this a realistic expectation? What needs to change so that caregiving work is no longer systematically devalued?

A good place to start is with our own reservations about giving real value to caring and caregiving. We are not used to thinking of these as prestigious, highly rewarded activities. Devaluing them as "women's work" is a dominator habit of thinking we've inherited. I know this from my own experience. At first, giving real value to caring and caregiving was a strange, uncomfortable idea to me.

I also had to deal with a question that's probably already come to your mind: If caregiving is linked with material rewards, will anyone want to do it for free?

But consider that caring begets caring. Consider also that if caring becomes a truly valued activity, people will emulate it, whether it's directly compensated with money or not.

Even now, people emulate behavior highlighted in the media as the way to be. If caring became the "cool" thing to do, if it were associated with peer acceptance, honors, and glamour, more people would want to do it. Think of how people, young and old, imitate the dress and behaviors of high-profile, highly paid actors and sports figures.

As caring skills are taught and modeled in both formal and informal education, more people will learn them. They will experience the biochemical rewards of pleasure our bodies give us when we care for others. When caring skills are taught through our educational system — which they must be — more people will also experience the pleasure of doing something well. As children receive better care, they will learn caring skills by example. They will imitate these behaviors, and themselves experience the pleasure that comes with caring.

More people will grow up valuing and practicing caring. They will be more caring parents, friends, employers, workers, and government officials. More people will volunteer for unpaid caring community work. At the same time, giving good care to children, the elderly, and the sick will rise in status and in pay. As a result, we will have more caring people, more caring homes, workplaces, and communities.

CARING ECONOMIC INVENTIONS

ALL THIS WILL TAKE TIME. As a first step, you can raise awareness about this pivotal issue of the real value of caring and caregiving. You can talk about it to your friends and colleagues. You can invite them to take a second look at the rules and models on which our present economic systems are based, and at what we can do to promote economic inventions that give real value to caring and caregiving.

Everything involved in our economic life is an invention — from stock exchanges and sweatshops to banks and social security. Laws that permitted slavery or male ownership of women's work were economic inventions to serve a dominator economic system. Laws prohibiting child labor and giving women property rights serve a partnership economic system. So do workplace safety regulations, unemployment insurance, laws against workplace discrimination, and parental leave.

In short, economic inventions are like any other human invention. They are created by people who want to achieve certain goals.

We already have a few economic inventions that give monetary value to caring and caregiving. In the United States, parental leave for both mothers and fathers, as well as flexible work options, are becoming more prevalent. In the Scandinavian nations, as well as in France, Germany, Great Britain, and other industrialized democracies, there is *paid* parental leave. There are also government subsidies for childcare and home elder care *(not* just tax credits), as well as community-service job programs for unemployed youths. All these enlightened developments are partnership economic inventions.

Some of the most interesting economic inventions are emerging on the community level. Caregiving work is recognized as economically valuable by many of the new local currency systems that bypass national monetary systems. These systems are used by people in a community to exchange goods and services locally. Childcare can therefore be valued as highly as tax preparation or other professional work. In Japan, there's an interesting caregiving exchange program between Tokyo and Kyoto. If someone takes care of an elderly person in a retirement or nursing home in one of these cities, that caregiver's parents in the other city can obtain similar services. In other words, economic credit for caring is transferred from one community to another. Local communities that offer free public transportation and other public services to volunteers have invented still another way to give caring work visibility and economic value.[19]

If we really value quality caregiving as much as we value quality legal counsel, for example, we must insist that the professionals who care for our children and elderly are well trained and certified. Does it make sense that we require training and licensing for drivers and cosmeticians, but that in many places there's no training or licensing requirement when childcare is provided in someone's home? We need high-quality training programs for caregivers. We also need certification programs that help parents choose the best caregiver for their child's particular needs. And we need community support to help parents pay for the best quality care. All of us can support these changes.

Community investment in caregiving will pay for itself in less than a generation. It will make a huge profit in the bargain. Consider the enormous community expense of *not* investing in good childcare — from crime, mental illness, drug abuse, and lost human potential to the economic consequences of lower quality "human capital."

Community investment in good training, pay, and benefits for caregiving work will raise awareness about the value of quality caregiving, whether it's performed at home or in the market economy. Again, giving economic value to caregiving at home might seem a strange idea. But what is, or isn't, economically rewarded is a matter of values, not of any fixed economic laws. These values are very different in a dominator or partnership context. New partnership economic models and rules will recognize the economic value of the work of those who stay home and care for their families. There will be new economic inventions, such as community-supported parenting education, caregiving education as part of the school curriculum, and tax rebates and old-age pensions for caregivers. (I deal with this issue in my article "Changing the Rules of the Game," which you can download from www.partnershipway.org.)

As I propose in *Tomorrow's Children,* caring for life — for self, others, and our Mother Earth — should be a thread running through the educational curriculum from preschool to graduate school. It should be an integral part of every child's education.

Isn't it peculiar that our schools teach everything except the essential life skills of caring? This too is part of our heritage from earlier societies based on domination, where empathy and caring would get in the way of fear-and-force-based rankings of "superiors" over "inferiors."

We need to change this. Seeing the win-win of partnership helps us give real value to caring and caregiving.

BECAUSE THIS MATTER OF CARING IS FUNDAMENTAL to relationships all across the board, I will return to it many times. But I'm not going to preach that we should be more caring. I'm always going to focus on what I have learned about *creating the conditions that encourage rather than inhibit or prevent caring relations.*

If we really want more caring, if we want safer streets and more loving homes, if we want a more humane and productive workplace, if we want our children to get the education that equips them to live good lives, we have to do a better job of supporting and rewarding caring in our homes, schools, workplaces, and communities.

It's all very well to talk about more caring communities. But if we want our children to be healthy, we need to work for better health care for all children. If we want less crime in our communities, we need to prevent crime by providing good nutrition, housing, and education for all, rather than pouring buckets of money into building more prisons to warehouse whole populations. If we want to end hunger, we must help build the social structures, culture, and social policies — including partnership rules and economic models — that prevent poverty and hunger.

Based on years of thinking, observation, and research, I know that recognizing and rewarding the work of caring and caregiving is essential to creating more sustainable, equitable, and humane workplaces and communities. But I also know that it will take a lot of ingenuity from a lot of people to make this goal a reality.

Sometimes progress will be slow, and we will become discouraged. I do at times. But I remind myself of the gains that have been made, and of how much harder it was to make progress during more rigid dominator times. I also remind myself that if enough of us become engaged, like pebbles that set in motion ever-widening circles in a pond, the ripples from our actions will spread.

As you become involved in this venture of transforming how we look at work and community, you will inevitably meet opposition and hostility. But you will also meet wonderful people and make new friends with whom you share common interests and concerns — people who care, who make you feel cared for, and with whom you feel good. The more involved you get, the better you will feel.

I know this from my own experience, from all the friends and colleagues I have met who so greatly enrich my life. It feels good trying out new ideas and testing them in action. It feels good knowing you're not sitting on the sidelines. You feel less alone. Your creative juices start flowing. You become more venturesome in all aspects of your life. And you become part of a growing national and international community of people who share your values and your commitment to bring partnership into all aspects of our lives.

PUTTING PARTNERSHIP TO WORK

Everything in our lives is a matter of relationships — whether it's with ourselves, with others in our families and communities, or with our Mother Earth. All these relationships are interconnected.

As you realize that dominator social habits stand in the way of personal change, you may feel there isn't much you can do about such "big things." I used to think this way. Then I began to stand up for what I believe in rather than just complaining about things not being right. That was one of the most exciting changes in my life. Seeing I really could have an effect felt great. Knowing that I was putting ideas I believe in into action gave my life greater meaning.

You may be too young to remember when we had a much more segregated society. Not only were restaurants, hotels, and even water fountains segregated by race, but newspaper employment ads were segregated into "Help Wanted Male" and "Help Wanted Female." The low-paying, dead-end jobs were in the female section, and the well-paying jobs with a promising future were in the male section. As an attorney, I was one of the women who worked to change this. I started the first legal program aimed at changing laws and practices that disempower women. Today, we take for granted laws that prohibit rather than promote discrimination against girls and women. But it took a lot of people — people just like you and me — working against a lot of opposition to get these laws enacted.

The point is that it doesn't take "special" people to bring about social change. It takes people like Jeffrey Wigand, who blew the whistle on tobacco company executives and their scientific hirelings who falsely testified they knew of no evidence that smoking causes cancer; people like Rachel Carson, who took on petrochemical companies and their scientists to stop the spraying of DDT on our food. There are countless people like them, some of whom you'll meet in this book. Every gain we've made was because people just like you and I challenged entrenched traditions of domination — from authoritarianism and slavery to men's "rightful" control over women and children.

Every one of us is special, every one of us can do our part, and every change is important, no matter how small.

ACTION CHECKLIST

FIRST STEPS

❑ Observe how you relate to your co-workers, family members, and others in your community. What kinds of behaviors bring the results you want, or don't want? Make yourself a note about a behavior you want to change. For example, if you tend to be critical, make yourself a post-it that reads "I praise people," post it on your bathroom mirror, and start a new habit of praising yourself for the good things you do.

❑ Take an inventory of dominator and partnership aspects of your workplace. How do they affect you and others? Think of ways you can move your job, family, and community culture toward partnership.

❑ If you're married, keep a running list for a few weeks of who does what work around the house. Is each of your work given equal value?

❑ Consider how partnership behaviors at home reinforce the changes you want to make in your workplace, and how dominator family interactions do the opposite.

❑ Jot down ways that caring work is valued or not valued in your place of work, your family, and your community. Think of what you and those around you can do to recognize and reward this work.

NEXT STEPS

❑ Talk about the partnership and domination models at work, at home, and with those around you who might be receptive. Get their ideas and suggestions, and plan how to implement them together.

❑ If you're in a decision-making position at work, plan to put the ideas in this chapter into practice. Get input from your staff and employees. Make it clear that what you're aiming for is a partnership organizational structure with clear lines of responsibility, not a laissez-faire workplace where everyone does what they want.

❑ Read more about partnership workplaces. (The newsletters of organizations such as the World Business Academy, Businesses for Social Responsibility, the Social Venture Network, and the Life-Family Alliance are good sources.)

❑ If you're a manager, model partnership behaviors and advocate them with those who can help change your company's structure and culture in a more productive, creative, humane, and pleasurable direction. Bring in people who can share their partnership knowledge and expertise.

❑ Form a study group on how moving toward partnership can help you and your community. (*The Partnership Way* is a good resource for discussion and experiential exercises.)

GOING FURTHER

❑ Support, join, and become active in organizations working to create partnership cultural changes and social structures.

❑ Work for the introduction of partnership education in your community's schools and universities (*Tomorrow's Children* is a good resource).

❑ Bring awareness of the need to recognize and reward caring work into your place of work, your family, and your community. Brainstorm creative ways to change the devaluation of caring and caregiving.

❑ Organize a public forum to raise awareness about the value of caregiving work. Show the link between good caregiving and reduced street crime, less domestic violence, and a stronger community.

Your Relationship with Your National Community

WHY POLITICS MATTER

What does it mean to have a relationship with your national community? You might not think you have one. But consider that a nation's beliefs, laws, and policies directly impact whether it's safe to speak your mind, whether your children are safe in their schools, whether your tax dollars are spent on needed social services, whether you can plan how many children to have, and a host of other fundamental matters that profoundly influence your daily life.

In this chapter, you will see that your relationship with your nation is a two-way street where you are not only influenced by national beliefs, laws, and policies but can also influence them. You will see why you will want to get involved in this process — and how you can make more of a difference with every step you take.

THE NAZI TAKEOVER of my native Austria nearly cost me my life. My parents were able to buy visas to Cuba, which along with Shanghai was one of the few places on earth with governments willing to take in refugees from the Nazis. Our bank account was frozen by the

Austrian authorities, and we weren't permitted to take anything with us except the suitcases we could carry. But we escaped the Holocaust in which six million Jews were murdered, including my grandparents and most of my aunts, uncles, and cousins. Naturally, this experience made it easy for me to see the tremendous impact national policies — and hence politics — have on our lives.

The impact of national policies on your life would also be obvious if you were a woman living in the Taliban's Afghanistan. If you were driven from your job, denied the right to educate your daughters, shut into a house where the windows must be painted black so no man can accidentally see you, forced to cover yourself from head to foot so you're reduced to a lump of walking cloth, and in danger of being stoned to death for just talking to a man who is not your husband or other relative, you would be all too aware that national policies have a lot to do with day-to-day life.

You can also see these connections in the United States if you live in a poor inner-city racial ghetto and your food stamps have been cut off. But if you live in a suburban neighborhood, busy every day coming and going from your job, taking care of your children, trying to relax in front of your television at the end of a long day, what happens on the national level may seem to have little to do with what happens to you and your family. And even if you realize that both the good and bad things in your life have a lot to do with the kind of nation you live in, you may think there is little you can do to bring about more enlightened policies, laws, and cultural attitudes.

In reality, just about all the good things we take for granted — from eight-hour workdays, workplace safety regulations, and social security to legal access to contraception and public education — we owe to people who realized they could make a difference. Even the right to vote was at one time denied not only to women and African Americans but also to white men who didn't own land.

That all this was changed we owe to people who decided to stand up against traditions of domination. They were people just like you and me: men and women such as Frederick Douglass, the self-educated former slave who became a leader of the movement to enfranchise African Americans; Mary Jones, the fiery union organizer whose crusade for safer working conditions earned her the name Mother Jones; Margaret Sanger, the middle-class woman thrown in jail for the "crime" of opening the first U.S. clinic dispensing contraceptives after she saw women die from too-frequent pregnancies.

The thousands of people who worked to make ours a more just and caring nation were of different races, classes, and ethnic backgrounds. But they all had one thing in common. They became aware that national policies, laws, and beliefs profoundly affect our day-to-day lives — and they decided to work for changes that hugely improved, and in some cases saved, our lives.

TODAY OUR NATION STANDS at a crossroads. Take a moment to inventory the things that make you worry about your future and your children's future, things that make you feel victimized and maybe even afraid. You will see connections between your fears and worries, and what happens on the national level. If popular culture continues to glorify physical and emotional violence, if hate and scapegoating continue to be justified as moral and right, if the gap between haves and have-nots continues to widen, if the protection of our natural environment continues to be weakened, if our government continues to arm repressive regimes and would-be regimes — in short, if regression to the domination model continues — no matter how hard you work and save, much that you hold dear will remain threatened.

One reason more of us aren't aware of these connections is that we are led to believe that our personal choices take place in a vacuum. Take the matter of food we looked at earlier. As you saw, for a healthy diet we first have to become aware of what kinds of foods are good or bad for us. Then we have to change our eating habits and eat more

vegetables and fruit instead of junk foods and other foods high in fats
and sugars. But, unfortunately, even making these sound choices isn't
enough.

As a recent issue of *Consumer Reports* pointed out, the spinach,
green beans, fruit, and other foods we tell our children to eat so they
will grow up healthy and strong often have high concentrations
of pesticides.[1] So if we're to make sure the foods available on our
grocery shelves don't contain toxic substances that will harm our children and us, we have to change national policies, laws, and practices.[2]

This is only one example out of many. The point is that as essential as it is to change our personal habits, if we want to have better
lives we also need to change the larger society around us, because of
its profound impact on almost every aspect of our lives.

THE FIRST STEP is changing just one habit many of us have: believing
that you and I cannot make a difference.

Ask yourself two basic questions. What kinds of relationships do our
national policies, laws, and beliefs promote? Are they relationships based
on the domination/control model or on the partnership/respect model?
Then support those policies and laws that promote relations based on
partnership and respect, and work to change those that are not.

It doesn't matter whether you think of yourself as politically conservative or liberal. Partnership is not about right or left; it is about
moving forward and serving the enlightened self-interest of all.

There is already a strong grassroots political movement toward
partnership — a movement in which young people are often leaders.
However, much of this movement is fragmented and scattered, caught
up in old debates about liberal or conservative, left or right, religious
or nonreligious. What is urgently needed is a unifying partnership
political agenda that can take us beyond conventional debates and
classifications.

The most important thing you can do is to help us move beyond party politics to a politics of partnership that broadens and deepens the American vision of a more just and caring nation. This chapter and "The Politics of Partnership" at the end of this book provide the background and practical tools to put this partnership political agenda into action.

POLITICS THROUGH A NEW LENS

WHEN YOU WATCH TELEVISION or read a newspaper, you may get the impression that politics is like a football game or TV game show, that what counts is who outmaneuvers whom in a contest between winners and losers. Whose tactics are more effective? Who can sway the undecided voter with a simple slogan? Who can sling the most mud? Who can raise the most money? Which candidate's personality has the most popular appeal?

When you look at politics through the analytical lens of the partnership/domination continuum, you see a deeper struggle. You see the struggle between those who hold the old view of power — the power to give orders, to control, to disempower others — and those who want to use their positions of power to empower the rest of us.

Indeed, this has been the underlying political struggle for a long time — even though this isn't what we learned about history in school.[3] Now, you may think that history doesn't matter because it's already happened. But, as the old saying goes, those who don't learn from history are doomed to repeat it. Reexamining history through the partnership and dominator lenses is eye-opening — and it is essential if we are to move forward.

In school, you were probably taught that modern democracy began with the "rights of man" movement of the seventeenth and eighteenth centuries. But you were not taught that what this movement challenged is a tradition of domination: the "divinely ordained" rule of kings over their "subjects." In the same way, you were not taught that the "rights of women" or feminist movement challenged another tradition of domination: the control by men over women and children in the "castles" of their homes. The nineteenth-century abolitionist movement and pacifist movement challenged other entrenched traditions of domination: the enslavement of one race by another, and force as a means for one nation to control another.

As you look at history through the partnership and dominator lenses, you can see that other seemingly unconnected movements are also challenges to traditions of domination. The movement to humanize the treatment of the mentally ill challenged the practice of beating and chaining them to tame their "antisocial instincts." Educational reform movements challenged corporal punishment to control children in schools.

The twentieth-century civil rights, anti-colonialism, women's liberation, indigenous peoples' rights, peace, and gay rights movements also challenge traditions of domination. So does the environmental movement, which challenges the once-hallowed conquest of nature.

Over the last three hundred years, these organized challenges to traditions of domination have brought many gains. Consider that child labor, unsafe and unsanitary workplaces, twelve-hour workdays, and other features of early "robber baron" capitalism would still be legal had it not been for the challenges of organized labor. Without the civil rights movement, racial discrimination would still be legal, and we would still have segregated water fountains, buses, restaurants, hotels, and even hospitals. Without the feminist movement, women in the United States today could still not go to universities, own or manage property, go into business on their own, or vote.

A new, and very important, movement addresses domination and violence in intimate relationships. It challenges such crimes as rape, wife-beating, child-abuse, and incest, which were not so long ago unspoken and unprosecuted acts of violence often blamed on the victims. As you will see, this recent movement against intimate violence is foundational to an integrated politics of partnership.

But the shift toward partnership has been fiercely resisted every step of the way. It has also periodically been set back by regressions to the domination model.

Even though on the surface they seem to have little in common, the most repressive regimes of modern times — from Hitler's Germany to the Taliban's Afghanistan — have been regressions to the core blueprint of the domination/control model. All have been a return to a brutally authoritarian structure. All have attempted to put women back into their "traditional" subservient place. All have advocated and used violence to establish and maintain top-down rankings of control by men over women and men over men.

There have also been periodic dominator regressions in the United States, although in milder form. And one reason we urgently need a new politics of partnership is that we are in such a period today.

THE PUSH BACK

AS YOU LOOK AT THE NEWS through the partnership/domination lenses, you will see that many of the things that disturb you both in this country and worldwide are part of a regression to the domination model. In the United States, demagogic leaders (often unfairly invoking religion) preach intolerance, which has led to increased violence against marginalized groups such as homosexuals. They call for a return to the family values of more authoritarian times — male dominance and punitive childrearing. At the same time, violence has increased against women and children to beat them back into submission.[4] Even the American separation of church and state, which our nation's founders included in our

Constitution to prevent the religious control and violence that was once prevalent (and in some places still is), is under attack. And a key part of this dominator regression is a massive reconcentration of economic power.[5]

Most of us are vaguely aware of the serious implications of these developments, even though they're rarely analyzed in depth in what we read in our newspapers or see on TV. Consider these economic statistics:

- Did you know that during the much publicized economic growth period leading up to the 1990s, the income of the middle fifth of the U.S. population actually declined, while the income of the top 1 percent skyrocketed? The income of the top 1 percent jumped by 78 percent. But the income of the middle fifth dropped by 5.3 percent.[6]
- Were you aware that there's a hidden story behind the widely publicized Census Bureau statistics that from 1995 to 1996 Americans' median income climbed 1.2 percent? These statistics conceal that while income for the richest 20 percent increased 2.2 percent, income for the poorest 20 percent actually *fell* 1.8 percent.[7]
- Did you know that in 1999 — nine years into the longest economic expansion in our nation's history — labor's share of the national income remained 2 to 4 percent below the levels reached in the late 1960s and early 1970s?[8]
- Did you know that the combined net worth of the 1999 *Forbes* list of the four hundred richest people in the United States was $1 trillion?[9]
- Were you aware that approximately five hundred billionaires in a handful of countries such as the United States, France, Mexico, Thailand, and Saudi Arabia have a combined wealth equal to the combined wealth of 52 percent of the billions of people on this planet?[10]

THIS RECONCENTRATION OF WEALTH[11] has enormous political significance, since with it comes the massive control moneyed interests wield over the politicians and the mass media that shape national policies. Many of the same enormously wealthy individuals and corporations who control most of the world's wealth also exercise enormous control over most of the world's governments. In some nations, this control is exercised through outright payments or bribes that are accepted as traditional practices. In the United States, this control is generally exercised through large campaign donations and lobbyists that influence such key matters as who gets tax breaks, which government programs are funded by tax dollars, which laws and regulations are supported or opposed by elected officials, and, of course, who gets elected.

Many corporations trade political contributions for political favors, which include subsidies and other forms of corporate welfare, as well as government protection for unfair, monopolistic activities. Consider the Archer Daniels Midland Corporation (ADM), one of the most prominent recipients of corporate welfare in recent U.S. history. ADM and its chairman, Dwayne Andreas, have given millions of dollars to both political parties, and in return have reaped billion-dollar windfalls from taxpayers and consumers in the form of federal protection of the domestic sugar industry, ethanol subsidies, subsidized grain exports, and various other programs.[12] Consider the enormous price hikes by companies such as Enron and Duke after California energy prices were deregulated. Duke raised its prices during early 2001 peak times to $3,880 per megawatt hour from the average of $76 in 2000. These high energy prices were then passed on to California consumers. Household and business utility bills doubled and tripled, with disastrous consequences for small businesses, poor families, and many elderly people living on pensions. But when President Bush came to California in May 2001, he refused to change his energy policy, which was crafted by advisers with close ties to natural gas giants such as

Enron, one of the largest contributors to Bush's 2000 presidential campaign.[13]

These aren't isolated cases. The point is that in the U.S. we have a legal form of political corruption. We have a system in which the purchase of politicians and government policies is lawful. But even though these patterns are there for all to see, political commentators rarely make this connection. In fact, you rarely see analyses of patterns of domination — from intimate to corporate — in the mass media.

MEDIA CONTROL AND THE MASS MIND

WHO GETS ELECTED to political office is obviously affected by the information available to voters, not only about specific candidates but about issues. Here we face another threat to democracy and our day-to-day quality of life: the increasing concentration of media ownership in fewer and fewer hands.

In many nations, for example fundamentalist Iran, newspapers that don't conform to official dictates are shut down. Any deviation from officially approved policies, beliefs, or religious dogmas is censored and severely punished. Thankfully, we don't have this kind of media control in the United States. But here too we're seeing a radical narrowing of sources of news and opinions.

More and more independent newspapers are shut down or swallowed by huge media companies that control many publications. Even the Internet is becoming more centrally controlled, as both access and content are recentralized in the hands of ever fewer commercial entities like AOL/Time-Warner and the Microsoft Network.

In the first edition of his renowned book *The Media Monopoly,* published in 1983, Ben Bagdikian shocked the nation by reporting that fifty companies controlled most of America's mass media — newspapers, magazines, books, films, radio, television, cable, and music. In the 1997 edition of the book, the number had shrunk to ten.

By the 2000 edition of the book, it was down to only six: AOL/Time-Warner (which also owns substantial print media, including 24 magazines, among them, *Time, Fortune,* and *People*); Disney (which owns 22 major subsidiaries, including its enormous theme parks, the Disney Channel, and ABC); Viacom-CBS-Paramount; Bertelsmann (which owns an international media empire that includes the giant U.S. publisher Random House and its many subsidiaries, as well as Bantam Books, Doubleday, and Dell); Rupert Murdoch's News Corp. (which controls another international media empire, including HarperCollins, Twentieth Century Fox, the Fox Channel, 132 newspapers, and 25 magazines, including a percentage of *TV Guide*); and General Electric (which counts RCA and its subsidiary NBC among its holdings).[14]

As you can see by just turning on the TV, these and other corporate giants are spreading destructive messages about what is normal and desirable in human relations. This doesn't mean that there are bad people in these organizations. Most are simply repeating, and all too often amplifying, the kinds of messages they have learned to accept. They are people who were raised and are now living by deeply ingrained dominator rules. Hence, they also often tend to filter, shut out, or deny information that contradicts their worldview.

Denial is characteristic of dominator personalities who learn this fear-driven pattern of shutting down and filtering their perceptions early on. But denial is also characteristic of people who seek to justify their beliefs, actions, and lifestyles. So what we're dealing with is not an evil conspiracy or a matter of evil people. It is a problem built into dominator systems, which, to maintain themselves, block out anything that threatens them.

I emphasize this because the information I'm outlining is not intended to blame media people, the wealthy, or even the corporations that control the media. It is to alert you to a dangerous situation that will only change if enough of us, including people in the mega-corporations that today wield so much power, become aware of what is happening to the media — and to us.

TODAY CHILDREN GROW UP in homes where televisions are turned on for an average of seven hours per day — more time than most children spend in school or with their parents. The average child is likely to have watched 8,000 screen murders and more than 100,000 acts of violence by the end of elementary school. So by the time they are adults, violence seems natural, and uncaring and abusive relations seem acceptable, even entertaining.

As the former Dean of the University of Pennsylvania Annenberg School of Communication, George Gerbner writes, all this "cultivates an exaggerated sense of insecurity, mistrust, and anxiety about the mean world seen on television.... Media violence demonstrates power and paves the way for repression."[15]

Simply put, media violence and the normalization of insensitivity support dominator politics. When we condone, support, and export violent media, we are helping to create mindsets receptive to "strongman" leaders who can get things "back under control" with punitive rather than caring policies.

The ratio of men to women on U.S. television further supports dominator beliefs, habits, and policies. It is a shocking two to one.[16] What does this massive imbalance subliminally communicate to children and adults? Isn't it that men are more important than women? Not only that, what is communicated by the fact that women are disproportionately cast as the victims of crimes and violence? Doesn't this too reinforce the message that men are active, women are passive, and that violence against women is natural?

And doesn't the low ratio of poor people on television and the casting of people of color disproportionately as criminals or victims of crimes also invalidate the actual experiences, dreams, and needs of people of color? The huge toll of energy and the heroic fortitude it takes to live day in and day out with the grinding stress of racism, and the poverty that often goes with it, is virtually invisible on TV.

In contrast, white males are frequently cast in heroic roles, including roles where they have a great deal of power. Also, these male characters often acquire and use power through violence, further reinforcing dominator stereotypes of masculinity and once again communicating that violence is normal, even desirable, in human relations.

This problem is particularly serious in children's television programs and movies, where violence is regularly presented as manly and fun. In *Teenage Mutant Ninja Turtles* and its sequel *The Secret of Ooze*, for example, there are an average of 133 acts of mayhem per hour. As Gerbner writes, in this kind of film, "males fight, torture, gorge themselves on pizza (brand names prominently displayed), burn, crush, mutilate, and kill." As for women, in *Teenage Mutant Ninja Turtles*, "one lone mini-mini-skirted sex object (intrepid reporter bossed by boorish editors) is assaulted, scared, victimized, and rescued at least three times" until finally "she, too, kills and earns an appreciative 'You're a natural, Sis.'"[17]

Consider how these vivid images of violence as normal, heroic, and fun influence the developing brains of children. As discussed in earlier chapters, the brain's neural and biochemical networks — and with this, habits of thinking and behaving — are largely shaped in childhood by what we experience, including what we see modeled for us. These vividly brutal TV programs and films have an impact on the developing brain of a child. Video games are even more brutal,[18] and rap songs often aim much of their cruelty and violence at girls and women — for example, albums of Two Live Crew, Ice Cube, NWA, Cannibal Corpse, and Eminem feature songs with titles such as "Get Off My Dick" and "Tell Yo Bitch to Come Here." Even in the news, the most prominent headlines are reserved for acts of violence.

All this violent "entertainment" — which is exported worldwide

— poisons the minds of not only children but adults. It gives the false impression that pain and violence are the most interesting and news-worthy events and human behaviors. It constantly communicates, on both the conscious and unconscious level, that what counts in life is who inflicts pain and on whom pain is inflicted — the staples of dom-inator politics.

THE MEDIA AND DEMOCRACY

I DIDN'T ALWAYS THINK OF THE MEDIA as political. I certainly didn't think the media spread a regressive political agenda, having often heard corporate and political figures complain that the media are "too liberal."[19] It wasn't until I began to analyze the content of mass media systematically that it became evident — despite all the talk about democracy, freedom, and equality — that the media often support the opposite.

Not only do the media tend to make relations based on domination, and even violence, seem the inevitable order of things. The mass media, with only a few exceptions, have also steadily "dumbed down" their con-tent. This is true not only of television, but even of the print media, where there also has been a massive consolidation of ownership in book, newspaper, and magazine publishing.

While this dumbing down is sometimes justified on commercial grounds (the idea being that this is what a mass audience wants), it is actually a way to dumb down the mass audience, making us more easily manipulated both commercially and politically. As was often evident in the debates between Bush and Gore during the 2000 U.S. presidential campaign, the media force political candidates to dumb down their speeches and other messages, and instead fool around like comedians on late-night shows. This effectively substitutes superficial sound bites for serious coverage of important ideas and issues.

Consider that during the same period that Aid to Families with Dependent Children was massively cut, the U.S. government gave away millions of dollars to huge corporations to help them advertise their products overseas: for example, $16 million to Gallo, $9 million to Pillsbury, $4 million to M&M candies, $1 million to McDonald's, $1.5 million to Campbell's Soup, and $2 million to Fruit of the Loom.[20] But the mainstream press did not point out that this corporate welfare was the direct outcome of political contributions made by corporate interests, who quite literally are writing their own laws.[21]

It is scandalous that when tobacco giants gave millions to politicians to do their bidding, this only got a little story in the back pages of most newspapers. It doesn't take a rocket scientist to figure out that the Republican defeat in 1998 of anti-smoking legislation, which would have raised $516 billion over twenty-five years to improve the quality of education and other social services, was directly related to donations to Republicans by the tobacco companies. During 1997–1998, Philip Morris gave $2 million to Republicans (versus only $490,000 to Democrats) and R.J. Reynolds gave the GOP $1 million (versus only $100,000 to Democrats).[22]

Similarly, political contributions from communications and electronic industry sources to federal candidates in the 1995–1996 election cycle totaled over $53 million. However, barely mentioned in the news was the obvious fact that these contributions had something to do with the passage of the 1996 Telecommunications Act, which legalized the largest concentration of media control in U.S. history.[23]

Another thing you won't find making front-page news is the despotic nature of some of the regimes and would-be regimes our government has been arming and training. Even after the September 2001 terrorist attack on the United States that killed over five thousand people, only the alternative media pointed out that during the 1980s the Reagan administration supported — indeed, helped create — the Taliban to push the Soviets out of Afghanistan. And only alternative news outlets noted the fact that many of Osama bin Laden's cohorts, and possibly bin Laden himself — the people the U.S. government now holds responsible for this massacre — received military

and financial support from the C.I.A. and U.S.-supported fundamentalist Pakistanis.[24]

THE NARROWING OF THE INFORMATION available to us goes beyond
the subtle, and sometimes not so subtle, internal censorship of the
media that has been thoroughly documented by Ben Bagdikian,
Robert McChesney, Dean Alger, and others.[25] As Sheldon Rampton
and John Stauber document in *Trust Us, We're Experts,* almost half of
our news is now generated by public relations firms in the service
of major corporate interests.[26]

A study by the *Columbia Journalism Review* found that in a typical issue of the *Wall Street Journal* more than half the news stories were
based solely on press releases from public relations firms. Not only
that, video news releases — entire news stories written, filmed, and
produced by public relations firms — are transmitted by satellite feed
or the Internet to thousands of TV stations around the world. These
public relations firms are hired specifically to put a positive "spin" on
corporate activities and images.[27] So it shouldn't surprise us that our
news is heavily filtered even before it gets into the hands of the people
who decide what's fit to broadcast or print.

The seriousness of our environmental problems is another topic that
is treated gingerly by the mass media. Scientists keep warning us about
global warming, holes in the ozone layer, the loss of biodiversity, and
other threats to ecological balance — and hence to the health of every
one of us and even to our survival as a species. But these warnings are
rarely on our front pages. For example, in 1992, 1,700 scientists, including the majority of Nobel laureates from the sciences, issued "World
Scientists' Warning to Humanity," which spelled out why "if not
checked, many of our current practices put at serious risk the
future... and may so alter the living world that it will be unable to sus-
tain life."[28] But this dire warning wasn't even reported by most newspapers and TV newscasts. And when it was, it was tucked away as a short

item with no details or editorial comment. On the day of its release, the *New York Times* instead found front-page space for a story about the origins of rock and roll, and the *Globe and Mail's* front page made room for a large photo of cars arranged in the shape of Mickey Mouse.[29]

The mainstream media are owned by giant corporations, and their advertising customers are giant corporations. So the media constantly push consumption of ever more goods — and rarely mention the environmental depletion and pollution caused by overconsumption. They also rarely mention that many of the products they advertise damage our health. For example, as long as cigarette ads were a major source of revenue, the media rarely reported on the link between cigarettes and cancer. In the same way, we rarely see reports that dairy products are actually harmful to many people because of allergies, or that there are data linking prostate cancer to high consumption of dairy products.[30]

When I first became aware of these trends, I became angry and alarmed. Angry, because we depend on the media for reliable information. And alarmed because filtered and dumbed down information makes it difficult for any of us — including government and business policymakers — to make adaptive choices, much less to effectively participate in elections and other democratic processes.

GETTING DOWN TO FUNDAMENTALS

Now you may ask, how did we let all this happen in a nation that prides itself on its credo of freedom, equality, and democracy? How did our elections become a mass-marketing circus in which outcomes can be controlled by big donors? How did the free flow of information become so strangled by those who have economic, and therefore political, control? Why do we increasingly find ourselves in a nation where rankings of "superiors" over "inferiors" are protected by government policies, regardless of the costs to our health or environment?

One reason is, of course, the mass media itself, which constantly distract us by focusing our attention on a lurid murder trial, a sex scandal, sports, or fashion, while offering only the most superficial and all too often slanted coverage of the things that matter in our lives. Another reason is that we're busy just making ends meet. Americans today work more hours than workers in any other industrialized nation, including Japan. When we come home tired and just want to spend some time with our families, or simply relax, it's hard to make the effort to find out what's really going on in the world.

But the problem goes far deeper. A major aspect of the contemporary dominator regression is a concerted push back to the kinds of parent-child and gender relations that promote acceptance of top-down rankings across the board. Indeed, one of the most dangerous aspects of the current dominator regression is the worldwide push to strengthen the kinds of family and gender relations that are the foundation on which the entire dominator pyramid rests.

You may think that politics has nothing to do with what happens in intimate relationships, and vice versa. But if that's the case, why do you think political regressions — be they rightist or leftist, religious or secular — have focused so much on pushing us back to domination and submission in the relations between parents and children and between women and men?

The reason is that these intimate relations are where we first learn to accept domination and control as normal, inevitable, and right or where we learn partnership ways of life. This is why many of the most repressive modern regimes — from Hitler's Germany and Stalin's Soviet Union to Khomeini's Iran and the Taliban of Afghanistan — have sprung up where family and gender relations based on domination and submission are firmly in place. It is also why, once in power, these regimes have vigorously pushed policies that have as their goal the reinstatement of a punitive father in complete control of his family.

WE SEE THIS PATTERN ALL TOO CLEARLY in one of the most serious aspects of the dominator regression of our time: the rise of so-called religious fundamentalism. I say *so-called* because, if we look closely, it's clear that what many fundamentalist leaders preach — be it in the Middle East or the United States — is not religious fundamentalism but the domination/control model with a religious spin.

If you look closely at the teachings and policies advocated by leaders of the Christian Right in the United States, you will see that they are often the polar opposite of the teachings of Jesus. Whereas Jesus challenged the rigid rule of the religious hierarchies of his time, these men (and occasional women) are bent on controlling all aspects of our lives — from our family relations to our political relations. Whereas Jesus taught caring, compassion, empathy, and nonviolence — in a word, the fundamentals of partnership — the leaders of the Christian Right preach the fundamentals of the domination model. They preach fear, as in "You've got to put the fear of God into people," guilt, as in "You're a sinner," prejudice, as in the vilifying of people of different races or sexual orientations, and scapegoating, as in "Feminists are out to destroy the family."

If you look at the Gospels, you will find that Jesus did not say anything about strengthening male power over women. On the contrary, when he preached against divorce, it was to protect women from being thrown out on the street by their husbands, as divorce was in his time the right of men only. He said nothing about keeping women out of the priesthood. Indeed, we know from the New Testament that many of the leaders in early Christian communities were women.[31] We know from the Gnostic Gospels that, rather than being a prostitute, Mary Magdalene was a major figure in early Christian leadership.[32] As for violence against women, Jesus prevented the stoning death of a woman accused of sexual independence.

By contrast, the aim of fundamentalist leaders — whether in the U.S., India, Iran, or Pakistan — is to push women back into their controlled place. In some Muslim nations, women are still publicly stoned to death. So-called honor killings by members of their own families of girls and women suspected of any sexual independence are socially condoned. In the United States, the bombing of family planning clinics and the murder of physicians, nurses, and volunteers who help women exercise their constitutional right to reproductive choice is incited by some fundamentalist leaders. In Afghanistan, Osama bin Laden and other fundamentalist leaders command that women who don't follow their oppressive dictates be killed. Indeed, one of the reasons for their anti-American rage is that they see the higher status of Western women as a threat to their regressive social order.[33]

If you look at the political agenda of fundamentalists — Muslim, Hindu, Jewish, or Christian — what really interests them is reimposing the system of rigid top-down control basic to the dominator configuration. This configuration consists of strong-man rule in both the family and the state, the ranking of the male half of humanity over the female half, and fear and institutionalized violence to maintain rankings — be they man over woman, man over man, race over race, or religion over religion. (This configuration is outlined in the "Partnership/Domination Continuum" in the "More Partnership Tools" section at the end of this book.)

A centerpiece of the fundamentalist political agenda is that women must be returned to their "traditional" place in a family where the authority of the father is unquestioned. Of course, women sometimes rule over men, but then they're seen as usurpers, as in the phrases "henpecking wife" and "she's wearing the pants in the family."

This goal of preventing gender equality is why the rightist-fundamentalist alliance in the United States rallied to defeat the proposed Equal Rights Amendment to the U.S. Constitution, which would simply have declared that federal and state laws may not discriminate on the basis of sex. It is why fundamentalist leaders in the U.S. are so fiercely opposed to reproductive freedom for women, why they are so virulently hostile to gays (who in their eyes violate the God-given order of a man never taking the subservient role of a woman), and why they have even opposed federal legislation to protect women from violence as well as government funding for shelters for abused women (as in former Senator Laxalt's so-called Family Protection Act). It is also why organizations such as the Promise Keepers offer men the false choice between neglecting or abandoning their families and "regaining control."

Another key element of the U.S. fundamentalist agenda is that children must, on pain of the most severe punishment, learn that their parents' will is law. This is why fundamentalists support programs such as those that claim to teach parents how to raise their child "God's way" that we looked at in chapter 2 — programs designed to terrorize babies into absolute obedience. And unfortunately, because this way of structuring relations is familiar and thus comfortable for people who carry the pain, frustration, and anger of dominator childrearing, such programs flourish.

YOU MAY ASK, what does all this mean for me? I don't have, and don't want to have, this kind of family. While this dominator agenda may not affect your family directly, it leads to regressive social attitudes, policies, and behaviors that counter the American credo of freedom and equality for all.

These trends in the U.S. and worldwide are dangerous to each and every one of us. They may seem to affect only those directly impacted by them. But they work to undermine the centuries-long movement toward partnership. They are designed to reinstate traditions of domination and submission in the parent-child and gender relations that are the foundations on which the entire dominator pyramid rests.

STRENGTHENING OR DISMANTLING THE FOUNDATIONS FOR DOMINATION

IF WE WANT A TRULY DEMOCRATIC SOCIETY, we can no longer afford to ignore the political importance of parent-child and woman-man relations, where we first learn, and continually practice, democratic or undemocratic relations. When children grow up in families where they learn that men are superior to women and parental orders must be obeyed at all costs, they learn to accept relations based on domination and submission as normal and right. Of course, not everyone remains caught in this trap. Some of us try our best to transcend our dominator upbringings. Some even try to change these patterns in the world around us. But many more pass on habits of domination and submission unconsciously from generation to generation.

The problem is that many people who have only experienced relations of domination and submission in their early years believe there is only one alternative: you either dominate or you're dominated. They can't imagine any other way. In their mental maps for relations, rankings of domination and submission are inevitable and even moral. Such people are extremely uncomfortable with anything that threatens this "natural order." During stressful periods of rapid change such as ours, they can be easily manipulated by demagogic leaders who promise to "get things back under control."

Just as their obedience, and even love, was harshly demanded by their punitive parents, many people who are brought up in the dominator way become enraged at those who won't "stay in their place." And just as abused children often repress their rage toward abusive parents (as they must to survive) and divert it against children they perceive as weak, these people often scapegoat groups they see as weak or feminine — and feminine is the same as weak in the dominator mind.

They express contempt for more sensitive men in popular phrases such as "sissy," "pussy-whipped," and "mama's boy." Racial and ethnic minorities, women, gays, and lesbians are often their targets for vilification and persecution. Caring people are contemptuously dismissed as "do-gooders" or "bleeding hearts." Government leaders who aren't "properly masculine" are demonized and hounded from office, if possible. On the other hand, leaders who stand primarily for control and punishment are respected, and even loved — in still another replay of the emotional habits learned in dominator families.

THE POLICIES OF LEADERS TRAPPED in dominator mindsets and emotional habits also follow a familiar pattern. Because nurturing and caring are associated with the "women's work" of mothering, a politics guided by a more stereotypically feminine definition of power as empowering rather than disempowering is unthinkable to the properly socialized dominator psyche.

How shocking this idea is to such people is illustrated by an article called "The Ideology of Sensitivity" in the rightist-fundamentalist journal *Imprimis*. In the view of its author, a more empathic and caring politics is dangerous, ridiculous, and un-American. It would, he sarcastically claimed, replace Big Brother with Big Nanny.[34]

What really lies behind this horror of sensitivity and caring in politics are deeply ingrained psycho-social dynamics rooted in dominator family relations. Just as the nurturing and caring parent is the metaphor for a politics of partnership, the punitive, distant parent is the metaphor for a politics of domination. I say nurturing or punitive parent, even though in dominator societies parental punitiveness is associated primarily with the father (as in, "Wait till your father gets home"), and parental nurturing is associated with mothering.

Following the politics of domination, politicians backed by the U.S. rightist-fundamentalist alliance always find money for the "men's work" of wars and bigger and costlier weapons systems such as the multibillion-dollar missile-defense shield.[35] And this despite the fact that the most serious threat to our national security today is from terrorism — from domestic flights flown into buildings, as in the horrible New York and Washington, D.C., hijackings of September 2001, and from biological agents or other portable weapons technologies — for which such a missile-defense shield would be useless (even in the doubtful case that it would actually work).

Also following the old role of the male head of the family, these kinds of politicians always find money to punish rather than to nurture (nurturing being the stereotypical female role). They have no trouble finding money to build more and more prisons, for example. But they can never find enough money to provide better care for children — even though high-quality childcare has not only been proven to prevent violence, but is foundational to human development.[36]

We need to change this. If we want to strengthen our democratic institutions, if we want relations of mutual respect and partnership in all aspects of our lives, we must help others become aware of these connections. We have to help them understand that what is often being promoted as religious fundamentalism today is not a matter of religion, but of ensuring that two of the cornerstones for a partnership society — partnership parent-child relations and partnership gender relations — do not replace the kinds of relations that are foundational to a dominator society.

Above all, we must regain the political initiative. If we are to become politically proactive rather than just reactive, we need to join together to develop and promote a new partnership political agenda that supports relations that are respectful of people's dignity and rights both nationally and internationally.

THE POLITICS OF PARTNERSHIP

HOW WILL FUTURE GENERATIONS SEE our time? Will they look back at it as a period when the United States was retreating from the vision that inspired its founders? Will they be living in a nation of glaring contrasts of poverty and wealth, of homelessness, hopelessness, and heartlessness? Will they see in the mass media and in much of reality a culture that is violent, polarized, and cynical? Will their families and education conform to traditions of domination rather than supporting real democracy? Or will they see a renewed flowering of the American vision of equality, democracy, respect, and freedom for all?

As you have seen, many gains already made are in jeopardy today. It's easy to get discouraged or, like the proverbial child with its finger in the dike, try to plug the rising waters of dominator regression one hole at a time, always from a defensive position. But this piecemeal approach doesn't help us build anything substantial for the future, or prevent more waves of dominator regressions.

It is precisely during periods of regression that we need to be proactive rather than just reactive. In the first stage of the modern partnership movement, the emphasis was primarily on the top of the dominator pyramid, on economic and political relations in the so-called public sphere. Very little emphasis was placed on the so-called private sphere of relations — the relations between parents and children, and between the female and male halves of humanity — which were seen as secondary "women's issues" and "children's issues." As a result, we still lack the solid foundations on which to base a truly democratic and equitable society.

Today we are at the threshold of a crucial second stage in the challenge to traditions of domination: a politics of partnership that encompasses *both* the public and private spheres of human relations.

This integrated partnership political agenda focuses on four cornerstones:

- Partnership childhood relations
- Partnership gender relations
- Partnership economics
- Cultural beliefs, myths, and stories that support partnership

There are key strategic building blocks to put each of these cornerstones in place — and every one of us can help with their construction.

ONE THING EVERY ONE OF US CAN DO IS RECLAIM emotionally laden words such as *tradition, morality, family,* and *values*. These words are being misused to drive us back to the "good old days" when

all women and most men knew their place in rigid rankings of domination.

When you're told we need to strengthen families, you can ask
what kinds of families — and explain that democratic families are
foundational to real democracy. You can point out that the phrase
"family values" has been used to push us back to a male-controlled
family where women can manipulate but cannot assert themselves (a
recipe for misery for both women and men), and where children are
taught early that love is conditional on absolute obedience to orders,
no matter how unjust or painful they may be.

When you're told we must be more moral, you can ask whether it
is moral to dominate others, and even to kill people of different beliefs
or lifestyles. When you're told we must go back to "traditional values,"
you can make people aware of older traditions — traditions of partnership rather than domination that date back thousands of years.[37]

The chart "The Vocabulary of Partnership and Domination" in
"The Politics of Partnership" at the end of this book provides partnership alternatives to these emotionally loaded phrases.

A major goal of the partnership political agenda is ending the violence against children and women that has traditionally been used to
maintain — and provide a basic model for — relations of domination
and submission. With the kinds of resources that have been put into
campaigns such as the "war on drugs," a national as well as international
campaign to stop intimate violence can have enormous impact. It can
help the millions who are beaten, raped, and at risk of being killed. It
can help both victims and perpetrators regain their essential human dignity. It can bring together people from all segments of the current political spectrum — religious and secular as well as conservative and liberal.
And it can help us dismantle two cornerstones on which the dominator
pyramid rests: dominator parent-child and dominator gender relations.

Encouraging organizations to unite behind such an anti-violence
campaign can be as easy as including a letter asking them to do this

with your contribution check. You can then give preferentially to organizations that cooperate.

You can invite community leaders to state that intimate violence is immoral, intolerable, and must be stopped. You can start by approaching religious leaders. Some religious organizations are already joining human rights groups in condemning family violence. For example, in October 2000, Imam Abdul Khan and other Muslim clerics joined Bonita McGee, a Muslim activist supporting battered women, in a meeting organized to address domestic violence among immigrants from the Middle East and Asia.[38]

Imagine what would happen if cardinals and bishops, as well as rabbis, pastors, priests, and mullahs, regularly preached from their pulpits that beating your wife or child is a sin. Or if antiviolence messages from movie stars like Clint Eastwood and Mel Gibson or sports heroes like Junior Seau and Tiger Woods disentangled "real masculinity" from violence? Or if Oprah gave top priority to a campaign to end violence against children and women? Our world might change dramatically overnight.

SOMETIMES JUST TALKING TO A FRIEND or colleague about the partnership political agenda can be a powerful step forward. You can do simple things, such as giving a friend an article you found interesting that exemplifies the partnership model in action. One place you can find a wealth of information is on the website for the Center for Partnership Studies, at www.partnershipway.org, where it is easy to find and forward articles to friends.

You can also point out that the terms *free enterprise* and *free market* are often code words for economic predation, worker exploitation, and environmental degradation — and that these practices are mainly the result of bad economic rules and models rather than bad people. Free enterprise is not free when megacorporations are writing their own rules. Corporate charters requiring social and environmental responsibility, campaign financing reform that prevents politicians from being legally purchased by large contributors, and economic inventions that recognize and adequately reward caregiving work can all help us build the third cornerstone for a partnership society: partnership economics.[39]

Without new corporate charters that require accountability not only to shareholders but all stakeholders — including employees, host communities, and the larger global community and natural environment that are impacted — we cannot expect to change dominator economic practices. Without real political campaign finance reform — that is, limiting not only campaign donations but also limiting campaign spending through public campaign financing — we cannot speak of real democracy.

Without community support for training and adequate economic rewards for the socially essential work of caregiving in both the formal and informal economy, we won't have the high-quality human capital needed for the postindustrial economy. Nor will we be able to end poverty and discrimination or ensure a better life for our children and grandchildren.

As you will see in the chart "The Four Cornerstones of the Partnership Political Agenda" in "The Politics of Partnership" at the end of this book, there is also a great deal you can do to help build the fourth cornerstone for a partnership society: cultural beliefs, myths, and stories that support partnership. For starters, you can work to persuade as many organizations as possible to back partnership education, which includes parenting and childcare classes in schools. You can enlist business leaders by pointing out that this education is needed to ensure our nation has the high-quality workforce required for the postindustrial economy. You can introduce partnership educational ideas and programs into schools and PTA meetings. You can become a partnership educator yourself, and inspire young people to do the same.[40]

AS YOU'VE SEEN THROUGHOUT this book, the first step for change is expanding awareness. When Thomas Jefferson and other framers of the U.S. Declaration of Independence met in Philadelphia in 1776 to affirm that "all men are created equal," they expanded the awareness not only of their contemporaries but of future generations to the possibility of partnership/respect in political relations. When Elizabeth Cady Stanton and other activists gathered in Seneca Falls, New York, in 1848 to formulate a more inclusive declaration of independence stating that "all men *and women* are created equal," they set in motion another major expansion of awareness. When Martin Luther King, Rosa Parks, and other civil rights activists defied the segregated bus system in Montgomery, Alabama, in 1956, they too expanded awareness. In all these cases expanded awareness led to purposeful action.

Countless other people whose names are not in our history books have also expanded our awareness and launched important actions. A former Boston socialite who took the name Laura X has devoted every cent she had to raising awareness about marital rape, launching a successful state-by-state effort to pass laws against these crimes of sexual violence. Mary Hernandez, an insurance auditor and mother of three children, and Sylvia Herrera, a mother of two children, organized PODER (People's Organization in Defense of the Earth and its Resources) and took on Exxon, Chevron, and other oil company giants to protect their children's health from toxic emissions.[41] Two high school students, Jeff Johnson and Margarita Herrera, organized a team of young people to turn weed-infested empty lots into vegetable gardens, bringing social entrepreneurship, good food, beauty, and income into their inner city neighborhoods.

Susanna Martin, a twenty-two-year-old bank clerk from the Bronx, founded one of the first centers for battered women in the United States after a friend was beaten to death by her husband. Morris Dees and Joe Levin founded the Southern Poverty Law Center, which has brought successful lawsuits against white supremacists and other hate groups. Belvie Rooks developed workshops to empower African American and Hispanic kids through real-life stories of young people who have what I call spiritual courage — the courage to non-violently stand up against injustice.

All these people — young and old, black and white, female and male — did something that changed our nation for the better. So you see that "ordinary" people like you and I have done, and continue to do, extraordinary things.

We need to work together. We need both more focus and more determination. We have to be in this for the long run. None of us can do everything. But all of us can do something.

Making the changes needed for a partnership culture will not be easy. Each step will be fiercely resisted. But by working together for the integrated partnership agenda described in this chapter (and in the chart called "The Politics of Partnership" at the end of this book), we can help realize the American dream of freedom and equality for all.

PUTTING PARTNERSHIP TO WORK

Whether we think of ourselves as liberals, conservatives, or neither, none of us profits when our nation drifts away from the ideals of democracy, equality, respect, and freedom that inspired its creation.

Think about political candidates. How do their policies support or oppose partnership relations? If none of them seems to understand partnership, vote for the one most closely aligned with partnership principles, even if you don't agree with everything they do or say. If you don't vote, you give a green light to regressive candidates.

It's hard to tell from the popular media if a candidate's politics support a partnership or a dominator agenda. You can get helpful information from the newsletters of organizations such as the League of Women Voters, Common Cause, the National Association for the Advancement of Colored People (NAACP), The Simon Wiesenthal Center, People for the American Way, the Children's Defense Fund, Children Now, the Older Women's League (OWL), the American Friends Service Committee (Quakers), the International Partnership Network (IPN), Greenpeace, Friends of the Earth, Rainforest Action Network, and Co-op America.[42] You can also subscribe to alternative publications such as *Women's International Network (WIN) News, Too Much, Ms., New Moon, E Magazine, The Utne Reader, Yes!, The Nation, Business Ethics, Mother Jones,* and *The Washington Spectator.*

The antitrust laws on our books must be used to break up media monopolies. You can play a part in seeing these laws enforced by persuading organizations you support to join a coalition to this end.[43]

You can tell your representatives that you want them to promote the partnership political agenda. As you get more involved in politics, you may want to run for office yourself. You can begin with your school board, water board, and city or county board of supervisors.

The main thing is to raise awareness, whenever you can, about the partnership alternative and to enlist others to work for a unified politics of partnership. The chart "The Four Cornerstones of the Partnership Political Agenda" at the end of this book is a useful tool. A second chart, "Exposing the Dominator Political Agenda," compares partnership and dominator politics. You can use these charts, other materials in "The Politics of Partnership," and this chapter to persuade organizations to support this unified political agenda.

ACTION CHECKLIST

FIRST STEPS

❑ Observe what comes to mind when you think of power. Consider how power in dominator relations is defined as power over others. Then jot down words and phrases that describe power in partnership relations.

❑ When you look at the newspaper or watch TV news, notice how your day-to-day life is affected by whether government and business decisions support dominator or partnership relations. Take note of domination model events and contrast them with partnership-oriented events.

❑ Consider how TV situation "comedies" promote relations based on put-downs, insults, and violence, making dominator relations seem normal and even fun.

❑ Consider how those who hold economic power control public debate and the flow of information, and how democracy is compromised by the unbridled influence of economic interests over politics and the media.

❑ Discuss your new perspective on politics and the media with your family and friends.

NEXT STEPS

❑ Move discussions past old categories such as right versus left, capitalism versus communism, liberal versus conservative, and religious versus secular. Encourage others to also look for dominator and partnership patterns.

❑ Form a group to discuss and act on the materials in this chapter. Use "The Politics of Partnership" material at the end of this book.

❑ Subscribe to journals, periodicals, and newsletters that offer independent views on contemporary issues.

❑   Work for a more democratic media and to introduce media literacy into schools and community study groups.

❑   In the next election, think about the candidates' positions from the perspective of the partnership-domination continuum.

❑   Promote the partnership political agenda through the Internet, by writing letters to the editor, calling into radio talk shows, and writing articles for newsletters of organizations and associations to which you belong or for newspapers, magazines, and other mainstream media.

GOING FURTHER

❑   Include this chapter and "The Politics of Partnership" material at the end of this book in letters to heads of organizations, and invite them to work for the four cornerstones of the partnership political agenda.

❑   Invite your friends, colleagues, and religious leaders to form a task force to end intimate violence. Invite celebrities, business leaders, and public officials to be participants and sponsors. Ask local, state, and federal officials to allocate money for this effort.

❑   Organize a public forum to raise consciousness about the need for a truly free press.

❑   Encourage organizations to form an alliance to support the higher economic valuation of caring and caregiving work as foundational to a more just, equitable, and caring economics.

❑   Meet with parents and teachers to discuss how schools can incorporate resources from this chapter in history and civics classes. Work with community leaders to introduce partnership education into schools. (*Tomorrow's Children* is a good resource. You can get more resources from the Partnership Education Institute of the Center for Partnership Studies at www.partnershipway.org.)

❑   Form a group to share ideas on how to build a partnership
    model of political organizing, and put these ideas into action
    locally, nationally, and internationally.

Your Relationship with the International Community

THE WORLD AROUND US

What does living in a "global village" mean for you? Does it really affect your life, or is it just another catchy phrase? And even if what happens fifteen thousand miles away has an impact on your security, your health, and your pocketbook, is there anything you can do about it?

In this chapter, you will see that because we live in an age when not only technologies of communication but technologies of destruction make distances irrelevant, a global shift from domination to partnership is urgently needed. You will also see that there is a great deal every one of us can do to help support and accelerate this shift.

MANY THINGS WE ENJOY in the United States were brought here from other places. We dance to Latin American and African music. We wear French and Italian fashions. We delight in Chinese and Mexican food. Because ours is a nation of people from many world regions, we can learn about different cultural traditions from our friends and acquaintances.

I know how fascinating it is to learn about different cultures from my own experience as an immigrant growing up in three different countries. Having to flee our home in Austria to escape the Holocaust was extremely painful for me and my parents. But moving from one culture to another also greatly enriched my life and my understanding of the world. I learned to love many musical heritages — Viennese waltzes and the classical music of Europe, the Spanish- and African-influenced music of Cuba, and later the folk and African-American music of the United States. I learned three languages — German, Spanish, and English — and a smattering of French and Italian. And I learned a great deal about how different cultural traditions affect how we see the world.

Having been born in Vienna, I was exposed to its cultural heritage of beautiful music, architecture, and art. At the same time, I felt the brunt of its cultural tradition of anti-Semitism. Growing up in a poor part of Havana, but going to the best private schools because my parents made my education their priority, I learned how different the beliefs and habits of the rich and poor can be, even in the same country. I came to love the warmth of many of the Cuban people, their tradition of hospitality, and their amazing *Comparsas,* when fantastically dressed dancers gyrated sensuously through the city streets during the yearly carnival. But living in a Cuba fomenting revolution against a sham democracy dominated by U.S. sugar- and tobacco-growing corporations and Cuban presidents who pocketed millions, I also learned about traditions of corruption. And I learned about traditions of violence from the battles between rival revolutionary factions as well as from the domestic violence that was common among our neighbors.

All this taught me two basic lessons that have served me well, both in my life and my scholarship. I learned that what people consider "just the way things are" is different in different places. And I learned that not every cultural tradition should be preserved.

Certainly, valuing difference is basic to partnership relations. We should value people from different cultural traditions. Whenever possible, we should preserve historical and ethnic traditions. But we also should look at cultural traditions in the same way we look at individual behaviors. We should ask if a cultural tradition promotes cruelty and abuse or caring and respect.

There is a huge difference between the deep sense of connection we feel with our ethnic or religious roots and the in-group versus out-group thinking and violence that is our dominator heritage. To see the difference, you only have to look at the "ethnic cleansings" of Bosnia and Kosovo, at the carnage of tribal warfare in Rwanda, and at the way religion is being used to spread hate and violence, as in the terrorism against children, women, and men by so-called Muslim fundamentalists, now even on American soil. When terrorists kill and maim innocent strangers in the name of God and tradition, as in the 2001 New York Trade Center and Pentagon attacks, when hoodlums dressed in western clothes gun down women for not shrouding themselves in traditional Muslim garb, when they blow up buses with children in them, what is being advanced in the name of religious or cultural traditions are traditions of domination and violence.

What I am talking about is not an "us versus them" attitude. It is applying the same standards of human rights and responsibilities provided by the partnership model to all cultures — our own and that of others.

This is not idealistic, it is realistic. In a world where technologies of communication and destruction span the globe almost instantaneously, creating a better world is a matter of enlightened self-interest. If we swallow whole cultural habits and practices that devalue and brutalize human life, we fail to help those who most need help. We also perpetuate entrenched power imbalances that can then explode not only in intranational violence but also in international violence — including violence against us.

Think about what kind of world your children will live in. Will it still be a place where behind the facade of the lovely travel ads — scenic beaches, expensive hotels, and exotic dancing girls — the vast majority of the world's children, women, and men live in abject poverty? Will it still be a place where the vast majority of nations are dictatorships or sham democracies? Will the U.S. continue to arm repressive and exploitive regimes that train future terrorists, as it did in Afghanistan with the fanatic mujahideen who are Osama bin Laden's cohorts?[1] Will our policies still fail to support family planning even as global population soars?

Think about the effect of our national policies. Think about the suffering — the hunger, poverty, and violence — many of these policies cause. Then think about how today there are more and more people in the world who see you and your children as the enemy simply because you are Americans.

Consider that some of these people are in governments that have nerve gas, biological weapons, or nuclear bombs, that some are terrorists who hijack airliners and blow up buildings, and that they invoke cultural and religious traditions to justify their brutal acts. Then think about whether you want to passively accept all this or help shift our world from dominator habits and relations to partnership habits and relations.

HELPING US AND THEM

WE LIVE IN A WORLD interconnected by new ecological, technological, and economic realities. Infectious diseases such as AIDS, mad cow disease, and tuberculosis quickly spread from continent to continent. Our economy is impacted by what happens in foreign countries, and vice versa, as we saw in 1998 when the Asian "little tigers" economies slumped and the U.S. bailed them out with our tax dollars. Whether a nation's air and seas are clean or polluted is also an international matter. As the preamble of the proposed Earth Charter states, today "everyone shares responsibility for the present and future well-being of the human family and the larger living world."[2]

We certainly can't solve all the problems of the world's peoples. But they are increasingly not just their problems, but our problems.

I didn't always think this way. There was a time when I didn't even want to think of all the injustice, violence, and suffering in our world. I told myself that there was nothing I could do about it and, anyway, it was too overwhelming. My personal life was more than enough for me to deal with.

Then I began to realize that many of my personal problems were connected with social problems, and that whether I liked it or not, I had to address both. As my awareness changed, I became a social activist, first in my community and nation, and later internationally.

In 1984, for example, I went to the former Soviet Union with a group of women from Europe and the United States to talk with Soviet women about nonviolent solutions to global problems. I found that, despite our differences, we all shared a deep desire for peace. In 1985, I went to Kenya with my husband to attend the third United Nations Conference on Women. Again, even though the people at that historic meeting came from different corners of the world, we all had common concerns and goals.

Being with thousands of women from all world regions who had also concluded that we must join together to make a better world, not just for our children but for all children, was an extraordinary experience. It powerfully reaffirmed what I already knew in my heart — that all the world's people are inextricably linked. It also heightened my awareness that most of the world's problems are the result of a domination model of relations — and that if enough of us join together to shift relations to partnership we can make a big difference.

THE FIRST STEP IS AWARENESS OF THESE INTERCONNECTIONS. From this new awareness, action follows. Our actions are cumulative, and no matter how small what we each do may seem in relation to the vast problems in our world, what each of us does — or does not do — is important.

You're undoubtedly aware of the ravages of intertribal warfare in places such as Rwanda and Sudan. But you might not be aware that most of the weapons that kill and maim millions of African children and adults have been exported by Western nations such as the United States, France, and Russia. Weapons manufacturers such as General Electric, General Dynamics, Lockheed, Hughes, and Thompson enrich themselves and their shareholders at the expense of this bloodshed. You might want to ask yourself if you're unwittingly contributing to this carnage by purchasing and holding shares in these companies or in mutual funds that hold such companies.

You can instead invest in socially and environmentally responsible companies. There are mutual funds that screen their investments, such as Calvert, Women's Equity, Domini, and Parnassus (you can find others on http://www.socialinvest.org/). Many of these funds do extremely well. For example, Domini outperformed most mutual funds in 1997, 1998, 1999, and 2000.

You can also ask yourself whether you support companies — by purchasing their products — that do not provide a living wage or safe working conditions. Many multinational companies manufacture products in Asian and Latin American sweatshops where workers — generally the young women dubbed "maquiladoras" — work for pennies an hour. You can stop buying products from them, and tell others to do the same.

These boycotts make a difference. A boycott against Nike forced its management to begin looking into the abuses of workers in their overseas sweatshops. Lists of socially and environmentally responsible companies are available from Co-op America and other organizations. You can use these lists to guide you in letting your money work for the kind of world you want.

You may also want to ask yourself if you voted for the politicians who cut funding for family planning. Or did you help put them in office by not voting at all? When U.S. legislators cut back funding for the U.N. Population Fund and other international agencies, they cause enormous human suffering. They also contribute to the extinction of many species. Think of all the wildlife disappearing as a consequence of the doubling of the human population in Africa every forty years.

As you look at the urban slums of the developing world on TV, you can think about some of the policies today driving economic globalization. What is the real effect of so-called structural adjustment policies that nations such as the United States demand through powerful international agencies? What happens to people when the International Monetary Fund (IMF) requires a debtor nation to cut essential government services for health, food, and education so that they can redirect more resources into private industry? What does this push toward privatization mean for families with barely enough to eat, no safe drinking water, and no money to buy medicines when their children get sick? What do these cuts mean for the lives of the homeless children wandering the streets of cities in the developing world? When these children grow up, will they see you and your children as the enemy because of U.S. policies that further enrich the rich and impoverish the poor?

According to United Nations figures, the majority of African children are malnourished and hungry. The policies of Western nations contribute to the suffering and untimely deaths of these children. For example, the bulk of international loans and technological aid is typically funneled to large landowners who grow crops for exports that often also enrich Western companies. But women — who in Africa do the subsistence farming — get hardly any help or support as they struggle to feed their families.

When you read about the hundreds of pairs of shoes (allegedly *three thousand*) owned by Imelda Marcos, the widow of the former president/dictator of the Philippines, or about the enormous wealth of the ruling Sukarno and Suharto families and their cronies in Indonesia, ask to what extent our foreign policies have helped line their pockets. Have you silently acquiesced to foreign aid and economic policies that maintain corrupt and exploitive regimes in power?3

By your inaction, aren't you in the long run endangering your life and the lives of your children, given the rise of anti-American terrorism? Since terrorism is often encouraged and funded by the ruling families of tyrannical regimes to deflect attention from themselves, is U.S. government support of such regimes to protect oil companies or other U.S. financial interests really in our best interests?

Once again, you don't have to passively accept any of this. When in May 2001 the Bush administration gave a gift of forty-three million dollars to the Taliban rulers of Afghanistan — the most virulent anti-American violators of human rights in the world today and the protectors of Osama bin Laden — what kind of signal did this send about our nation's real position on human rights?4 And what particularly did it say about our position on the human rights of women, which are nonexistent under the Taliban? You can tell your elected officials you want more humane and sensible foreign policies, and vote for those who will implement these.

You can also exert pressure on corporations that enrich despotic regimes by refusing to buy their products or use their services, and writing to their CEOs to let them know exactly why. This kind of feedback is very effective if enough people do it.

WORKING FOR HUMAN RIGHTS

AS YOU CAN SEE FROM these examples, what we do or fail to do in the United States influences much that happens in the world. But the point is not to blame the world's problems on the United States.

The constant finger-pointing at the West as the world's villain is both unfair and unsound. The reality is much more complex.

Traditions of domination are still strong all over the world. At the same time, movement toward partnership is also strong, both in the United States and abroad. There is a constant sparring between old habits of domination and new partnership habits. Anything you can do to help those who value human rights can tilt this contest toward freedom and equality.

Unfortunately, the TV show *Star Trek*'s prime directive of noninterference on other planets doesn't work for earthbound cultures. (I'm not sure the directive is suitable in *Star Trek* either). The reality is that we cannot afford to let old dominator patterns elsewhere continue without comment or action.

None of this means judging other cultures by what is considered normal in our culture or subculture. Quite the contrary. It means understanding the conditions that lead people to embrace traditions of domination, and working to change those conditions.

We need standards for what traditions should be strengthened or left behind. Slavery, serfdom, and public stonings of women once were, and in some places still are, cultural traditions. They are cultural traditions appropriate to maintain dominator relations. So when we look at cultural traditions, the key question is *what kinds of relations do they maintain?* Do they maintain relations of domination/control or relations of partnership/respect? Do they protect human rights? Or do they condone or even command human rights violations?

Promoting human rights standards worldwide is central to an integrated partnership political agenda. Without these standards we cannot develop the new personal and political ethic needed to transform these dangerous times. Every one of us, not just policymakers, can help support the development and implementation of these standards.

At the same time that we empathize with those who have been

taught to accept unjust and violent traditions, it is essential that we encourage them to move toward more peaceful, equitable, and pleasurable ways of relating. Rather than being divisive, working for universal human rights can unite us across the widest geographic and cultural barriers.

During the 1993 United Nations World Conference on Human Rights, a number of nations, including China and Iran, argued that charging nations with human rights violations was an interference with national sovereignty and cultural tradition. Fortunately, these arguments were rejected in the resolutions that came out of that meeting, largely due to the leadership of the U.S. delegation sent by the Clinton administration.

One of the most important events at this conference, however, was the result of actions by people like you and me. At a Global Tribunal on Violations of Women's Human Rights organized by women's groups, women from twenty-five countries testified to atrocious human rights abuses. These included mass rapes of women by Serbs, Bosnians, and Croats; Muslim fundamentalists burning down a widow's house (causing the death of her baby son) to "cleanse the neighborhood" of the "impurity" of women living alone in their community; economic discrimination depriving women of legitimate income and property rights; the sale of girls and women into the international sex trade; female sexual mutilation; and beatings and other forms of family violence that blight the lives of millions of women worldwide.[5]

This tribunal, and the persistent lobbying of women's groups, led to a landmark ruling by the war crimes court based in The Hague, Holland. In February 2001, for the first time in history, an international court ruled that mass rape is a crime against humanity. Until then, the military tradition of mass rape had been accepted as a natural occurrence in war. Mass rapes and other forms of sexual violence against women, such as forced prostitution by victorious armies, were never prosecuted by the international war crimes courts established after World War II. In sharp contrast, the 2001 ruling proclaimed that mass rape is the second most serious category of international crime after genocide.[6]

This historic ruling would never have happened had it not been for grassroots women's groups all over the world. It highlights the fact that each of us can make a difference. It also highlights the need for the integrated partnership political agenda described in chapter 4 that places the human rights of the majority — women and children — in a central rather than peripheral place. We need an integrated politics of partnership that affirms freedom from violence, cruelty, and want as primary rights for all of humanity.

WHEN WE WORK FOR THE HUMAN RIGHTS of women and children, we work for a better life for everyone. The violations of women's and children's human rights are the most pervasive human rights violations in our world. This obviously causes enormous suffering to women and children. But it does more than that.

If we are to finally put an end to the prejudices and persecutions that have caused so much bloodshed and suffering, we have to leave behind cultural traditions that justify violence and abuse in the foundational relations between parents and children and between women and men. The acceptance of these violations provides a model for accepting human rights abuses across the board.

I have found a great deal of satisfaction and meaning in participating in these efforts. I have also found the community rallying around this work a source of wonderful friendships.

One of my dearest friends was a woman from Pakistan, a political refugee who was tortured, raped, and almost killed for the "crime" of working for women's human rights. She eventually died in exile from the physical and emotional effects of this brutality. She might have died even earlier, had she not assumed the fictitious name Abida

Khanum (*khanum* meaning "woman") to escape the *fatwah* or death
sentence imposed by mullahs who claimed she blasphemed against
Islam. Her "blasphemy" consisted of a public statement that passages
in the Koran commanding violence and cruelty against women
cannot legitimately be attributed to the Prophet Mohammed because
of his great love for his young wife Ayesha.7

On the surface, Abida and I were from different worlds: one an
Asian woman of color, a poet brought up in the Sufi/Muslim tradition; the other a European woman, a cultural historian and systems
scientist of Jewish background. Abida was married off at age fourteen
to a man more than twice her age and lived in Africa and Asia, while
I did not marry until my twenties and lived in Europe and South and
North America. But despite these very different backgrounds, the
insights, yearnings, and passions we shared were so powerful that we
felt like sisters.

Both of us were immigrants who were forced to flee our home-
lands, persecuted and hated by those in power. Both of us had a great
zest for life and learning. Both of us shared the need to do what we
can to build a better future. And both of us had come to see that helping girls and women gain equal rights and equal access to food,
healthcare, and education worldwide is a prerequisite to creating this
better future.

"WOMEN'S ISSUES" AND HUMAN ISSUES

WORKING FOR THE HUMAN RIGHTS OF WOMEN worldwide is one of
the most effective actions you can take to protect yourself and your
family in our "global village." Consider that the fundamentalist
"schools for terrorism" in Pakistan and Afghanistan teach boys that
women are evil and dangerous, and must be terrorized into submission — and that this model for dealing with groups that are labeled
evil and dangerous can then easily be generalized to justify terrorism
against the West and even other Muslim sects.

Of course, moving from domination to partnership in the relations between men and women will not by itself take us to a more just and peaceful world. However, it is an essential change that has vast repercussions from our living rooms to our international relations.

The reason is simple. The structure of the relations between the female and male halves of humanity provides a basic mental map for all other relations between people who are different — people of different races, ethnic origins, religions, and so forth. If we don't reject the old view that one half of humanity is entitled to dominate, and even brutalize, the other half, all of us face a bleak future.

Unfortunately, this view is still deeply entrenched in cultural traditions worldwide. Consider that the sexual mutilation of millions of young girls and women is still condoned by cultural traditions, as well as by the governments of many nations. This traditional practice involves cutting off all or most of the clitoris and/or sewing the vaginal labia together so tightly that they must be cut before marriage for intercourse and still further for childbirth. It is designed to prevent sexual intercourse, and even to take away any pleasure women have from sex.[8] One hundred million African and Asian women living today suffered this practice, and millions are added every year.

Yet human rights organizations have only recently started to bring this form of torture to public attention. And even now, it is far from being a major focus for human rights action. There is still the notion that, as cultural outsiders, we shouldn't interfere with ethnic or religious traditions — when in fact only outside support made it possible for people in these cultures to themselves finally struggle against this horrific human rights violation.[9]

Another practice in many world regions is discrimination on the basis of sex in food, health care, and education for children. This is justified by cultural traditions that value the male half of humanity more than the female half. Since women are the primary caregivers and educators for babies and little children, the fact that the mass of the world's illiterate are women obviously has very negative repercussions not only for women but for the whole of society. Even worse are the repercussions of allocating more food and health care to boys than girls in some of the poorest regions.

Despite the well-known fact that women as a group have longer life spans than men, there are in some countries fewer than 95 women for every 100 men. In China and South and West Asia, there are only 94 females for every 100 males. The Nobel prize–winning economist Amartya Sen has estimated that more than 100 million women across the globe are "missing."[10]

Female infant mortality rates are also considerably higher than those for males. For instance, according to statistics released in 1995 (the year of the Fourth United Nations Conference on Women), deaths per year per thousand in Bangladesh were 15.7 for girls age one to four versus 14.2 for boys. In Pakistan, the ratio was 9.6 for girls versus 8.6 for boys. In Guatemala, it was 11.3 for girls versus 10.6 for boys. In Egypt, it was 6.6 versus 5.6. And even in Singapore, which at that time had a strong economy, the ratio was 0.5 for girls versus 0.4 for boys.[11]

When I look at these numbers, I don't just see statistics. I see the hollow eyes of little girls, too listless from malnutrition even to cry. I see girl babies, neglected and starved, slowly dying without even the comfort of caring mothers or fathers. And I recoil in anger at the horror of cultural beliefs that can make a child's own parents treat her so cruelly simply because she was born female.

IT'S HARD FOR ME to write about these things — and I know it isn't "easy reading." But it needs to be said: This terrible suffering that is still so widely perpetrated could be avoided with simple caring. I realize that most people who treat their children so cruelly have experienced cruelty themselves. But my empathy for them is even more reason for my determination to help stop these cycles of abuse and suffering. All

I know is that I refuse to stand by, that I have to make others aware of this suffering — and of how it ultimately affects us all.

I know that it sometimes seems easier to shut our eyes to suffering so we don't have to deal with our feelings of pain and sadness. But I have found that when I allow myself to confront these feelings, I free energy for constructive actions — actions that help not only those directly affected, but help all of us. Because today what happens in the world, wherever it happens, affects the welfare and security of everyone.

A dramatic example of a human rights violation that affects us all is the deliberate denial of food to female children. Evidence of nutritional deprivation among women and girls is clearly apparent in many world regions. In Bangladesh, for example, 77 percent of pregnant women from middle-income households, and more than 95 percent of those from low-income households, weighed less than the standard of 50 kilograms. In India's rural Punjab, 21 percent of the girls in low-income families suffered from severe malnutrition compared with only 3 percent of boys in the same families. Low-income boys actually fared better than upper-income girls.[12]

The classification of such matters as "women's issues" — a code phrase signaling that these issues should take second place to more important ones — is in itself a commentary on how entrenched the devaluation of the female half of humanity still is. But this label is also an effective way of blinding us to what otherwise would seem obvious: the malnutrition of girls and women profoundly impacts the development of both boys and girls, and with this, economic, social, and cultural development, and our chances for a more humane and peaceful world.

It has long been known that children of malnourished women are often born with poor health and below par brain development. This obviously has enormous implications for the entire world. It affects such vital issues as global poverty and hunger, difficulty in adapting to new conditions, level of frustration, and propensity to use violence. In short, discrimination against girls and women not only robs children, whether they are male or female, of their birthright — their potential for optimal development — but it potentially affects us all.

Yet were it not for the efforts for over thirty years of women's organizations worldwide — of people such as you and me — this information would not be gaining currency. And even then, because of the strength of cultural traditions that view discrimination against girls and women as normal and right, government leaders are only now beginning to consider these obvious connections.

LOVING AND VALUING CHILDREN

THERE IS NO QUESTION that the effects of women's lower status are more visible in poorer areas. But there is also strong evidence that when the status of women is low, this adversely affects the quality of life for everyone — not only women, but also men and children.

One of my projects at the Center for Partnership Studies was a three-year study of statistical data from eighty-nine nations comparing quality of life measures with measures of the status of women. We found that the status of women profoundly affects the quality of life for all.

For example, Kuwait and France had almost the same levels of per capita gross domestic product, or GDP (the conventional measure of a nation's wealth). But the infant mortality rate in France and Kuwait were very different. France is a democracy in which the status of women is higher and which, accordingly, conforms more to the partnership configuration. Here the infant mortality rate was 8 infants per 1,000 live births. In Kuwait, a monarchy where the status of women is much lower, the mortality rate was 19 infants per 1,000 live births — more than double the rate of France.[13] Similarly, the GDP of Finland and Singapore were almost identical. But the maternal mortality rate in Singapore, a dictatorship in which the status of women is much lower, was more than double that of Finland, a democratic society where, as in other Scandinavian nations, women have made strong gains.[14]

In short, what we found is that the material wealth of a country doesn't necessarily translate into a high quality of life for its people. It certainly doesn't translate into real caring for children. Much depends on whether the distribution of wealth and the governing system orients to dominator or partnership values. And a great deal depends on the status of women.[15]

There are many reasons for this. Where women have higher status and, with it, education and access to job opportunities, they tend to have fewer and healthier children, which leads to a higher quality of life in their nation or region.

But the main reason for the correlation between a low quality of life and a low status for women is this: where the status of women is low we also find the greatest devaluation of traits and activities stereotypically associated with women — activities and traits such as caring, caregiving, and nonviolence. This means that less money goes into supporting the values and activities that make for a high quality of life for everyone, including feeding and caring for children.

DESPITE THE RHETORIC about valuing and loving children, most of the nations of our world — both wealthy and poor — have failed to invest their economic resources in ensuring that children are safe, well-fed, and cared for. Not only that, most nations still have deeply embedded traditions that view children as the property of their parents. Hence, in most world regions, violence by parents against their own children is considered normal and right.

This violence is a major obstacle to a world of peace. Children are literally beaten into the belief that those who are stronger can legitimately use force to impose their will on those who are weaker. Once learned, this lesson is applied to all relations — whether intertribal or intratribal, international or intranational.

The chronic abuse of children worldwide is only now beginning to come to the fore — once again, only because of the organized efforts of people like you and me through nongovernmental organizations working for the human rights of children and women. The most heinous crimes against children — from brutal beatings to forced marriages that are little more than the sale of girls by their own parents — are still accepted as culturally and economically justified in some regions, with no hint of moral, much less legal, censure despite occasional laws that prohibit them.

TO BRING REAL PRESSURE to end these traditional practices and help people worldwide learn partnership parenting, the Nobel Peace Prize winner Betty Williams and I have called for a global campaigns to end violence and abuse in childhood. You can read more about The Spiritual Alliance to Stop Intimate Violence (SAIV) at www. partnershipway.org under the "Relationships" link. We can all be part of such campaigns. They are urgently needed if we are to move to a more caring and peaceful world. They will protect those who can't protect themselves. And because the childhood years set the foundations for all of life, they will help pave the road to a partnership future.

We also need global campaigns for nonviolent and equitable gender relations. There are already many organizations working on this in bits and pieces. Again, each one of us can support efforts such as the annual "Take Back the Night" vigils.

Particularly since the girl child is the most vulnerable and abused of children, if we unite behind these two simple issues, we can do a great deal to help create what my friend Raffi, the beloved children's troubadour, calls a child-honoring society. He writes that in such a society:

Addressing the universal needs of young children would employ unprecedented human initiative.... Clean air, water, and soil would be protected as sacred heritage rights.... Guiding principles for living would be oriented toward long-term, inter-generational concerns. An explosion of purpose would grip young and old and bring them together in count-less new ways to everyone's enrichment. And happiness wouldn't be pursued — it would be embedded in the play of daily life.[16]

We have the economic resources to create a child-honoring soci-ety. All we have to do is change our global priorities.

Of course, as long as domination and conquest prevail, we still need adequate military capacities to defend ourselves. But we must stop investing so much of our world's economic resources in arma-ments — if only so they're not one day turned against us.

A far more effective way of making the world safe for ourselves and our children is to invest our resources in ensuring that all chil-dren are fed and cared for. This is not only essential but doable. For example, the cost of just one ballistic submarine would double the education budgets of eighteen poor countries, offering millions of children a better chance in life.[17] World military budgets are roughly $800 billion per year.[18] Only a fraction of this could easily provide food and health care for all the world's children. But the issue is not one of economic resources. It is one of economic priorities and eco-nomic rules.

ECONOMIC RULES AND SOCIAL PRIORITIES

THE UNITED NATIONS *Human Development Report 1998* reported that the world's 225 richest people have a combined wealth of over $1 trillion, or equal to the combined annual income of the poorest 2.5 billion people — 47 percent of the world. It also reported that less

than 4 percent of the combined wealth of these 225 people ($40 bil-
lion) would not only provide adequate food, safe drinking water, and
sanitation for all, but would also ensure basic health care for all, universal access to education, and reproductive health care for all
women.[19]

Once again, these figures aren't just statistics. They tell us about
the unnecessary suffering of babies with empty, swollen bellies. They
tell us about orphaned children whose malnourished mothers died in
childbirth. They tell us about eight-year-old Manuel Ortega, whose
family can't afford the medicines he needs to treat his tuberculosis.
They tell us about homeless children roaming crowded city streets, of
teenagers like Toma Kiburu, who crawls on her belly because in her
African village, where women walk miles to fetch water and children
have barely enough to eat, a wheelchair for her crippled body is an
impossible dream.

Clearly there is something wrong with an economic system in
which so few have so much more than they could ever spend and
so many have so little that they barely survive and all too often die.
But the problem isn't only the misdistribution of resources that
results from the massive concentrations of wealth characteristic of
dominator economics — be they ancient or modern, Western or
Eastern. It is rooted in a fundamental imbalance: the fact that most
present economic systems, whether tribal, feudal, capitalist, or
communist, still give little or no value to the work of caring and
caregiving — work that is foundational to the welfare of children,
and hence to us all.

I BRING US BACK to this matter because the economic devaluation
of work traditionally considered women's work — such as caring for
children and the elderly and maintaining a clean and healthy home
environment — is a cornerstone of dominator economic rules.
These rules are supported by bizarrely unrealistic systems of global

bookkeeping that fail to include the most socially essential work — the work of caregiving — in calculations of economic productivity such as GDP (Gross Domestic Product). These measures don't even reflect the fact that it's women who do the farming, hauling of firewood, and bringing in water in many African nations, as this work is not part of the quantified market economy.

This omission of "women's work" from measurements of "productive work," together with the failure of economic development policies to support this work, in large part accounts for the massive gap between haves and have-nots. Who are the have-nots? Women and children worldwide are the mass of the poor — 70 percent, according to U.N. figures. Women and children are also the poorest of the poor. Yet most people are unaware of these shocking facts. And because this knowledge is ignored by both our media and our policymakers, current economic policies not only fail to effectively deal with poverty, but they often make things worse.

For instance, the Structural Adjustment Policies (SAPs) imposed by wealthier nations such as the United States through the International Monetary Fund (IMF) and World Bank require debtor nations to sharply cut expenditures on social services such as food subsidies, childcare facilities, and healthcare. And who bears the brunt of these cuts? Women and children, although this too is rarely noted in mainstream publications.

As Lois Woestman writes in a recent briefing paper for the European Network on Debt and Development, "what is regarded as increased efficiency in the adjustment process is actually a transfer of costs from the paid to the unpaid economy — in effect from the government to women and girls. . . . It is women and girls who take up the slack: they take on the care of ill family members when healthcare charges are introduced. It is women and girls who set up soup kitchens and childcare cooperatives when food prices skyrocket and childcare facilities are closed. SAPs increase the amount of unpaid work women and girls have to do."[20] And to top it all off, these added hours of unpaid work for women, overtaxing their health and stretching their already long working hours even more, are not included in calculations of GDP or other measures of economic productivity — ensuring that they remain invisible to policymakers and the public at large.

There has been some movement toward substituting "Quality of Life Measures" for GDP and GNP. This is an important step in the right direction. But these measures by and large still fail to include gender-specific data that reflect the invisible economic contributions of women, and this needs to change.

Gender-inclusive Quality of Life Measures have been proposed in Marilyn Waring's *If Women Counted* and the Center for Partnership Studies' *Women, Men, and the Global Quality of Life*, which I wrote with the social psychologist David Loye and the sociologist Kari Norgaard. These gender-specific quality-of-life measures are needed to make visible the essential work of caregiving and maintaining a clean and healthy home environment in systems of national and international accounting. As Hazel Henderson writes, "it is now imperative for the common good that national accounts in all countries and the United Nations System of National Accounts (UNSNA) include caring unpaid work to maintain family and community life."[21]

One of the most effective ways you can help raise living standards worldwide — thereby protecting yourself and your family here in the United States — is to work for the inclusion of "women's work" in systems of national and international accounting. We all know that when things are not counted they are not taken into account. Only through changes in accounting can we encourage the development of new economic rules.

Just as it's absurd to talk of taking care of the world's children when caregiving is not considered real work in measures of economic productivity, it's absurd to talk of economic equity as long as we have economic systems based on the notion that one half of humanity was put on earth to serve the other half. If women must be subordinate because they are different from men— if they are meant to serve, to work hard and not be recognized or paid — other groups can also be forced into subordinate roles because they are of a different race or ethnicity.

Ultimately violence keeps rankings of domination in place. So as long as relations of domination and submission in these foundational relations are considered normal, peace cannot be more than just an interval between wars. Unless we change this, we can't realistically expect to eliminate terrorism as a means of imposing another sect's or nation's will — as is so tragically illustrated by the Muslim fundamentalist terrorists who come from cultures where women are routinely terrorized into submission.[22] And as long as "women's work" is considered less valuable than "men's work," talk of a more equitable and caring economy will be just that — talk.

TOWARD AN ECONOMICS OF CARING

To change today's imbalanced economic relations, we need new economic models and rules. Fortunately, more and more people are thinking in these terms.

There are proposals for new accounting systems that put on the profit or plus side only those business activities that promote environmental health. Strange as it sounds, business activities that create environmental despoliation, along with the costs of repairing the damage, are still in current accounting systems included on the plus rather than minus side.

There are also proposals for "environmental sin taxes" that transfer the health and environmental costs of pollution to the companies responsible for them — instead of having them borne by us, the public. These taxes could eventually be a substitute for taxing productive work, which would benefit us all.

Local, national, and global charters requiring that corporations live up to minimal standards of accountability are also attempts to change economic rules.[23] Organizations such as the Social Venture Network are working to implement standards for corporate social responsibility. Such standards have already been introduced in some parts of the world. For instance, some industries in Germany have adopted standards developed by Monika Griefahn of the German Green party.

These standards are steps toward economic rules that promote job creation while also improving our quality of life and protecting our environment. Powerful international organizations such as the International Monetary Fund (IMF), the World Bank, and the World Trade Organization (WTO) should support, rather than oppose, such standards.

For trade to be really free, we need economic inventions that make business ownership more inclusive, not only of employees but of community members. For example, Jeff Gates proposes in his book *The Ownership Solution* that utility users should become utility shareholders, with a say in rates.[24] Community currencies that encourage purchases of local goods and services not only help prevent the concentration of economic power but also promote more caring and responsibility, since large corporations are usually headquartered far from the communities they service. Inventions such as Sergio Lub's "Friendly Favors," an Internet community that follows the partnership model, allows people to exchange gifts rather than money for services and products they want.[25]

We don't have to replace all economic rules. We certainly don't want to create more bureaucracies, much less another dominator pyramid, as in the Soviet Union's "dictatorship of the proletariat." But through a politics of partnership we can unite to support these and other economic inventions appropriate for a less centralized, less controlled partnership economics.

ECONOMIC INVENTIONS THAT GIVE GREATER VALUE to caregiving work are crucial if we want to move toward a more equitable and caring economic system. Parental leave for both mothers and fathers and flexible work options are becoming more popular. France gives government assistance to mothers through its *crèche* programs. Canada gives its workers a year of parental leave at half salary. Most industrialized countries provide universal healthcare as an investment in their human capital. Great Britain's healthcare system pays people to take care of their elderly family members, rather than just paying if they're put in convalescent homes.

These are all good starts. But to move toward a truly more caring and compassionate world, we have to go further.

For example, every nation has government-funded programs to train soldiers to effectively take life. Most provide pensions for them. This fits perfectly into dominator economics, which values conquest and domination. But where are the government-funded programs to train women and men to effectively care for children? Where are the pensions for this kind of work? Through partnership economic inventions, we can create ways of financing, training, and providing pensions for this foundational work, along with means of administering them without a large bureaucracy.

Of course, there will be opposition. Some will argue that we cannot accurately measure the effectiveness of training for caregiving. But we also do not have accurate measures for the effectiveness of combat training, and yet we still invest in it.

We need to take a close look at what kinds of activities are supported by our present economic rules and priorities. This is not something we can leave to policymakers. We all need to become more aware of this key economic issue, and do what we can so that, as the saying goes, we put our money where our mouth is.

We are not talking about top-down change. Obviously we want to enlist people in positions of power. But every one of us can be a leader by raising awareness and initiating and supporting specific actions.

YOU AND THE FAMILY OF NATIONS

GRASSROOTS GROUPS ALL OVER THE WORLD are peacefully changing customs, institutions, and practices in a partnership direction. They are working to preserve our environment, promote nonviolent conflict resolution, and protect the human rights of children, women, and men.[26] These groups aren't being organized by specially trained or specially endowed people. They're being organized by "ordinary" people — young and old, black and white, female and male — people just like you and me.

Andrea Guellar, a twelve-year old Bolivian girl who works as a domestic servant to survive, leads a group of children in her poor Santa Cruz neighborhood who meet to help each other as well as other children. Called Defensores del Pequeño Mundo (Defenders of the Little World), this "children's brigade" conducts its own anti-violence campaign, going to the homes of children who are abused to talk to their parents, explaining why it's important not to beat children, pleading with them not to use violence against their children. When they were fifteen and sixteen, Ocean Robbins and Sol Solomon formed YES (Youth for Environmental Sanity), which has enlisted thousands of high school and college students into environmental activism.[27] Patricia Cane, a former nun, founded CAPACITAR to help poor women and children in the United States and Central America.[28] Ella Bhatt formed SEWA, the Self-Employed Women's Association, which pioneered small loans to women entrepreneurs. SEWA now has its own bank and lobbies for women's rights across Indian society. Wagari Maathai founded the Green Belt Movement in Kenya to conserve the environment and improve women's lives. Millions of trees have been planted through this movement, which has spread to other African nations.[29]

You may not want to start an organization. And you may not have a lot of free time to volunteer. But you can join or send donations to organizations working for human rights, peace, democracy, economic equity, and freedom.

UNICEF is the United Nations agency devoted to helping children. The Children's Defense Fund, Defense for Children International, and the Inter-American Children's Institute work for the rights of children. These and other groups are trying to end the abuse of children worldwide, including the killing of children simply because they are homeless. (A powerful documentary showing how these abuses are often carried out with the complicity of those in authority is *Innocents Lost* by filmmakers Kate Blewett and Brian Woods,[30] whose earlier work *The Dying Rooms,* an exposé of the mistreatment of abandoned girls in Chinese orphanages, also won critical acclaim.)

The U.N. International Development Fund for Women (UNIFEM) and the U.N. International Research and Training Institute for the Advancement of Women (INSTRAW) are United Nations agencies formed to help women. Organizations such as the Women's Environment and Development Organization (WEDO), the Feminist Majority, the American Association of University Women (AAUW), and the Women's International Network (WIN) News are also dedicated to the empowerment of women as one of the foundations for a better society.[31] The Global Fund for Women gives grants to grassroots women's groups worldwide. The Hunger Project is dedicated to eradicating hunger by empowering women.

Planned Parenthood International, Population Action International, and Pathfinder International work to stem the tide of unwanted children and at the same time empower women. Organizations such as the Union of Concerned Scientists and the Environmental Defense Fund are working to protect our natural environment. The International Partnership Network (IPN) links people committed to the shift to a partnership world, and the Center for Partnership Studies (CPS) develops and promotes partnership education.

One of the most important things you can do is ask organizations to which you belong or donate money to support the partnership political agenda. This agenda is described in the previous chapter and outlined in "The Politics of Partnership" at the end of this book.

Another important action is to introduce partnership education into schools. We need to ensure that our education is gender-balanced and multicultural, and the resources available from the Center for Partnership Studies can be helpful in these efforts. We also need to close the huge education gap between boys and girls in much of the developing world, so that girls and women have equal access to literacy and basic knowledge and skills — an essential step toward a truly developed world.

THERE ARE MANY OTHER THINGS you can do. You can lobby your senators to ratify the United Nations Convention to Eliminate All Forms of Discrimination Against Women (CEDAW) and the United Nations Convention on the Rights of the Child. Although both these agreements have been ratified by many nations, neither has at this writing been ratified by the U.S. Senate.[32]

You can change your purchasing habits. For your long distance telephone service and Visa credit card you can choose a company called Working Assets, which donates a percentage of profits to organizations working for social justice and protection of the environment. You can buy clothes from companies such as Levi Strauss (the makers of Levi's), who pay workers (both in the U.S. and overseas) a living wage and don't use child labor.[33] You can buy environmentally safe products from companies such as Real Goods and Seventh Generation, both of which sell items through their catalogs and websites (www.realgoods.com and www.seventhgen.com). You can buy cosmetics from the Body Shop stores, which employ indigenous peoples and sell natural products that haven't been cruelly tested on animals.

You can ask relatives or friends to make a donation to an organization working for peace, human rights, or partnership education at Christmas or other occasions instead of giving you a gift. If you're a writer, artist, or filmmaker, you can write articles, use art to raise consciousness, make documentaries, feature films, videos, or create new television programs. If you're a teacher, you can bring in speakers from groups working for social equity and environmental sustainability. You can make arrangements with these groups for student internships for your school's service learning programs.

You can buy videos from the Media Education Foundation, or the Center for Partnership Studies, including my video *Tomorrow's Children: Partnership Education in Action,* or you can ask your community's schools and universities to purchase them. You can ask your municipal government to form city-to-city partnerships, like Sister Cities, a worldwide citizen diplomacy program.

These and many other actions you can take in the course of your daily life are building blocks for the road to a partnership future. Every one of these building blocks advances the partnership political agenda.

We have a choice. We can futilely try to protect ourselves and our families behind high walls, electric gates, and "Star Wars" missile shield technologies, and turn a blind eye toward chronic human rights violations and an economic globalization that is not accountable to anyone. Or we can join with people and organizations from all the world's nations to lay the foundations for a world of peace, to ensure workers are protected by international standards, and to find ways of giving value to caring and caregiving.

Rather than putting corporate profits ahead of human welfare — and even, as is happening, exporting our radioactive waste to developing nations — let us work to ensure that there are environmental safeguards worldwide and that everyone's basic material needs are met. Rather than turning the other way, let us join to protect children, women, and men from human rights abuses. Let us remember that unless every child is safely cared for in our global village, no child is safe.

It is time to realize that we need a global partnership: we're all together on one planet, one single support system. We have to work in partnership to ensure the security and health of everyone, and the safety and opportunities for the generations to follow.

This requires governments, corporations, and the rest of us to do what we can to create a sustainable world, to work with respect with all our resources, including every child and adult on earth.

PUTTING PARTNERSHIP TO WORK

I have already suggested many ways you can put partnership relations into practice. You have also seen that there is movement toward partnership relations all around you. In families, more empathic parenting styles are beginning to take hold. Women are entering professions that were once restricted to men, and many men are no longer ashamed to take care of babies or exhibit other so-called feminine behaviors. Many companies are discovering that a partnership leadership style that empowers others is more effective than the old-fashioned autocratic leadership style. The idea of nonviolent conflict resolution is beginning to change the old idea that you have to out-shout or beat up or kill your opponent. The idea that we should try to live in harmony with our Mother Earth is beginning to change the "conquest of nature" mentality.

You may ask, can whole countries move toward the partnership model? The answer is emphatically yes — many countries have already made huge advances toward the partnership model. Scandinavian countries such as Sweden, Norway, and Finland have created much more equitable societies with a good living standard for all.

The Scandinavian nations pioneered experiments in economic democracy that did not result in another dominator system, as happened in the former Soviet Union. They were the first nations to move toward more industrial democracy, pioneering teamwork by self-directed groups to replace assembly lines where workers are mere cogs in the industrial machine. In these societies there is much greater partnership between women and men, as well as a much greater acceptance of women in leadership positions: women have held the highest political offices and a larger proportion of legislators are female than anywhere else in the world.[34]

These societies also show a greater acceptance of "feminine values." Consequently, caring and caregiving have become a key part of their social policy, and the Scandinavian health-care, childcare, and eldercare systems have become models for other industrialized nations.

The Scandinavian nations also pioneered nonviolent conflict resolution. They established the first peace academies when the rest of the world only had war academies, and in Scandinavia there is a strong movement by men against male violence toward women.[35] Rather than increasing the violence against nature presently ruining so much of our world, Scandinavian nations have pioneered more environmentally sound manufacturing approaches, such as the "Natural Step," where materials are recycled even after they reach the consumer to avoid pollution and waste.

These nations are not "pure" partnership societies. As I said, there is no such thing as a "pure" domination model or partnership model in practice. Most families, organizations, and societies lie somewhere between these two poles. But the Scandinavian nations show how more partnership-oriented structures, beliefs, and relations support less violent, more caring, more environmentally sustainable ways of living.

Every culture has partnership elements that can be strengthened and built upon. If we really want a more peaceful world — a world where we and our children can feel safe — we will help in this process.

By helping spread the partnership political agenda (described in chapter 4 and "The Politics of Partnership" at the end of this book) to other world regions, you can play an active part in this urgently needed enterprise. We can't wait for governments to take the lead. If enough of us start, government leaders will eventually follow.

You can start by working for the human rights of women and children worldwide. You can urge your governmental representatives to stipulate in foreign aid grants that one-third be used for children's nutrition, healthcare, and education, with special emphasis on the girl child. You can urge them to channel this aid directly to grassroots organizations such as the Hunger Project or the American Friends Service Committee (Quakers) that work with local groups of mothers to prevent this funding from being diverted into the pockets of those in power. You can write letters to heads of governments that still condone the brutal subordination of women in the Middle East, Asia, Africa, and Latin America, and urge international human rights organizations to take a stronger stand on human rights violations in these regions. You can urge religious leaders to actively work to end violence against women and children worldwide.

Just pick one or two of the actions described in this chapter or in the action checklist that follows, and get some of your friends or colleagues to join you. This is how change starts.

ACTION CHECKLIST

First Steps

☐ When you hear about millions of children starving in some corner of the world, think of each as a hungry, bewildered child, not just a faceless statistic.

☐ When you hear what is being done to women under the guise of religious tradition, imagine what life would be like if you could not let a square inch of your skin be seen in public, could not attend school or have a job, and could not drive a car or even get into one without a male member of your family. When you read of girls and women publicly flogged, hanged, and stoned to death by the Taliban in Afghanistan or other regimes led by religious fundamentalists, imagine yourself and your mothers, daughters, and sisters living under a religious fundamentalist regime.

☐ Reexamine Christian, Muslim, and Jewish fundamentalist teachings in terms of the core dominator configuration of rigid male dominance, top-down rule, and the religiously condoned use of violence in families, communities, and the world. Consider how these teachings violate the core of their religious teachings: caring, nonviolence, and empathy.

☐ Think about how the current rules for economic globalization are widening the disparity between the developed and developing world — and how most of the world's poor are women and children.

☐ Consider the effect on poor families worldwide of congressional cuts in domestic and international family planning funds, and vote for people who understand the need for policies that support family planning.

☐ Visualize yourself living in a society where the work of caring and caregiving is highly rewarded, and imagine how this would affect your life and that of your children.

NEXT STEPS

❏   Buy products and services from socially and environmentally responsible companies, and do not buy from those that are not.

❏   Invest in stocks of socially and environmentally responsible companies and mutual funds.

❏   Share the materials in this chapter with others, both one-to-one and by forming a discussion group.

❏   Contact international human rights organizations and government agencies, urging them to actively work for human rights in both the private and public spheres, focusing particularly on the long-ignored human rights of women and children.

❏   Speak up against prejudice and hate in radio talk shows and letters to the editor.

GOING FURTHER

❏   Raise the awareness of your family, friends, and business associates to global partnership as a necessity in our age of instant technologies of destruction.

❏   Help move political discussions past old categories such as right versus left, East versus West, capitalism versus communism, liberal versus conservative, and religious versus secular to the underlying issue of attitudes and policies that support domination or partnership.

❏   Ask organizations to which you belong or to which you donate to sponsor a campaign to end violence against children and women worldwide.

❏   Introduce and support partnership education in schools and universities.

❏   Work for political candidates who support a national and international politics of partnership, or run for office yourself.

Your Relationship with Nature

FROM MOTHER EARTH TO BIOTECHNOLOGY

What does a clean and healthy environment mean for you? Does it mean the air you breathe and the water you drink are safe some of the time — or all of the time? Does it mean the food you eat is full of nutrition — or radiation? Does it mean that your grandchildren will enjoy the wonders of nature — or just read about them in old books?

In this chapter, you will see that to answer these questions we have to look at a much larger picture than only "environmental issues." You will see connections between how we think, how we live, our politics, our economics, our technology, and how all this relates to our Mother Earth. You will also see how we can more effectively protect our environment and our health.

UNTIL A FEW YEARS AGO, it never occurred to me that I have a relationship with Mother Nature. But of course I do — we all do. Even if you are in the middle of an urban jungle, ten miles from the nearest tree, six hundred feet above the ground, ensconced in concrete, sitting on a polyester chair, you still have a relationship with nature. We all depend on this relationship for our survival. We breathe nature's air. We drink her water. We soak up her sun. We move about on her soil and we live off her products. Wherever we live — in a city, out on a farm, deep in the woods, or along the coast — we are living in relationship with Mother Earth. And whether we know it or not, the role each of us plays in this relationship is of the same dominator or partnership cloth as all our other relationships.

You've seen how the partnership model is more conducive to meeting our most basic emotional and material needs, how it transforms our relationship with ourselves, our intimate relations, and our relations in our communities and our world. What may not be as apparent is that the same principle applies to our relationship with nature.

If you look at the mass media, you may get the impression that there's no need for concern about our natural environment. You'll read occasional stories about an environmental crisis. But you'll also see stories telling you that all that's needed to solve our global problems is a free market of more production, consumption, and ever bigger and better technologies.

How do you evaluate these conflicting messages? And why should you even try?

One reason is simple self-protection. How would you like to find yourself one of these days purchasing oxygen to breathe more easily? You might think this is an extreme example. But nobody used to buy bottled water at the grocery store; today more and more of us do.

Another reason is that our environment is irreplaceable. If we don't preserve it, we endanger our own life-support. We also endanger the unique wonders of nature. Every year thousands of species are being lost. Every month thousands of acres of wilderness are disappearing — from our national parks to the tropical rainforests that are the lungs of our planet.

I want my grandchildren to enjoy the seals and sea otters in the ocean near where I live and the whales that migrate here every year. I want the lush canyons near their homes to still be there when they grow up. I don't want them to be exposed to holes in the ozone layer that let in cancer-causing ultraviolet radiation. I don't want them to be imperiled by polluted air, water, and food.

It's scary to think about these huge environmental threats. They seem overwhelming, and you might feel there's nothing you can do. But once you become aware of why our relationship with nature is so out of balance, you can do a lot.

Our natural life-support system is at risk because advanced technology and a dominator value system are a potentially lethal mix. In this value system, the life-supporting services of nature are as undervalued as the life-supporting services of women. Dominator cultures treat the Earth much the way they treat women: exploiting and at the same time denying the essential importance of giving and maintaining life. This mindset shapes economic rules, policies, and business practices that lead to irresponsible uses of advanced technology to further "man's conquest of nature."

Again, matters such as economic rules, business practices, and uses of advanced technology may seem too huge to change. But in fact, they change all the time. Any trend can be stopped by a change of ideas, and all of us can spread new ideas.

All of us can disseminate accurate information about the environmental dangers of "business as usual." All of us can work to strengthen cultural values that support partnership rather than domination. And all of us can help spread the understanding that to protect our environment and health, we can't just focus on the environment: we need an integrated agenda that also addresses the cultural and economic factors that brought us to this place where our very life-support system is at risk.

DOMINATOR PSYCHOLOGY AND THE ENVIRONMENT

MANY PEOPLE — including people in political and business policy-making positions — are trapped in old dominator mindsets. These mindsets make it hard to accurately assess reality, since dominator thinking is so heavily based on denial.

How deep does the river of denial run? Very deep.

In 1992, the Union of Concerned Scientists published a statement by 1,700 leading international scientists (including over 100 Nobel laureates) urging the adoption of a new global ethic to avert the growing threats to our survival.[1] But this warning had no significant effect on policy.

In 2001, some of the world's top environmental scientists — including the executive director of the U.S. government committee studying the effects of climate change on the United States — reported that the impact of global warming is already more severe than scientists had thought earlier. They predicted that 200 million people in the world's coastal cities will be severely affected by rising sea levels, unless there is a radical drop in the buildup of greenhouse gases from unregulated industrial processes. They warned that unless global warming is halted, many regions will suffer from severe water shortages, crop failures, famines, tropical diseases, droughts, and floods. They emphasized that these are not remote threats: already in the Himalayan and Tian Shan mountain ranges of Asia, two-thirds of the glaciers are melting, and in the Arctic and Antarctic sea ice has decreased 10 to 15 percent in about twenty years due to gases such as carbon dioxide from burning oil and coal.[2]

How then can politicians tell us we don't need to worry about global warming? Why don't they address this and other large-scale threats to our safety and health? Why, even in the wake of nuclear plant accidents such as Chernobyl and Three Mile Island, are we again told that we should build more nuclear plants? How can these politicians tell us we should drill oil wells in national parks and burn more coal instead of investing in alternative energy sources? And why have the mainstream media failed to take our environmental problems as seriously as Tom Cruise's next movie?

Why don't those in charge of industry change practices causing irremediable damage to our environment and our health? Instead, they pay millions for ads that paint them as dedicated environmentalists. Some of this "happy propaganda" comes from oil companies and other business interests who make major financial donations to political candidates and are big advertisers and owners of the mass media. But don't they too have children and grandchildren, and don't they too worry about the future?

How can anyone believe that there is no environmental crisis, that the Earth can support infinite numbers of people, that all that's needed is a market economy where unbridled selfishness will somehow lead to the greater good for all? How can anyone believe that the road to a cleaner, healthier environment is more production, consumption, and high technology, when high-consumption "free market" economies such as the United States contribute a disproportionate share to pollution and other environmental problems?

You can start answering these questions by reminding yourself that one way people with dominator mindsets deal with the world is through denial. As we saw in chapters 1 and 2, dominator upbringing produces denial. It makes it hard for adults brought up this way to question, much less challenge, powerful economic interests on whom they feel dependent — the way they depended on powerful adults as children.

People who have been brought up in dominator ways also tend to have difficulty looking at the long-range future. As the emphasis on the short-term bottom line suggests, they're stuck in a defensive mode of protecting themselves and what they have. On top of this, people who were subjected to dominator childrearing often have trouble dealing with change.

Change is stressful for everyone. But it's particularly stressful for people who associate change with pain because in their families stressed adults took out their anxieties and fears on the children.

Change re-stimulates childhood hurts unconsciously associated with top-down abuse and violence. If you've grown up with adults who handle the stress of change by abusing those who are less powerful, you've learned that you're safest if nothing threatens those who dominate — and hence if nothing changes.

All this of course happens on a deep unconscious level. But it affects perceptions, beliefs, and attitudes profoundly.

People trapped in these dominator psychological patterns sometimes call their stance "conservative." But what they promote is the opposite of natural conservation. What they're actually trying to conserve are dominator power structures. Their agenda for exploiting nature is part of a larger agenda we have to understand, expose, and counter if we are to protect our natural environment and our health.

THE DOMINATION OF NATURE — AND OF US

WHAT IS THE POLITICAL AGENDA of "conservative" think tanks such as the Hoover Institute, the American Enterprise Institute, the Federalist Society, and the Heritage Foundation? They are against environmental regulations for big business — despite the damage "business as usual" is doing to our natural habitat. They are against arms-control treaties such as the ban on land mines, international small arms proliferation control, and other "interference" with unbridled weapons development and trade — despite the dangers this poses to our lives and environment. They are against laws that "interfere" with top-down control in families — despite the enormous personal and economic costs of child abuse and violence against women. They are dead-set against gender equality — despite the ongoing domination of men over women.

In short, they are determined not only to continue full-speed with the "conquest of nature," but also to defend the domination/command model in parent-child, gender, economic, and international relations. Theirs is an integrated agenda designed to maintain rankings of domination — be they man over woman, parent over child, race over race, or man over nature.

Obviously these people don't say — and probably don't consciously admit — that their real agenda is one of unhampered control by those in power. What you hear and read in the mass media are emotionally appealing code words such as "free enterprise, "decentralization," and "less control." But behind this rhetoric are policies that place greater control in the hands of those who have traditionally wielded power — in families, education, economics, politics, and religion.

Once you begin to connect these dots — and you have to connect them yourself because the mass media don't connect them — you see that what's being sold as "noninterference" is actually designed to maintain existing power imbalances. In this politics of "noninterference," those who hold power have the advantage. Since there is no legal or other interference, the status quo is maintained.

When opponents of environmental regulations talk about a free market, free enterprise, and freedom from environmental regulations, what they actually mean is freedom for those in economic control from any curtailment of their power.[3] What they are against is any real say by the government, which is supposed to represent the people's interests, in how big business impacts our natural environment and our lives.[4] Since regulations by the federal government are most potent in dealing with big corporations, they keep talking about state's rights and trusting the people. But their real goal is to take regulatory power away from the national agencies that can most effectively protect us and our environment.

Notice that while well-funded think tanks and the politicians they support seek to protect those who wield power from government controls, these same people and organizations advocate strict government control over those they want to keep "in their place." They have no problem with government interference when it comes to denying

women reproductive choice or quashing street protests against powerful economic interests. On the contrary, here they vigorously push
government controls that curtail freedom. They often even approve of
violence, as in police violence against environmentalists and other
nonviolent protesters.

So you see that the anti-environmental-regulation agenda is not
isolated: it is part of a larger social and political agenda. This agenda
seeks to dismantle not only environmental regulations but other progressive gains — from economic safety nets, more economic democracy, and government help for the needy to greater gender and racial
equity, less punitive and controlling child care, and a more humanis-
tic education. (For an outline of this agenda, see the second chart in
"The Politics of Partnership.")

If we want to protect our natural environment and our health, we
cannot just focus on environmental issues. It's not good enough just
to recycle or save the whales. We need an integrated political agenda
that is systems-wide to successfully resist the systems-wide agenda of
those who view rankings of domination as inevitable and right.

This partnership agenda, I want to emphasize, is not an agenda of
"us" versus "them." It is an agenda that will benefit us all, including
those who think that dominating or being dominated are the only
alternatives. It is not an agenda to fight "bad people," but to change a
fundamentally imbalanced system of beliefs, values, and relations that
makes it impossible to effectively address our environmental woes —
or even to see them clearly.

POPULATION AND THE ENVIRONMENT

ONE OF THE MOST PRESSING ENVIRONMENTAL PROBLEMS is overpopulation. Yet time and time again, the bastions of American "conservative" politics — actually, dominator politics — publish books and news
releases telling us that there is no population problem. Just look around
you, they say, there's plenty of space.

But world population is doubling approximately every forty-five years — growing by a staggering 90 million people each year. Every day, one-quarter of a million people are added to our planet — the equivalent of a good-sized city. As the Club of Rome study *Mankind at the Turning Point* warned, unless growth rates are drastically lowered, *in just one year in the middle of the twenty-first century more people will be added to world population than during the 1,500 years after Jesus' birth.*[5]

In the United States, population is increasing by 2.6 million people every year. This growth rate is considerably lower than in developing countries. But it too is unsustainable, considering the tremendous rate of consumption and industrial pollution of the United States. As the developing world industrializes and increases its rates of consumption, the damage to the environment by its exponentially growing populations will also exponentially increase. Already exploding population has led to ever more encroachment on wild land and wildlife, pollution, desertification, and other forms of resource depletion — not to speak of poverty, hunger, and armed violence.

So how can we defuse this "population bomb"? The answer to this question has been known for some time. Study after study shows that the only way to reduce population growth — other than by famine, war, and disease — is free access to family planning and raising the educational and economic status of women.

But here's the problem — and it's once again a deeply embedded cultural and social problem. Because of barriers inherent in dominator cultures, millions of women still lack access to family planning, even though they are often desperate to escape the slavery of enforced pregnancy. "Look at me," lamented a woman interviewed for *Third World Women Speak Out.* "I am nothing but a beast working in the fields and bearing all these children. I don't want any more children...."[6]

In many places where population is soaring, men still oppose the use of contraceptives. They argue that contraception makes it too easy for "their" women to have sexual relations with other men. Since polygamy and unilateral divorce by men is legal in some of these places, a man can easily replace a wife with a more submissive woman. In some Muslim societies in Africa, Asia, and the Middle East, women have no right to leave their homes. Even where women can move around more freely, they're forbidden to go to clinics with male doctors, again because this violates a man's sense of exclusive possession of "his" woman.

It's hardly surprising then that in rigidly male-dominated cultures women "choose" to have many children. If a woman has no sons, she has to keep breeding until she does. If her children die — which they all too often do in the developing world — her survival chances in old age are endangered. So, despite the devastation to their health of constant pregnancies — sometimes six or seven before they are in their mid-twenties — women are often afraid to stop having children.

By contrast, in cultures that are moving toward equality for women, there are lower birth rates.[7] We see the same within countries where the overall birth rate is high. For example, birth rates are lower in the Indian province of Kerala, where women's status is higher than in other parts of India.

Over thirty years ago, Kathleen Newland showed that if we want to reduce birth rates, women have to have alternative sources of status, income, security, and satisfaction.[8] Many studies and reports — for instance, Population Action International's report *Closing the Gender Gap: Educating Girls* — have since come to the same conclusion.[9]

We have to stop the population explosion if we want a clean and healthy environment for our children. The only way to stop it humanely is to ensure women free access to birth control and life options other than having child after child. But again, to accomplish this, we need to change embedded cultural beliefs, values, and social and economic structures.

TECHNOLOGY, VALUES, AND THE CONQUEST OF NATURE

SOME PEOPLE CLAIM that technology is the cause of our environmental ills. There is no doubt that present industrial technologies cause environmental damage. But industrialization also gave more people access to manufactured goods, so that living standards rose. Going back to a less technologically advanced economy is not the answer. The issue is the beliefs and values that guide the development and use of technology.

There was no intrinsic reason industrial technology had to destroy our natural environment and endanger our health. This happened because these technologies were developed guided by a dominator ethos. Guided by a partnership ethos, industrial processes that avoid waste and pollution have recently been developed. I've already mentioned the Scandinavian manufacturing process known as the Natural Step that ensures that virtually all materials, both raw and finished, are recycled. The same partnership ethos has brought us laws and regulations that protect our environment and health.

The history of industrialization could have been very different. In a partnership rather than dominator context, industrialization could have developed with respect for both humans and nature. Ever more advanced technologies would not have been used for domination and conquest, or caused all the misery we are told comes with progress.

If we believe in "man's conquest of nature," we will do irreparable harm. If we learn to seek harmony with nature, technological breakthroughs could vastly improve our lives.

Think about what will happen if recent breakthroughs in biotechnology are guided by a dominator ethos. There are already concerns that programs designed to eliminate "undesirable" genes could eventually be used to eliminate "undesirable" people, even whole populations. Scientists warn that selective elimination of genes could eliminate the positive mutations that have played such a major role in the evolution of life.[10] Many people worry that cloning and other new technologies could unleash new life forms that will create serious problems.

So some people argue that we should prevent any use of these new technologies. But historically, once a technology is discovered, it has been used. A technological breakthrough is like letting a genie out of the bottle. Once it is out, it cannot be forced back in. The real question is how new technologies will be developed and used.

An editorial in the influential magazine *The Economist* recently gushed about the commercial opportunities for business and consumers offered by biotechnology. "Should people be able to retrofit themselves with transmitters, to enhance various mental powers?" they enthused. "Or to change the color of their skin? Or to help them run faster? Or lift heavier weights. . . . The proper goal is to allow people as much choice as possible about what they do. To this end, making genes instruments of such freedom, rather than limits upon it, is a great step forward."[11]

But what will really happen if commercial interests determine our genetic agenda? We have already seen what can happen when bioengineering is used purely for commercial gain: scientific reports that genetically modified foods may not be as safe as claimed were suppressed. When the renowned scientist Arpard Pusztai reported that genetically modified potatoes weakened the immune system of rats and damaged their vital organs, he was forced to retire from the Rowell Research Institute. This apparently happened due to pressure from Monsanto, a major producer of genetically engineered crops, which had earlier donated a quarter of a million dollars to the institute.[12]

You may ask, isn't this suppression of information against the law? Yes it is. But people get around laws. In the infamous Nestle's case, executives knowingly sent watered-down baby formulas to developing nations. They were later prosecuted. But prosecuting a few people does not prevent the suffering caused by commercial interests that put monetary profits above people's health, even people's lives.

Just dealing with corporate abuses on a case-by-case, after-the-fact basis doesn't address the skewed values reflected by many business practices and government policies. In the same way, U.S. training of health providers to recognize anthrax poisoning symptoms doesn't address the mindset that makes it possible for governments and terrorists to even think of using biotechnological breakthroughs for weapons that will infect "enemy" children, women, and men with smallpox and other terrible diseases.[13]

Our only hope for a more humane and environmentally sustainable future is changing dominator mindsets and the cultural values they reflect. As David Orr writes in *Earth in Mind,* the crisis in global ecology is first and foremost a crisis in values.[14]

CHANGING ECONOMIC RULES AND BUSINESS PRACTICES

IT'S UP TO YOU AND ME TO CARE for the place where we all live — our natural environment. As you will see, there are many things you can do to this end. The first, and simplest, is to help those around you understand that our environmental problems cannot be solved by the same system that's creating them.

Our present economic system comes out of more rigid dominator times. It depends largely on a cycle of overconsumption and wastefulness by some, exploitation of others, and environmental despoliation. This cycle is at the root of many environmental woes.

Overconsumption and waste by those on top is a perennial feature of dominator societies, whether pre-industrial or industrial, ancient or modern. In these societies, conspicuous consumption is a symbol of power. Control over possessions and other humans is a substitute for the emotional and spiritual fulfillment missing from a system rooted in fear and force.

Today's mass marketing capitalizes on these unmet human needs by telling us that our yearning for love, fulfillment, and joy will be met if we buy and buy and consume and consume. In a Häagen-Dazs ad, Bernadette Peters practically has an orgasm eating ice cream. The implied promise of sex with gorgeous women is used to sell everything from soft drinks to cars. Love is promised in ads for deodorants, diamonds, and so forth. So the rich buy ever more costly luxury goods and the poor jam the aisles of discount stores to buy ever more gadgets.[15] And all these useless, even harmful, objects clutter up our planet, while depleting our finite natural resources.

We have to make people aware of how our most basic emotional needs are manipulated by commercial interests. We have to change the economic rules that encourage pathological cycles of overconsumption, exploitation, and environmental despoliation.

AGAIN, I WANT TO EMPHASIZE that the issue is not bad people. It is bad economic rules — rules that come out of, and help maintain, dominator economic relations.

Certainly, some corporate executives are aware of the damage they cause, and deliberately conceal this knowledge as long as they think they can get away with it. There have been well-documented cases in the petrochemical, utilities, and other industries. The movie *Erin Brockovich* tells a true story. Pacific Gas & Electric executives deliberately deceived families about the health and environmental consequences of plant operations in their neighborhood. They said that an epidemic of failing health, including high rates of cancer and serious respiratory problems, had nothing to do with PG&E — until Ms. Brockovich exposed them. Bill Moyers's documentary *Trade Secrets* tells how executives at Dow Chemical, Chevron, Ethyl, Conoco, and other petrochemical giants deceived their employees. They never informed them of studies showing that working in petrochemical plants was slowly killing them, causing brain tumors, bone disintegration, and cancer.[16] As the tobacco company scandals demonstrate, unfortunately this kind of deception is not uncommon.

Still, I believe that most people are well-meaning and would like to make a living for themselves and their children without causing harm to others. But all too often they are caught in dominator economic rules. And these rules effectively support psychological predispositions to denial and fear of change.

For instance, current rules governing profits and losses for businesses do not include in the cost of manufacturing what economists call "externalities," such as the cost to our health and to our natural environment of many old industrial processes. Until we change these rules, we can't effectively curtail activities that pollute our air and water, since these activities are rewarded rather than penalized.

We need a different system of accounting. Calculations of profit and loss should include the costs to our environment and health caused by industrial processes and products. As it stands, consumers and taxpayers pay these costs, and there is little incentive for business to be more responsible. Taxes on "externalities" such as environmental and health damage, and tax credits for companies that change to more environmentally and socially responsible processes and products, can also make a huge difference.

As you saw in chapter 3, economic rules and business practices are human creations — and hence can be changed. We need rules that support relations of partnership/respect. We need corporate charters that require environmental and social responsibility. We need international treaties that protect nature. And we need new economic rules that recognize and accord real value to the work of caring and caregiving — including caring for Mother Earth. These economic policies are set forth in the partnership political agenda outlined at the end of this book.

You can promote partnership economic policies by talking with your friends and colleagues. You can start by pointing out that economic rules and business practices depend on human choices, and it's up to us to change the cultural values that determine these choices. You also can point out that technology itself is not the problem: the real issue is what kinds of technologies are funded, developed, and used.

You can promote partnership business practices such as the Natural Step that follows a "flow through" method where raw material is recycled and recyclable.[17] Ray Anderson's Interface, Inc., a carpet manufacturer in Atlanta, Georgia, has adopted this method. Because customers lease rather than buy their carpets, there is no waste. Like other environmentally responsible companies, Interface is doing well financially. As Amory and Hunter Lovins and Paul Hawken point out in *Natural Capitalism,* environmental responsibility is sound business.[18] But economic rules such as tax incentives for companies that are environmentally and socially responsible could greatly accelerate adoption of sounder manufacturing and business practices.

The solar oven is another effective new technology, particularly for the developing world. With a minimum of training, it can be used as a substitute for cooking with fossil fuels and wood. It is far less environmentally destructive, as it does not produce greenhouse gases. It uses a renewable resource — the sun — rather than depleting forests or requiring more tree planting in areas where farmland is already scarce. It is easy to produce, and costs less than ten dollars to buy, a huge savings for poor Third World families that often spend half the household income on fuel. Unlike wood and fossil fuels such as coal and oil, the solar oven does not produce the smoke that causes women (who spend a great deal of time cooking) lung disease and contributes to the death of millions of children. Larger solar ovens for villages can bake fifty loaves of bread in an hour — feeding hungry people, preserving wood supplies, improving health, preventing pollution, and creating jobs.

Yet in the present economic system, big companies do not push solar ovens. Under narrow dominator rules for calculating profit and loss, there's hardly any profit in this cheap technology. And, unlike power plants and nuclear reactors, the solar oven does not lend itself to centralized control.[19]

THIS MATTER OF CENTRALIZED CONTROL is a recurrent theme in dominator economics. Consider that most of the world's economic aid, through the World Bank, the International Monetary Fund, and from governments such as the United States, still goes to large enterprises owned by a few corporations and individuals. And much of it still goes to fund technologies of destruction and domination rather than technologies that support and enhance life.

Weapons developed and then exported by the U.S., France, Russia, and other nations heavily involved in "defense technology" fuel bloody conflicts, keep dictatorships in power, and clutter up our Earth with shells, mines, and other dangerous debris. The United States is the world's largest arms exporter. And much of U.S. foreign aid goes to governments so that they can buy weapons from U.S. companies, often helping dictators maintain control over the people in their countries. (As a side note, in Russia, South Africa, Colombia, and Angola, criminal gangs use weapons of war to wage turf battles. The same is going on in the gang wars of the U.S. around the drug trade. The United States also has by far the most small arms in the world — by one estimate, enough to arm every adult and child in its civil population.)[20]

These technologies of destruction not only kill and maim millions of human beings; they are a menace to our environment. Besides their toxic effects, these weapons are increasingly used to kill endangered species. In Africa, elephant poachers use automatic, large-bore military weapons to slaughter herds and intimidate guards at nature reserves.

Nuclear and bacteriological weapons threaten our planet on a larger scale — and they too are proliferating. Iraq has already used biological warfare against its Kurdish population. India and Pakistan have joined the nuclear club. Yet materials for nuclear and bacteriological weaponry are still exported for commercial profit, with no regard for the human and environmental consequences.

It does not have to be like this.

RECONNECTING WITH NATURE

SOME PEOPLE WILL TELL YOU that since time immemorial we humans have used technology to dominate and destroy. But the belief that this is human nature is not well founded. There are millions of people who honor others and nature. In many prehistoric societies nature was revered; for example, the Minoan civilization that flourished on Crete until approximately 3,500 years ago had a more partnership-oriented ethos described by archeologist Nicolas Platon as "an ardent faith in the goddess Nature, the source of all creation and harmony."[21] In some tribal societies, Mother Earth is revered to this day.

The awareness that we are all part of an exquisitely interwoven web of life is part of a resurging partnership consciousness. I think that deep inside we all carry this consciousness, that it lies behind the profound connection many of us feel with nature.

I remember vividly when my mother took me to visit my grandparents in the country. I was five years old, and I had often walked along the tree-lined avenues of Vienna, gone to parks, and seen gardens with brightly colored flowers. But I had never been to a place where woods and fields spread out as far as the eye could see, where rivers shimmered between groves of towering trees, where you could ride horses for hours across vast expanses of wild green land. I still remember the joy of that first deep connection with nature.

Since then, I have been privileged to visit some of the great natural wonders of our planet. I have traveled through the Rift Valley of Africa, where the sky is bluer than anywhere else on earth. I have been to the Iguazu Falls of South America, where miles of waterfalls cascade through lush tropical foliage alive with brilliant butterflies. I have seen elephants and lions roaming free in their natural habitat, monkeys swinging on trees along tropical rivers, the wildebeest migrations when millions of buffalo-like creatures travel every year across the African veld.

I want my grandchildren — and all children — to know nature. I want there to be a Nature for them to know. I want them to experience the awe and joy I have felt in nature. I want them to live in a world that is sustainable, a world that honors both humans and our Mother Earth.

If you think about it, every one of our environmental problems — from air and water pollution to global warming — is of our making. Our relationship with nature is terribly out of balance. As in any good relationship, there needs to be give and take. Too much of the twentieth century has focused on the taking, on using advanced technologies to further "man's conquest of nature." Hopefully, the twenty-first century will focus on a more balanced give and take — on partnership rather than domination.

In the next few pages you will find many things you can do to accelerate the shift to partnership with nature. Remember that you are not alone, that thousands of groups all over the world are working to restore our Earth.[22] But remember also that we cannot just tack on environmental balance to a fundamentally imbalanced system where control is the primary mindset — be it control over other humans or over nature. If enough of us join together, we can counter the integrated dominator political agenda and move toward the world we want for ourselves, our children, and generations to come.

PUTTING PARTNERSHIP TO WORK

When you look around our world, it sometimes seems like we need to change everything. Actually, it comes down to one thing: relationships. As we shift our relationships from the domination to the partnership model for our families, communities, and world, as we relate more in partnership to ourselves, others, and our natural habitat, we have better lives and a better world.

If you pick one item from this section and one from the action check list that follows, you will help change habits that are making us and our planet ill.

Buy biodegradable soaps and pesticide-free produce. Use energy-efficient lightbulbs and drive a car with low emissions. Ask your school district to replace diesel-burning school buses with buses that use natural gas, or better still, with electric school buses.

Write your representatives to support the Kyoto Protocol, the international treaty to reduce emissions of the heat-trapping gases that cause global warming. Write them asking that genetically engineered products not be sold until tested for long-range effects, and that they be clearly labeled.

Work to educate elected officials about new rules that protect our health and environment. European Union countries require manufacturers to provide for the recycling and disposal of the packaging of products. This has led to more environmentally-friendly packaging, including the elimination of Styrofoam inserts and plastic wraps for many products sold there.[23]

Obtain a list of environmentally and socially responsible

companies from Co-op America, an organization based in Washington, D.C. that publishes a newsletter with practical ideas on how to work for social justice and the environment.[24] This information will help you use your purchasing power to reward socially and environmentally responsible companies.

Support organizations working to bring appropriate technologies and technological know-how to women and men worldwide. UNESCO sponsors the distribution of solar ovens and training for their use in refugee camps in Zimbabwe, where it has been a lifesaver, particularly for women and children, who are the majority of the world's refugees.

Help halt the population explosion by supporting groups such as Planned Parenthood International, Population Action International, Zero Population Growth, Pathfinder International, and the Population Institute.[25] These and other organizations provide family planning technologies, both barriers to conception and herbal or chemical methods of contraception, as well as reproductive health counseling to women worldwide.[26]

Support organizations dedicated to raising the status of women, such as the Ms. Foundation, the Global Fund for Women, NOW, the National Women's Political Caucus, Women Living Under Muslim Laws, the Feminist Majority, and Women's International Network. These organizations help accelerate the cultural shift to partnership.

Vote for public officials who support funding for family planning at home and abroad. Use your voice, and your vote, to get those who oppose this funding out of office. Write legislators to support the United Nations Population Fund (UNFPA), which under the leadership of Dr. Nafis Sadik mounted a massive educational campaign linking overpopulation with environmental and human rights issues, particularly with the rights of women and children.[27]

Support environmental education by interesting your friends and colleagues in partnership education. Introduce partnership education in your community's schools. (You can download information about partnership education from www.partnershipway.org.)

Discredit the claims of think tanks and politicians who oppose environmental regulations by exposing their dangerous denial of reality. Organize a public forum about what actually lies behind the current roll-back of environmental regulations in the name of freedom and free enterprise. Call phone-in talk shows. Write editorials for the mainstream press.

Gather support for the integrated partnership political agenda outlined in chapter 6 and in "The Politics of Partnership" at the end of this book.

ACTION CHECKLIST
FIRST STEPS

❑ Think about the implications for your health and our natural environment when science and technology are influenced by commercial profit and loss.

❑ Think about the connection between science and technology, on the one hand, and cultural beliefs and social and economic rules and structures, on the other.

❑ Think about the connections between our environmental problems and overpopulation, and how raising the status of women is a key to solving these problems.

❑ Think about the mindset that allows people to use scientific knowledge to develop weapons such as poison gas or biological weapons that kill children, women, and men. What conclusions can you draw about how values of empathy and caring, conscience and social justice, are severed in the service of dominator goals?

❑ Imagine what it would be like to live in a world where our Mother Earth is honored and revered.

Next Steps

❑ Think about the integrated agenda of those trying to push us back to more rigid dominator times, and the need for an integrated partnership political agenda where respect for — not control over — humans and nature is key.

❑ Share the information in this chapter with your friends and colleagues.

❑ Subscribe to publications such as *Nucleus* (published by the Union of Concerned Scientists), *WIN News* (published by Women's International News Network), and *Popline* (published by the Population Institute).

❑ Form a discussion group to share the materials in this chapter.

Going Further

❑ Talk to parents, teachers, and local school boards about introducing partnership education so young people develop an ethos of caring and respect for one another and our natural habitat.

❑ Organize a conference on partnership standards for the use of technological breakthroughs. Document and share what you do, so it can be replicated in other communities and universities.

❑ Enroll local grassroots groups and other organizations to support the partnership political agenda, and use the Internet as an educational tool and means of communication to gain support for it.

Your Spiritual Relations

PUTTING LOVE INTO ACTION

What are partnership spiritual relations? Is spirituality something above and beyond us, something for just a few elevated beings? Or is it something we can all access every day of our lives?

Like many of us, you may be troubled by the greed, selfishness, excessive materialism, and violence in our world. You may be searching for a more spiritual and truly moral way of living. But when you look at both traditional and new spiritual teachings, you find a maze of contradictory messages. In this chapter, we will use the lens of the partnership/domination continuum to sort these messages. You will see how partnership spirituality can bring us deeper meaning, purpose, and joy.

I REMEMBER SEEING AN AD for a well-known New Age spiritual work called *A Course in Miracles* that said, "Seek not to change the world, but to change your mind about the world." Many traditional spiritual teachings, both Eastern and Western, have the same message. What is needed, we are told, is to transform ourselves internally, not the world outside.

Actually, we need to do both. Doing both inner and outer work gives greater meaning to our lives. It helps us live more fully. It makes it possible to integrate spirituality into our day-to-day lives. It inspires us with the spiritual courage to work for a world where the teachings of love found in all religions are put into action.

My mother had this spiritual courage, and it saved our lives. She had the courage to stand up to the Nazi thugs that came to loot our home and drag my father away. She could easily have been killed when she demanded my father's release. I don't know if it was that my mother (who was Jewish) looked Aryan with her blue eyes and blond hair, but by some miracle she prevailed, and we escaped the Nazis.

There were others who had this spiritual courage, people who helped Jews hide even though it meant risking their lives and the lives of their families. When they were asked afterward why they did it, they often said simply that they had to.

I believe all of us are born with an inner voice that tells us to be caring, not cruel; that it is the essence of what makes us human. Unfortunately this empathic inner voice is often stifled, even silenced, by the dominator elements in our culture — including the dominator elements in some of our religious traditions.

I know that questioning one's own religious tradition is wrenching. It can turn your whole existence upside down. But it can also be a deeply enlightening and, in the end, deeply spiritual experience.

This is what happened to me, and why I want to share my spiritual journey with you.

MY SPIRITUAL JOURNEY

LIKE MANY OF US, I grew up taking God for granted. After we fled to Cuba, every night at bedtime I repeated after my father the Jewish evening prayer, the *Shema*. I didn't understand the Hebrew words, and I don't think my father did. All I knew was that this was a special rite of bonding between us, this reaching out to a greater spiritual power in which we placed our trust. After the *Shema,* I always said my own prayer asking God for protection and help. As children will, I always made sure I didn't forget anyone, that I didn't omit a single name of those in our family left behind in Europe. It was a long list: my grandparents, aunts, uncles, cousins.

Then World War II ended, and I saw the newsreels of the concentration camps: the carelessly thrown piles of the dead, the skeletal bodies of the survivors with their hollow, haunted eyes. I found out what happened to those I had so faithfully prayed for, the cruel horror of their lives and deaths.

I still cry when I think of it. There are no words to describe what I felt as I grieved not only for the dead of my family and my people, but for the faith I lost. How could any God let this happen?

It was a long time before I ever thought of spirituality again. I went through the motions of going to synagogue on high holidays to please my parents. Later, I went to their home with my children to celebrate Passover and Chanukah. I never rejected my Jewish identity — I was, and am, a Jew.

I still found comfort in biblical passages such as Isaiah 11:6–9 and Hosea 2:18, predicting a world with no more war and no more killing. I still cherished the poetry of some of the Psalms. But I also began to open my eyes to things in the Bible I had never thought about — the commands in Numbers 31 and Deuteronomy 20 to raze cities and kill every living being in them lest God be angry that some were spared; the laws in Deuteronomy 22:20–21 that order the stoning of women to death; the double standard for men and women in sexual morality and the treatment of females as male property, as "thy neighbor's wife, . . . ox, . . . ass." I woke up to what was communicated about human relations in stories like the "moral" tale of Lot, who offered his daughters to be raped by a mob to protect two male guests — and got rewarded instead of punished when his guests turned out to be angels sent by God.[1]

Awakening to this side of my religious heritage was both shocking and illuminating. I was horrified by these teachings of violence, cruelty, and inhumanity — and appalled that they had been there in plain sight, yet I'd never reflected on what they taught. At the same time, I still found value in those parts of the Bible that teach empathy, respect, and caring. These biblical teachings, and the Jewish tradition of helping the less fortunate modeled by my parents, were — and continue to be — extremely important to me.

IT WASN'T UNTIL YEARS LATER, after a long search for new faith and decades of research into the history of religion, that I again began to use the word "spirituality." Except now it had a very different meaning for me. It was no longer associated with a specific deity, but with a larger reality beyond human comprehension. Neither was it associated with sitting on a mountaintop meditating, or joining a monastery to withdraw from the pains and pleasures of this world. Spirituality was now associated with a simple word, a word that, not coincidentally, is at the core of all the world's religious traditions: love. But it was no longer love in the disembodied, abstract sense found in so many religious texts. It was love in the very immediate, concrete sense of caring connection in this life on this Earth.

I became aware that my most illuminating spiritual experiences have come when I feel at one with nature or with others of our kind — when I see a glorious sunset, when I look into my grandchildren's sparkling eyes, hear the beloved voices of my children, or touch my husband's hand. I became aware that these experiences in one way or another involved loving, reaching out beyond myself. I also became aware, although I had never thought of it this way, that in trying to help make this world a more caring place, I was spiritually re-educating myself.

Now when I think of spirituality, I think of our profound human capacity for love, our striving for justice, our hunger for beauty, our yearning to create. This is a partnership spirituality, a spirituality that helps us be in partnership with what is called our higher selves.

Partnership spirituality is both transcendent and immanent. It informs our day-to-day lives with caring and empathy. It provides ethical and moral standards for partnership relations as alternatives to both lack of ethical standards and the misuse of "morality" to justify oppression and violence.

SPIRITUALITY — AND PAIN OR PLEASURE

WHEN YOU THINK OF SPIRITUALITY, what comes to mind? What images do you see? Are they images of pain or pleasure?

Questions about pain and pleasure may strike you as strange for spirituality. But they are key questions. They help us find our way through the maze of religious teachings that alternately preach love and hate, caring and cruelty, nonviolence and violence.

Have you ever wondered why museums house so many paintings of people suffering hideous tortures in Hell, of so many saints killed in the most terrible ways? Why were Christians in the Middle Ages taught to think of the world as a "vale of tears"? Why were mystics encouraged to show their devotion by wearing hair shirts, lying on beds of nails, and other ways of tormenting their bodies? Why are Hindus still taught that their only hope lies at the end of a long cycle of reincarnations that brings them back to this world again and again, always doomed to suffering?

Consider for a moment the message of these teachings — the Christian doctrine that our only hope lies in some better life after death, or the Hindu dogma that the caste system is divinely ordained. Isn't the message that pain and suffering are our inevitable lot? Aren't we being told to accept what is and just hope for a better afterlife? Isn't there another message, too: Don't do anything to change the status quo — no matter how cruel, painful, or unjust?

Consider also the story of Job, how God afflicted him with every conceivable pain just to win a bet with the Devil. Consider the Christian teaching that if we don't obey the Church's commands, we're doomed to the fires of Hell for eternity.[2] Why are control and pain so prominent, and freedom and pleasure so forbidden in much of Eastern and Western religious dogma? Why is this, when what we humans most want is to avoid pain and feel pleasure?

When I first began to ask these questions, I felt very uncomfortable. I was, after all, dealing with matters I'd been told to take on faith, and it frightened me. Somewhere inside I still feared divine punishment for daring to question what I had been taught was God's will.

Only later did I realize that asking these questions was the first step toward finding my own spiritual way. I had the analytical lens of the partnership/domination continuum. So I could see that the reason for teaching that we should just accept control and pain wasn't religious. These teachings are designed to maintain power imbalances.

Simply put, there are two basic human motivations. One is seeking pleasure. The other is avoiding pain. A society that motivates people mainly through pleasure tends to be more partnership oriented. By contrast, pain and fear of pain is the glue that holds together rigid rankings of domination — man over woman, man over man, race over race, nation over nation.

Understanding this finally helped me understand why so many of our sacred stories and images — both Western and Eastern — link the sacred with the infliction of suffering or pain. It also helped me understand why there is so much emphasis on control and obedience.

Most of our written history carries a heavy dominator stamp. Consider many of the religious teachings on sex. Men are taught to think of sex in terms of control over women. The Bible has rules that require men to stone to death women suspected of sexual independence. For hundreds of years, the Church condemned every sexual position except man on top and woman on bottom — what came to be known as the "missionary position." This too subconsciously programs women to accept subordination and men to think of domination as normal, sexually exciting, even moral.

Making matters worse, for century after century the pleasures of the body were linked with sin and punishment. Saint Augustine, whose views were accepted by the Church, is a classic case. For him, the act of sex — the act that gives us life and pleasure — was the "original sin" of Adam and Eve that transmits humanity's sinfulness from generation to generation. So, not surprisingly, the medieval Church decreed that sex for pleasure is sinful even within marriage. As Pope Gregory the Great put it, if a couple has sex that is not strictly for the necessary act of procreation, without "the admixture of lust," they "besmirch the conjugal bond."[3]

While the medieval Church condemned sex for pleasure as a horrible sin, it never said that sexual violence against women is a sin. Instead, in the *Malleus Maleficarum,* the medieval handbook for persecuting and burning "witches" blessed by Pope Innocent VIII, the Church labeled woman as more carnal, and hence more sinful, than man.

Nor did the Church condemn the constant warfare of medieval kings and nobles. On the contrary, the Church itself unleashed terrible hate and violence. It instigated the Crusades and the Inquisition. It blessed the witch hunts, during which, by the most conservative estimates, 100,000 European women were tortured to death. Given the small population of Europe in those times, this slaughter of women was a holocaust comparable to the killing of six million Jews by the Nazis.[4]

You may think this is just history: what does it mean for my life? But dominator elements in religious traditions — Eastern and Western — affect our lives profoundly. They are a major obstacle to the movement toward a partnership way of living and loving.

FORTUNATELY, THERE IS A POWERFUL PARTNERSHIP voice at the core of all world religions.[5] A spirituality that tells us to accept things as they are, to unquestioningly obey "higher authorities" — including punitive, angry deities — is not the spirituality of the great religious visionaries of history. Isaiah and Jesus, Gautama and Hildegard of Bingen did not ask us to tolerate injustice and cruelty. They tried to change things — Jesus stopped the stoning of a woman and Hildegard stood up to a pope.

At the core of the major faiths — Hindu, Buddhist, Muslim, Hebrew, Christian, Confucian — are the partnership values of sensitivity, empathy, caring, and nonviolence. These are the spiritual values many of us are striving to reclaim. These are the values that support the relationships we yearn for. They are the values we can use to develop a partnership spirituality that infuses our day-to-day lives with empathy, caring, and responsibility — a spirituality focused on joy, life, and love rather than pain, death, and hate.

You may say, wait, pain is part of life — we all get sick, old, and eventually die. Of course, partnership spirituality recognizes pain as part of the human experience. It recognizes the pain of birth, death, illness, sadness, rejection, and other inevitable hurts — and when possible, comforts us. Partnership spirituality also recognizes that pain can bring about psychic growth. But it does *not* hold that suffering is necessary for spiritual development. On the contrary, when people are truly loved rather than abused, they are more likely to be empathic, caring, creative — to develop their noblest spiritual qualities.

So pleasure, not pain, is sacred in partnership spirituality. Pleasure, however, isn't self-centered, frantic "fun." It isn't the escape from pain mistaken for pleasure in dominator societies. It's certainly not pleasure at someone else's expense. It is the joy of love, the fulfillment of kindness and sharing, the wondrous awe at the miracle of life and nature, and the ecstasy of heightened states of consciousness.

GOD AS MOTHER AND FATHER

YOU MAY BE SHOCKED BY THE IDEA that pleasure can imbue our day-to-day lives with the sacred. But this view is gaining currency among theologians. Carter Heyward, Carol Christ, Elizabeth Dodson Gray, Matthew Fox, and Judith Plaskow all write about an "embodied spirituality."

In dictionaries, body (or embodiment) and spirit (or spirituality) are as separate as they are in our society. However, we're all familiar with one aspect of an embodied spirituality. Many of our images of deity are embodied. But here, too, there's a hidden dominator message: the deity is pictured in a *male* body.

In Western tradition, God appears exclusively in male form. In Eastern tradition, the more powerful divinities are male — except for an occasional bloodthirsty deity such as the monstrous Hindu Kali.

Partnership spirituality sees the divine in both female and male form. And it does not focus on the power to inflict pain and kill, but on the power to give life and pleasure.

Again, you may find this idea new and radical. Actually, it is very ancient.

Many prehistoric images of deity emphasize the life-giving and nurturing aspects of woman's body — the aspect we today call God as Mother or Mother Goddess. Alexander Marshack, James Mellaart, and other scholars point out that the 30,000-year-old Stone Age nude figures that nineteenth century archeologists mislabeled "Venuses" are the first Western Goddess representations. Twenty thousand years later, in the agricultural societies of the Neolithic (circa 8000 to 3500 B.C.E.), female images still predominated, indicating what Mellaart calls a remarkable, millennia-long cultural continuity.

There were also male deities in these earlier societies. They were, however, not associated with thunderbolts (like Jehovah or Wotan) or weapons (like Zeus or Thor), strongly suggesting that masculinity was not synonymous with domination and conquest.[6]

But then came a massive cultural shift. In the Babylonian *Enuma Elish,* an epic poem written over four thousand years ago, a war god called Marduk dismembers the living body of the Mother Goddess

Tiamat to create land and sea. This myth idealizes Marduk's violence and demonizes the Mother Goddess. But earlier myths from that region are very different. They credit a Mother Goddess, not a violent male deity, with creating the world. This Mother Goddess was often described not only as the source of life but also of love, wisdom, and prosperity.

Archeological excavations from the Neolithic indicate that the first art idealizing armed male force came late in Western cultural evolution.[7] In Europe, this art dates from the Indo-European invasions (circa 4000–3000 B.C.E.), which brought an ethos of conquest and domination. In *The Chalice and the Blade in Chinese Culture,* a work that tests my cultural transformation theory in Asia, scholars at the Chinese Academy of Social Sciences in Beijing show that this shift also took place in China.[8] Anthropologist June Nash's study of the Aztecs shows a similar shift in the Americas.[9]

While this information is still not widely disseminated, if we know what to look for, we find traces of more partnership-oriented cultures in all world traditions — often in plain sight. In the Bible, when the prophet Jeremiah rails against the Hebrew people for backsliding from the worship of Jehovah, they respond that there was peace and prosperity when women baked cakes for the Queen of Heaven (Jeremiah 44:15–17). Ancient Greek, Indian, and other mythological traditions are full of female deities, even though most are already subservient to male ones. The most popular Chinese deity to this day is Kuan Yin. The Christian Mary is also known as the Mother of God. And like Kuan Yin, she is associated with love and compassion.

SINCE THE VENERATION OF FEMALE DEITIES originated in more partnership-oriented times, it's no coincidence that female images of the divine are reemerging in our time of partnership resurgence. As theologian Sallie McFague writes, in Judeo-Christian tradition, the

Father God has been pictured more as redeemer from sins than as giver of life. His love has been understood as "disinterested," involving no need or desire or feeling for the objects of his love. By contrast, God as Mother is associated with feeling and nurturing, adding a dimension of caring.

McFague asks us to consider what happens when we think of God as both Mother and Father: Doesn't the image of God as Mother expand and deepen our conception of God? "A theology that sees God as the parent who feeds the young and, by extension, the weak and vulnerable, understands God as caring about the most basic needs of life in its struggle to continue," she writes.[10]

Seeing God as both Mother and Father has direct consequences for what we think is normal and moral. It impacts whether we really value democracy and caring or value authoritarian control. As we have seen, the nurturing parent — the stereotypically feminine role in dominator mindsets — is the metaphor for a politics of partnership. The punitive parent — the stereotypically male role in dominator mindsets — is the metaphor for a politics of domination.

How we see God also directly affects how we view the most basic aspects of life: sex, birth, and death. Many Western sacred stories and images vividly portray acts of killing and dying — but images of the act of giving birth are totally absent. In earlier, more partnership-oriented societies where the deity was embodied in female form, birth-giving images are prominent. For example, in the Neolithic site of Catal Huyuk in Turkey, we find an 8,000-year-old figure of a seated Goddess giving birth.

When I first looked at these images, it seemed natural to me to make giving life, rather than ending it, sacred. But I was still taken aback by Neolithic and Bronze Age art that pictured sexuality as a sacred part of life and nature. Of course, this too makes sense in a spirituality, and society, where pleasure rather than pain holds relations together.

LOVE, SEX, AND THE SACRED

NOT SO LONG AGO, pregnant women could not teach school. It was deemed improper for children to see their swelling bodies. Even today, many people think sex education is wrong. They think it's wrong to even talk about sex to children — although they think exposing them to violent stories, images, and games is perfectly normal. Small wonder we were never taught about ancient art and myth dealing with sex.[11]

The earliest deciphered writings of Western civilization, the cuneiform tablets of Sumer, tell of the sacred union of Inanna, the Sumerian Queen of Heaven and Earth, and her lover, the King-God Dumuzi.[12] Inanna's breasts are described as pouring out plants and water, combining sexual imagery with portrayals of the Earth's fecund beauty. Other passages describe sensual pleasure:

> He put his hand in her hand.
> He put his hand to her heart.
> Sweet is the sleep of hand-to-hand.
> Sweeter still the sleep of heart-to-heart.[13]

Thousands of years later, in the biblical Song of Songs, we still find traces of this earlier spiritual tradition.[14] The beautiful Shulamite, the Rose of Sharon, sings to her lover, "I am my beloved's and my beloved is mine . . . a bundle of myrrh is my well-beloved unto me; he shall lie all night betwixt my breasts."[15]

Mystical writings, particularly Eastern ones, contain innumerable clues to a time when woman's body, man's body, and sexuality were part of the sacred. Spirituality is frankly erotic. We read of passion, intense feeling, and tantric yoga teaches explicitly that sexual union is a path to the divine. But in these writings, we already see signs of the shift to a dominator way of life.

In tantric yoga, woman's body is imbued with divine energy. But, unlike the Hymns of Inanna, most tantric writings focus on the spiritual experience of the man. The woman is a mere vehicle for his bliss. Moreover, the human body is considered of a lower order than the spirit.[16]

In Western mystical traditions, there are even more drastic changes. The sacred union between a female and male deity now becomes a union between God and one of his "earthly flock" — usually another male. The female deity has been eliminated from this "mystical marriage." And, tellingly, the emphasis is no longer on pleasure, but on pain.[17]

Mystics flagellate themselves. They lie on beds of nails. They tattoo their bodies with hot irons. But they write about this masochism, this cruel domination of their bodies, as an ecstatic road to oneness with God.[18]

So we see that a transformation of both myth and reality has taken place. Ancient myths and symbols have been radically changed to meet the requirements of a system that elevates male over female, and is primarily held together by pain and fear rather than pleasure and caring.

This then is the dark side of our religious heritage — the dark and indeed the sick side of spirituality diverted from its higher purpose by the dominator ethos. It's understandably hard for many of us to come to grips with this. But if we don't, we unthinkingly accept a system that continues to cause enormous suffering.

UNRAVELING AND REWEAVING OUR SPIRITUAL HERITAGE

ALL AROUND US, WE SEE MORAL AND SPIRITUAL CONFUSION. On one side are those who incite scapegoating and violence under the guise of religious morality. On the other side are those who consider ethical and moral standards nothing more than cultural constructs that vary from time to time and place to place. If we seek counsel in our traditional religious scriptures, we are confronted by massive contradictions.

How can we make sense of the biblical commandment "Thou shalt not kill," when passage after passage contradicts this commandment? In Numbers 31 and Deuteronomy 20, we are led to believe that God approves of massacres of whole populations. In Leviticus 20:9, we are told that children who curse their parents must be killed. How do we take biblical passages approving of slavery (Leviticus 25:44–46) and even of a man selling his daughter into slavery (Exodus 21:7)? What should we make of Jesus' teaching that we should love one another and live in peace, when in Revelations 12:19 angels pour out "the wrath of God upon the earth," and terrible horrors are unleashed on everybody — except the chosen "hundred and forty and four thousand," who, according to chapter 14:3, "were redeemed from the earth"?

If these contradictions distress us and we're tempted to flee East, like many people in New Age circles, we find the same problem. As in Judeo-Christian tradition, there are teachings in Hindu, Muslim, and Buddhist scriptures about honesty, respect, and love. But there are also contradictory teachings, some very brutal. For instance, one of the most celebrated Hindu stories tells us that when the great god Vishnu was a baby his father set out to kill him — but that a girl baby was put in his place to be killed instead. The Muslim Koran tells us that a disobedient wife should be beaten by her husband. In epics such as the Hindu *Mahabharata,* violence and cruelty are presented as divine attributes in bloody battles between deities.

What do these teachings tell us about how men should treat women? What do they say about the value of a girl's life compared to a boy's? What do they teach about killing girls and women with impunity? What do they teach about human relations in general — about the "morality" of using force to impose one's will on others, about the "morality" of killing human beings considered less valuable than others?

STORIES PROVIDE MODELS FOR BEHAVIOR. When these are religious stories, they carry enormous moral authority. So do rules and commands found in sacred scriptures. If we turn a blind eye to stories and rules that justify injustice and brutality, can we realistically expect a better world?

Looking at our spiritual traditions through the partnership/domination lens makes it possible to find our way to the spirituality and morality we need. We *can* retain the healthy, truly moral teachings in our religious traditions and discard the unhealthy, inhuman ones.

Sorting out partnership from dominator teachings in our scriptures is one of our greatest challenges. It isn't easy. There is much opposition, both inside and outside of us. But if we do nothing, we can't successfully counter the religious hatemongering regaining strength today in both the East and West. Nor can we counter the rudderless view that there are no moral or ethical standards — that to insist on standards is being "too judgmental."

A morality for partnership relations has basic standards rather than a patchwork of contradictory rules. Its primary standard is the moral imperative of moving through our lives with awareness, empathy, and respect. This standard fosters the sense of oneness that is at the core of partnership spirituality.

Obviously, this standard cannot be tolerated in domination-oriented cultures. If we are sensitive to others, how can we enforce rigid rankings backed up by fear and force? Moral sensitivity has to be repressed, or at least fragmented. It has to be completely suppressed in relations with "out-groups," as when religious demagogues preach hate against homosexuals and terrorists kill "enemy" children in "holy wars."[19] It also has to be suppressed in relations between "superiors" and "inferiors" — be it in families and workplaces or politics and economics.

We need to expose those who use the name of God to perpetuate cruelty, violence, and pain. We need to counter those who would indiscriminately discard all religious teachings. At a time when we humans have the power of total destruction once associated only with

God — technologies that can wipe us out — we need moral clarity more than ever before.

LOVE AND SPIRITUAL COURAGE

WE HAVE A CHOICE. We can do nothing and sit by on the sidelines. Or we can cultivate the spiritual courage to challenge religious stories and rules that are inhuman.

Though it may sometimes seem impossible, religious teachings can change. They have changed in the past. But the only reason they changed is that people took it upon themselves to make them change. For example, determined people eventually succeeded in stopping the Church's holy wars, inquisitions, and witch burnings.

We don't have to accept a spirituality that merely helps us cope with chronic injustice and misery, that teaches us to accept anything and everything as the manifestation of divine will. Every one of us can lead the way to a partnership spirituality. Men and women from both established religions and New Age communities are already taking leadership roles. To give just a few examples: theologians Hans Kung, Carter Heyward, Rosemary Radford Ruether, and Walter Wink from Christian tradition; the Dalai Lama, Thich Nhat Hanh, and Gelek Rinpoche from Buddhist tradition; rabbis Zalman M. Schachter-Shalomi, Laura Geller, and Michael Lerner from Jewish tradition; Abdul Hadi Palazzi, Secretary General of the Italian Muslim Association, and religious scholar Dure Ahmed, from Muslim tradition; Marianne Williamson, Neale Donald Walsch, Barbara Marx Hubbard, Thom Hartmann, Starhawk, and John Robbins from the "new spirituality" camp.

You, too, can initiate change. You can persuade others that faith should not mean accepting injustice and oppression as God's will. You can talk to your rabbi, priest, or mullah and enlist them in speaking out against stories and rules that lead people to persecute and kill in the name of God. You can introduce partnership spiritual and moral education in churches, synagogues, mosques, and other places of worship. (The section at the end of this chapter outlines the core elements of this education.)

Rather than remaining silent, we can each speak out against what is cruel, unfair, and immoral. Rather than looking for another prosperous guru and following his commands, we can each help identify, and support, the partnership core of our world's religious traditions.

I believe the voice of love is the real voice of God, of that mysterious cosmic energy that brought us the beauty of stars and sunsets, of caring and creativity, of all that gives joy and meaning to our lives. I believe that we all have this inner voice of love, and that we all can help build a world where love is embodied, nature is respected, and our human need for fairness and caring is honored.

All we need is spiritual courage. This is the lesson my mother taught me. Because ultimately spirituality is not just talking about love. It is putting love into action.

PUTTING PARTNERSHIP TO WORK

PARTNERSHIP SPIRITUAL AND MORAL EDUCATION

What does spiritual and moral education mean? How do we educate young people for spirituality? How do we help them understand that hurting and killing others in the name of God and morality is immoral? How can we teach them a morality based on empathy and caring? What behaviors do we need to model so children learn to be ethical and responsible?

There are four components of partnership spiritual education.

WE NEED TO DEVELOP THE CAPACITY TO LISTEN TO OUR INNER WISDOM.

Meditation and prayer combine intense concentration and "letting go." They can take us past the noise of the old dominator tapes to connect with what is most evolved in us — our capacity for love. However, looking inward is not enough. Looking outward is equally important.

BECOME FULLY CONSCIOUS OF OTHERS AND WHAT'S HAPPENING AROUND US.

Being sensitive to others enables us to live our spirituality. Without this mindfulness, spirituality becomes little more than self-indulgence.

LEARN PARTNERSHIP MORAL STANDARDS OF EMPATHY, CARING, AND RESPONSIBILITY.

The analytical lens of the partnership/domination continuum makes it possible to sort and evaluate the contradictory rules and commands we've inherited from more domination-oriented times. This lens is a powerful tool for spiritual education. It helps us navigate through the moral confusion of our time, and distinguish between partnership moral sensitivity and dominator moral insensitivity.[20]

PUT PARTNERSHIP MORAL STANDARDS INTO PRACTICE.

Partnership spirituality is transcendent *and* immanent. Partnership spiritual education helps young people learn skills and habits for relations based on empathy and respect rather than control and submission.

Children learn by imitation. If we want to educate young people to be truly moral, we need to model moral behaviors. This doesn't mean we have to be saints. It does mean that we adults also need to educate ourselves spiritually and morally.

Children learn from stories. They need partnership fables and stories. Unfortunately, some stories routinely used for moral education — such as the stories of Cain and Abel, Abraham and Isaac, Joseph and his brothers, or Samson and Delilah — do not model partnership behaviors. Certainly children should study the Bible as a foundation of Western culture. But they need tools to sort out the dominator and partnership elements; the lens of the partnership/domination continuum gives them this analytical tool.

Children learn by doing. In *Tomorrow's Children,* I propose that caring for life — for self, for others, and for Mother Earth — be part of the curriculum, from preschool to graduate school. These are essential spiritual and moral skills.

Educating adults and children in partnership parenting is a key to caring for life. Partnership or dominator relations begin at home. Not just in your home, but in homes all over the world. Education for empathic, responsible parent-child and gender relations is foundational to partnership morality and spirituality.

Teaching boys and girls empathic, responsible parenting will break cycles of violence that escalate from homes to intertribal and international violence. International violence won't stop until we stop intimate violence. The United Nations, at least in principle, promotes a culture of peace. But we need to move from declarations of principle to partnership practices.

Much of the current school curriculum conflicts directly with teachings about nonviolence, empathy, and caring. Look at all the emphasis on wars and conquests. In a curriculum informed by the partnership model, young people still learn about this part of history, but it isn't idealized. They learn about evolution from a larger perspective that includes, and highlights, the evolution of love and spirituality. This gives them a more complete, accurate, and hopeful view of what being human means.[21]

ACTION CHECKLIST

FIRST STEPS

❑   Celebrate the beauty and miracle of love and life.

❑   Spend five minutes a day in meditative or reflective mode. Sit quietly, focusing on the sensations in your body, on your surroundings, and the interconnection of all beings and energy in the universe. Reflect on how all elements are in one great partnership — interconnected in manifold subtle, mysterious ways.

❑   Think about your most profound spiritual experiences. Did they involve an experience in nature? With a loved one? A child? Perhaps an unexpected expression of caring from a stranger? What do these experiences teach you about yourself?

❑   Think about what you've been taught to associate with morality. Consider whether it promotes or inhibits empathy and caring. Sort these teachings into partnership and dominator morality. Write them down in two columns that you can share with others for further discussion.

❑   Consider how partnership spirituality does not place man and spirituality over woman and nature.

❑   Consider the legacy of Jesus as a teacher of "feminine" values of caring and empathy, and how, in a partnership-oriented world, these values can be put into action by both men and women.

❑   Consider how the image of God as both Mother and Father

expands and deepens our conception of God, and what this means for our day-to-day lives.

❑ Consider how integrating the erotic and the sacred leads to a worldview in which both giving and receiving pleasure and love become the highest expression of sacred living.

NEXT STEPS

❑ Promote partnership teachings such as honesty, caring, and nonviolence as expressed in your religious tradition.

❑ Support efforts to adopt human rights standards as cornerstones of religious morality.

❑ Collect stories from all religious traditions showing that being spiritual doesn't mean making no judgments or standing above political and social issues. For example, Jesus challenged the authorities of his time.

❑ Practice spiritual work not only as "inner work" but in having the courage to speak up for justice.

❑ Find the spiritual courage to challenge dominator stories and rules as expressed in your spiritual or religious tradition.

GOING FURTHER

❑ Form a study group in your church, synagogue, mosque, or other religious group to identify and discuss partnership and dominator themes as expressed in the stories and rules of your religion.

❑ Use the section "Partnership Spiritual and Moral Education" above to start a partnership Sunday school group.

❑ Ask the leaders of your denomination to participate in a campaign to end violence against women and children.

❑ Involve your religious denomination in supporting the partnership political agenda outlined in "The Politics of Partnership" at the end of this book. Urge them to counter the dominator

political agenda of fundamentalist religious groups that have
influenced politics in the United States and other world
regions.

❑ Ask theologians and departments of religious studies to use
the analytical lens of the partnership/domination continuum to
identify stories and teaching that support either partnership or
dominator ways of thinking and living.

Partnership Living

IT BEGINS WITH YOU

I JUST CAME HOME FROM A WALK by the ocean. A little girl was running on the sand, and I thought of my five year-old granddaughter's last visit. On these late afternoon walks I often think of my grandchildren, of their joy running on the beach, and of my joy watching them against the backdrop of majestic blue waves and beautiful green hills rising into the sky.

When I think of my grandchildren, I think of what I wish for their lives. I'm thankful that they're blessed with wonderful parents who give them enormous love. I'm thankful that through partnership parenting they're learning how to become caring, responsible, accomplished adults. I'm thankful that at home and at school they're encouraged to develop their unique potentials, and that chances are good that they'll find meaningful work and loving life companions. But then I think about the kind of world they will inherit.

Will the beach where we love to walk when they visit be here for them and their children? Or will it be drowned under the rising seas of global warming predicted unless environmental policies change? Will they be faced with the diminished living standards and shortages predicted if the world's population keeps doubling every generation? And what about the biological terrorism experts predict will escalate? What will happen to them if these trends aren't halted? What will happen if the religious fanaticism sweeping our world isn't arrested? With their free-thinking upbringing, will they be targets? And even if they aren't, what kind of life can they have in a world of so much hate and violence?

When these thoughts come, I remind myself that in many ways our world is better than it was only a hundred years ago. I remind myself of all the gains we owe to women and men who acted to make their visions of better things come true. I remind myself that, despite the current regression, there is strong movement toward partnership worldwide. I remind myself that I am not alone, that millions of people are already on the partnership path, without giving it that name. This spurs me on to turn my fears into purposeful action.

YOU CAN MAKE A DIFFERENCE

AS WE'VE SEEN IN THIS BOOK, many dysfunctional personal and social habits are products of a dominator/control way of life. These habits cause a great deal of damage in how we relate to ourselves, our loved ones, our co-workers, our local, national, or international communities, and our Mother Earth.

As we've also seen, habits can be changed. I have certainly changed many of my habits of thinking and feeling. I have learned to question much that I was taught about "human nature" — including my own. I have changed many of my ideas and behaviors. And time and again, I found that the first step to change is awareness.

When you become aware of the difference between the partnership/respect and domination/control models, you see that you have choices in every moment of your life. When you use this new language to describe what really happens in families, workplaces, and nations, you automatically think of the consequences of your choices for yourself, those you love, those you work with, and all those with whom you interact, as well as those you'll never meet or interact with directly.

When your awareness changes, your habits of thinking and feeling change. You begin to focus on relationships as key to your individual growth and to the kind of world you live in. You question harmful habits of relating you never noticed.

When you begin to change these habits, you gain even greater awareness of the difference between partnership and dominator relationships in every aspect of life. As your awareness deepens, you in turn make more changes in how you think, feel, and act. So the more you change, the more your awareness grows. And the more your awareness grows, the more you initiate change in your life and the lives of others, helping them express in their actions the truths they hold in their hearts.

At first, the changes you make may be subtle, sometimes barely perceptible. But it is enough that you are making the effort to start a process that will empower you and those you care about to make a true and lasting difference in the world. None of us will always be in a partnership mode. But the more you help those you love and those with whom you interact to choose awareness and partnership over denial and domination, the better for us all.

What each of us does and thinks truly matters. Be bold, be persistent, and be patient. Be focused, and do not give up. Remember that cynicism leads to depression and feelings of powerlessness, robbing us of the energy and will to make changes. Remember that by not doing anything you're actually doing something that perpetuates cruelty and injustice. Remember how much we owe to people just like you and me, people who chose to take a position, envision a better way, and act to attain their goal. And remember that in ever widening circles over the years your purposeful actions will spread — and inspire others to act in their turn.

THE CHALLENGE AND THE OPPORTUNITY

THE SIMPLE MESSAGE to take from this book is that change begins with small acts and thoughts. You can initiate changes both in your life and the lives of others.

If every month you focus on just one item from one action checklist in this book, change will start. If you send "The Politics of Partnership" section at the end of this book to one organization a month, if you enlist one organization every six months to work for the partnership political agenda, change will start.

The problem is not "human nature." It is not science and technology. The problem is that the domination/control model leads to imbalanced relations with ourselves, our planet, and those with whom we share the planet. Viewing our challenges from the perspective of partnership is the first step. By expanding our awareness and helping expand that of others, we begin the long journey home to the kind of society we need to survive and thrive.

As we become aware of the unnecessary suffering in our world — our own and that of others — we feel sad and angry. I am sad and angry that there is so much injustice in the world, that so many people are deprived of the most basic sustenance, respect, and caring, that there is so much abuse and violence. But I have learned that the way to handle these feelings — which otherwise might eat me up — is to transform them into positive action. One positive action I have taken is to write this book. If this book helps others become more aware of the domination-partnership choice, the sadness and anger that fueled my desire to write it will have had a positive impact.

I encourage you to channel your anger and sadness into positive action. Reading this book is already a start. Imagine what would happen if a thousand new people embraced partnership thinking and living every month. Imagine if this happens all over the world. In a few years, the number of people focusing on partnership as a viable alternative would be in the hundreds of millions.

Imagine what would happen if a hundred Partnership Political Action committees formed every month, if thousands of people shared the Partnership Political Agenda with colleagues, students, family, and friends, if they organized workshops, conferences, and public forums to discuss it, and presented it at universities, churches, and through web sites. Imagine what would happen as the Partnership Political Agenda gets wider media coverage, and this in turn enlists more organizations and individuals to unite in support of the personal, social, and economic transformation needed to move to partnership relations.

What a profound change this would make in the world we share. The change would be felt on every level. Families would change, corporations would change, local organizations and governments would change, national governments would change, international corporations would change, international religious groups would change.

None of this change will happen overnight, and some of this change will challenge individuals and organizations to stretch to their limits. But these challenges will enrich those who meet them with unimaginable rewards.

We can each play a part in creating a world that supports the virtues of joy, pleasure, sacred communion, creativity, trust, and equality. A world in which such virtues are everyday, commonplace occurrences is within our grasp. We can begin today. Embracing the sustainable and life-enhancing partnership way in our own lives is the key — the pebble that sends ripples throughout humanity in ever greater waves.

You are already on the path to partnership. Join with us who are part of the partnership movement. We can all be leaders in this movement. Young people can form Youth for Partnership groups. Older people can form Elders for Partnership groups. Partnership groups can be formed by homemakers, teachers, nurses, engineers, scientists, physicians, and so on. Together we can help others discover partnership principles and incorporate them into their lives. Together we can build a more just and joyful society.

The new science emerging from breakthroughs in physics, biology, psychology, and metaphysics reveals what spiritual sages have long told us: we are all interconnected even when we cannot perceive connections. Science also shows that we humans are unique in our capacity to envision and create new realities — we can direct our own evolution.

Every moment of our lives is an opportunity, a potential moment for partnership and the sharing of love, achievement, growth, and accomplishment. Contrary to what we're taught, life is not a zero-sum game. Energy is never destroyed, and love does not decrease in the giving — the more we give, the more of it we have to give.

The dominator habits we have inherited linger. They threaten us, our loved ones, our world. But the movement toward partnership offers grounded hope for the better life and world we all want. Every one of us, no matter who we are or where we are, can become part of the partnership movement.

It is my prayer for my children and grandchildren that each succeeding generation inherits fewer habits based on unhealthy beliefs and structures. I pray that this comes true for every child. May our children and grandchildren rewrite this book in future decades filled with the insights they have gained from a world that has found the partnership way.

More Partnership Tools

You have permission to reprint the following boxes and charts and share them with others. The resources in this section will help you bring partnership into your life and our world. You can also give or refer people to this book.

The Center for Partnership Studies website www.partnershipway.org provides additional resources. To bring partnership education into schools and universities, you can give interested parents and educators a copy of the books *Tomorrow's Children* and *Partnership Education in Action*. The video on partnership education, "Tomorrow's Children," is available from the Media Education Foundation or from the Center for Partnership Studies. The Partnership Education Institute of the Center for Partnership Studies is a resource for workshops and consulting assistance.

From *The Power of Partnership* by Riane Eisler (New World Library, 2002)

The Partnership/Domination Continuum

The tables that follow provide an overview of the basic blueprints of the partnership model and the domination model that are at the two ends of the partnership/domination continuum.

From *The Power of Partnership* by Riane Eisler (New World Library, 2002)

TABLE 1

BLUEPRINTS FOR THE DOMINATION/CONTROL AND THE PARTNERSHIP/RESPECT MODELS

COMPONENT	DOMINATION MODEL	PARTNERSHIP MODEL
One: Social Structure	Authoritarian structure of rigid rankings and hierarchies of domination.*	Egalitarian social structure of linking and hierarchies of actualization.*
Two: Gender Relations	Ranking male half of humanity over female half. High valuing of traits and activities such as control and conquest of people and nature associated with so-called "masculinity."**	Equal valuing of female and male halves of humanity. High valuing of traits and activities such as empathy, nonviolence, and caregiving in women, men, and social policy.
Three: Violence and Fear	High degree of fear and socially accepted violence and abuse — from wife and child beating, rape, and warfare, to emotional abuse by "superiors" in families, workplaces, and society at large.	Mutual trust and low degree of fear and social violence, since these are not required to maintain rigid rankings of domination.
Four: Belief System	Relations of control/domination presented as normal, desirable, moral.	Relations of partnership/respect presented as normal, desirable, moral.

---

*   What I have called a *domination hierarchy* is the type of hierarchy based on fear of pain and/or force. This kind of hierarchy is different from the hierarchy I have called an *actualization hierarchy*, where leadership and management are empowering rather than disempowering, and the goal is higher levels of functioning.

**   "Masculinity" and "femininity" in this context correspond to gender stereotypes appropriate for a dominator society and *not* to any innate female or male traits.

From *The Power of Partnership* by Riane Eisler (New World Library, 2002)

TABLE 2

INTERACTIVE DYNAMICS

As the diagrams that follow indicate, the relationship between four major systems components is interactive, with all four mutually reinforcing one another.

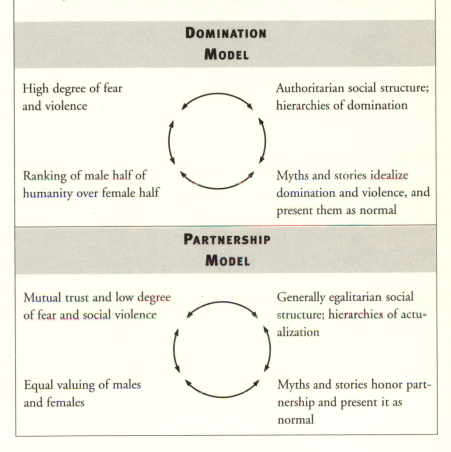

DOMINATION MODEL

High degree of fear and violence

Authoritarian social structure; hierarchies of domination

Ranking of male half of humanity over female half

Myths and stories idealize domination and violence, and present them as normal

PARTNERSHIP MODEL

Mutual trust and low degree of fear and social violence

Generally egalitarian social structure; hierarchies of actualization

Equal valuing of males and females

Myths and stories honor partnership and present it as normal

From *The Power of Partnership* by Riane Eisler (New World Library, 2002)

The Politics of
Partnership

In the charts that follow, you will find strategies that promote the integrated partnership political agenda, a comparison of the dominator and partnership agendas, and suggestions for reclaiming emotionally charged words such as family, values, and tradition.

From *The Power of Partnership* by Riane Eisler (New World Library, 2002)

TABLE 3

THE FOUR CORNERSTONES OF THE PARTNERSHIP POLITICAL AGENDA

One: Childhood Relations	*To build a partnership future the people who populate that future — today's and tomorrow's children — must understand, experience, and value partnership.*
	Stop violence against children so they don't learn that it's right to impose one's will through violence. Unite behind local, national, and international campaigns to stop violence against children, and promote partnership parenting.
	Work to end child poverty and to provide good nutrition and healthcare for all children, regardless of race, creed, or ethnic origin. Unite behind educational campaigns showing the personal, economic, social, and environmental benefits this will bring.
	Bring partnership education into schools. Unite to promote child-centered, multicultural, environmentally conscious, and gender-balanced curricula that help young people learn to respect themselves, others, and our natural environment.
	Work for high-quality childcare, and for training, status, and good economic rewards for this essential caregiving work, whether done by women or men.

From *The Power of Partnership* by Riane Eisler (New World Library, 2002)

Two: Gender Relations	*An equitable and peaceful future requires family, social, economic, and political institutions based on partnership between the male and female halves of humanity.* Change cultural beliefs that the male half of humanity is entitled to control the female half in families and societies. Help change mental maps of domination as normal by unlinking masculinity from domination and violence, and femininity from subordination and obedience. Unite to stop violence against girls and women through local, national, and international campaigns. Bring gender-balanced education into schools to change mindsets that value one kind of person over another. Unite to support partnership education as foundational to ending sexism, racism, and other dominator "isms." Bring partnership-oriented women and men from diverse racial and ethnic groups into policymaking positions to support more caring and empathic policies, including family planning and reproductive choice. Change social priorities so activities stereotypically associated with women are valued as highly as those associated with men. Teach that caring and nonviolence are essential in men, women, and social policy for a more peaceful, just, and caring world.

From *The Power of Partnership* by Riane Eisler (New World Library, 2002)

Three: Economic Relations	*For a good quality of life, we need economic measures and systems of reward that encourage empathy and creativity and give real value to caring for self, others, and nature.*
	Promote public campaign financing and other means of ending economic control of politics to free policymakers to work for an equitable, environmentally sustainable, and caring economic system.
	Promote socially and environmentally responsible business standards and rules. Work for partnership charters for domestic and international corporations, and for partnership standards in economic and environmental treaties.
	Work for new measures of economic productivity that focus on quality-of-life indicators — indicators that accurately report the needs and problems of the poor, that include the work of caregiving as productive work, and that include environmental impacts in cost-benefit analyses.
	Form coalitions to support an economic system that promotes empathy and creativity. Highlight the economic effectiveness of the partnership model. Give real value to the socially essential work of caring and caregiving — for self, others, and nature — whether in the workplace or at home.

From *The Power of Partnership* by Riane Eisler (New World Library, 2002)

TABLE 3 (CONTINUED)

THE FOUR CORNERSTONES OF THE PARTNERSHIP POLITICAL AGENDA

Four: Beliefs, Myths, and Stories	*To build a partnership culture we need to reexamine beliefs, myths, and stories — strengthening those that promote partnership and discarding those that do not.*
	Support cultural traditions that promote partnership, and work to discard those that promote domination. Strengthen the understanding that human nature is flexible and includes a powerful capacity for creativity and caring.
	Unite to break up media monopolies and change media policies and management so that the voice of partnership and diversity is heard in the media.
	Bring partnership education into schools and universities. Offer young people tools to recognize beliefs, myths, and stories that promote domination or partnership. Help them see the consequences of domination and the benefits of partnership.
	Work to bring partnership into religious organizations to promote partnership moral sensitivity and help them discard dominator "morality." Nurture the spiritual courage that will sustain us on the journey to make partnership a reality for our children and generations to come.

From *The Power of Partnership* by Riane Eisler (New World Library, 2002)

TABLE 4
EXPOSING THE DOMINATOR POLITICAL AGENDA

We can expose the dominator political agenda for what it is underneath appealing catchwords such as "family values" and "free market." A good way to do this is to contrast the dominator and partnership political agendas point by point.

AGENDA	DOMINATOR	PARTNERSHIP
Children	Go back to "spare the rod and spoil the child" as necessary and moral. Reinstate punitive, fear-based parenting to teach unquestioning obedience to authority.	Delegitimize violence against children as immoral and dysfunctional. Unite behind campaigns to end violence against children, and promote partnership parenting.
	Oppose funding for universal healthcare, good nutrition, and other measures that protect children.	Provide health care and good nutrition for all children regardless of race, creed, or ethnic origin. Unite behind educational campaigns that show the personal, economic, social, and environmental benefits this will bring.
	Reimpose rote teaching-to-the-test to rank and humiliate children, teachers, and schools, and squeeze out education that teaches gender balance, multiculturalism, peace, and environmental sensitivity.	Support child-centered, gender-balanced, multicultural, environmentally conscious education to help young people learn to respect themselves, others, and our natural environment.
	Oppose support for childcare. Give little or no economic value to the "women's work" of caregiving.	Work for high-quality childcare and for training, high status, and good economic rewards for the essential work of caregiving, whether done by women or men.

From *The Power of Partnership* by Riane Eisler (New World Library, 2002)

TABLE 4 (CONTINUED)
EXPOSING THE DOMINATOR POLITICAL AGENDA

AGENDA	DOMINATOR	PARTNERSHIP
Gender	Strengthen cultural beliefs that women must be controlled by men as heads of families and policymakers. Relink masculinity with domination and femininity with subservience. Oppose funding for programs that offer real protection from violence to girls and women.	Change cultural beliefs that the male half of humanity is entitled to control the female half in families and societies. Unlink masculinity from domination and violence, and femininity from subordination and obedience. Unite to stop violence against girls and women.
	Reinstate traditional curricula that focus on the male half of humanity, reinforcing mindsets that one kind of person is more valuable than another.	Bring gender-balanced education into schools to change mindsets that value one kind of person more than another. Unite to support partnership education as foundational to ending sexism, racism, and other dominator "isms."
	Fill policymaking positions with men (and token women) who support those who have economic control and want to take away rights to family planning and reproductive choice.	Unite to bring partnership-oriented women and men from diverse racial and ethnic groups into policymaking positions to support more caring and empathic policies, including family planning and reproductive choice.
	Reinforce social priorities that value activities stereotypically associated with men over those associated with women. Denigrate men who are nonviolent and caring as "sissies" or "wimps."	Change social priorities so that activities stereotypically associated with women are valued as highly as those associated with men. Teach that caring and nonviolence are essential in men, women, and social policy for a more peaceful, just, and caring world.

From *The Power of Partnership* by Riane Eisler (New World Library, 2002)

TABLE 4 (CONTINUED)
Exposing the Dominator Political Agenda

Agenda	Dominator	Partnership
Economics	Oppose meaningful political campaign financing reform to maintain control of laws and social and economic policies by powerful economic interests.	Promote public campaign financing and other means of ending economic control of politics to free policymakers to work for an equitable, environmentally sustainable, and caring economic system.
	Oppose socially and environmentally responsible business standards under the guise of a "free market" and "globalization."	Promote socially and environmentally responsible business standards and rules. Work for partnership charters for domestic and international corporations, and for partnership standards in economic and environmental treaties.
	Oppose changes in measures of economic productivity, pass on costs of environmental and health damage to consumers and taxpayers, and maintain the devaluation of the "women's work" of caregiving.	Work for new measures of economic productivity that focus on quality-of-life indicators — indicators that accurately report the needs and problems of the poor, that include the work of caregiving as productive work, and that include environmental impact in cost-benefit analyses.
	Develop agencies, rules, and policies that demand lack of empathy, such as international agencies that cut back social services, maintain top-down economic control, and increase availability of cheap labor.	Form coalitions to support an economic system that promotes empathy and creativity. Highlight the economic effectiveness of the partnership model. Give real value to the socially essential work of caring and caregiving — for self, others, and nature — whether done by women or men.

From *The Power of Partnership* by Riane Eisler (New World Library, 2002)

TABLE 4 (CONTINUED)
EXPOSING THE DOMINATOR POLITICAL AGENDA

AGENDA	DOMINATOR	PARTNERSHIP
Beliefs, Myths, and Stories	Preserve cultural beliefs that human nature is selfish and violent, and hence that people must be rigidly controlled through fear and punishment. Discredit partnership-oriented beliefs, attitudes, and myths as "unrealistic."	Support cultural traditions that promote partnership, and work to discard those that promote domination. Strengthen the understanding that human nature is flexible and includes a powerful capacity for creativity and caring.
	Filter out information that questions the status quo, and use media monopolies to discredit partnership possibilities.	Break up media monopolies and change media policies and management so that the voice of partnership and diversity will be heard in the media.
	Use schools to make rankings of domination seem normal, natural, and divinely ordained.	Bring partnership education into schools and universities. Offer young people tools to recognize beliefs, myths, and stories that promote domination or partnership. Help them see the consequences of domination and the benefits of partnership.
	Promote a "morality" of fear, intolerance, violence, and punishment.	Bring partnership into religious organizations to promote partnership moral sensitivity and help them discard dominator "morality." Nurture the spiritual courage that will sustain us on the journey to make partnership a reality for our children and generations to come.

From *The Power of Partnership* by Riane Eisler (New World Library, 2002)

TABLE 5
THE VOCABULARY OF DOMINATION AND PARTNERSHIP

DOMINATOR/CONTROL	PARTNERSHIP/RESPECT
Family values	Valuing families
Pro-life	Pro-living
Educational accountability	Educational responsibility
Capitalist economics	Economics of caring
Free market	Fair market
Compassionate conservative	Politics of caring
Traditional values	Humane traditions
Globalization	Global responsibility
Traditional morality	Moral sensitivity
Women's work	Caring work
Politically correct	Personally caring

You can add your own ideas to this short list.

From *The Power of Partnership* by Riane Eisler (New World Library, 2002)

Useful Publications and Organizations

A PLACE TO BEGIN

The resources that follow are by no means exhaustive. They represent a sample of publications and organizations that have a partnership orientation. Most are mentioned in this book, so that this section also serves as a partial bibliography. They are organized by topics in the following order: Children, Women and Men, Health, Education, Media, Work and Business, Economics, Human Rights, Politics, Environment, Prehistory and Cultural Transformation, and Spirituality. The Center for Partnership Studies website, at www.partnershipway.org, is also an excellent source for information and resources.

From *The Power of Partnership* by Riane Eisler (New World Library, 2002)

CHILDREN

BOOKS

Ariés, Phillipe. *Centuries of Childhood.* London: Cape, 1962.

Edelman, Marian Wright. *Guide My Feet: Prayers and Meditations on Loving and Working for Children.* New York: HarperCollins, 1996.

Eisler, Riane. *Tomorrow's Children: A Blueprint for Partnership Education for the 21st Century.* Boulder, Colo.: Westview Press, 2000.

Gopnik, Alison M., Andrew N. Meltzoff, and Patricia K. Kuhl. *The Scientist in the Crib: How Children Learn and What They Teach Us about the Mind.* New York: HarperTrade, 2001.

Gordon, Thomas. *Parent Effectiveness Training.* New York: Three Rivers Press, 2000.

Hyman, Irwin A. *The Case against Spanking: How to Stop Hitting and Start Raising Healthy Kids.* San Francisco: Jossey-Bass, Inc., 1997.

Leach, Penelope. *Children First: What Our Society Must Do — and Is Not Doing — for Our Children Today.* New York: Random House, Inc., 1994.

———. *Your Baby and Child.* New York: Knopf, 1997.

Pipher, Mary. *Reviving Ophelia: Saving the Selves of Adolescent Girls.* New York: Ballantine Books, 1995.

Sears, Martha, and William Sears. *The Baby Book: Everything You Need to Know about Your Baby from Birth to Age Two.* New York: Little, Brown & Company, 1992.

PAPERS AND ARTICLES

Embry, D. D., D. J. Flannery, A. T. Vazsonyi, K. E. Powell, and H. Atha. "Peacebuilders: A theoretically driven, school-based model for early violence prevention." *American Journal of Preventive Medicine,* vol. 12 (1996).

Leach, Penelope. "The New Thinking on Violent Toys, Toilet Mastery, Positive Discipline, and More." *Child* (April 1998) .

Mattaini, Mark A., and Christine T. Lowery. "Youth Violence Prevention: The State of the Science," PEACE POWER! Working Group, 1999. Accessible at http://www.bfsr.org/violence.html.

Perry, B. D., R. A. Pollard, et al. "Childhood Trauma, the Neurobiology of Adaptation, and 'Use Dependent' Development of the Brain: How 'States' become 'Traits.'" *Infant Mental Health Journal,* vol. 16 (1996): 271–91.

Rosen, Margery D. "Is it Ever Okay to Spank Your Child?" *Child* (September 1997).

Rosin, Hanna. "Critics Question Extreme Childrearing Method," *Washington Post,* 27 February 1999. Accessible at http://pages.ivillage.com/cl-yokopoko/ezzo4.html.

From *The Power of Partnership* by Riane Eisler (New World Library, 2002)

Scheck, Raffael. "Childhood in German Autobiographical Writings, 1740–1820." *Journal of Psychohistory,* vol. 15 (Summer 1987): 391–422.

Taylor, Karen J. "Blessing the House: Moral Motherhood and the Suppression of Corporal Punishment," *Journal of Psychohistory,* vol. 15 (Summer 1987): 431–54.

VIDEOS

Eisler, Riane. *Tomorrow's Children: Partnership Education in Action,* Media Education Foundation. Order online at http://www.mediaed.org/catalog/.

Pipher, Mary. *Reviving Ophelia: Saving the Selves of Adolescent Girls.* Media Education Foundation. Order online at http://www.mediaed.org/catalog/media/.

MAGAZINES

Child. To subscribe, see the following link: http://www.child.com.

New Moon. To subscribe, call (800) 381-4743 or go to http://www.newmoon.org.

Parenting. For a free trial issue, see the following link: http://www.parenting.com/parenting/magazines/subscriptions/index.html.

ORGANIZATIONS

The Children's Defense Fund
25 E Street NW
Washington, DC 20001
Tel: (202) 628-8787
http://www.childrensdefense.org/

Children Now
1212 Broadway, 5th Floor
Oakland, CA 94612
Tel: (510) 763-2444; Fax: (510) 763-1974
http://www.childrennow.org/

Defence for Children International
P.O. Box 88
CH 1211 Geneva 20, Switzerland
Visitors: 1 Rue de Varembé
Tel: (+41 22) 734 05 58; Fax: (+41 22) 740 11 45
http://www.defence-for-children.org/

From *The Power of Partnership* by Riane Eisler (New World Library, 2002)

Reiner Foundation: "I Am Your Child: The First Years Last Forever"
P.O. Box 15605
Beverly Hills, CA 90209
Tel: (310) 285-2385; Fax: (310) 205-2760
http://www.iamyourchild.org

The Troubadour Institute
610 Fernhill Road
Mayne Island, BC, Canada V0N 2J0
Tel: (250) 539-3588; Fax: (250) 539-3589
http://www.raffinews.com/about/about-ti.html

United Nations Children's Fund (UNICEF)
UNICEF House
3 United Nations Plaza
New York, NY 10017

WOMEN AND MEN

BOOKS

Barstow, Ann Llewellyn. *Witchcraze: A New History of the European Witch Hunts.* London and San Francisco: Pandora, 1994.

Bart, Pauline B., and P. H. O'Brien. *Stopping Rape.* New York: Pergamon Press, 1985.

Bleier, Ruth. *Science and Gender.* New York: Pergamon Press, 1984.

Brod, Harry. *The Making of Masculinities: The New Men's Studies.* Boston: Allen & Unwin, 1987.

Callahan, Mathew. *Sex, Death, and the Angry Young Man.* Ojai, Calif.: Times Change Press, 1991.

Eisler, Riane. *The Equal Rights Handbook: What ERA Means to Your Life, Your Rights & the Future.* Lincoln, Nebr.: iUniverse, Inc., 1999.

————. *Dissolution: No-Fault Divorce, Marriage, and the Future of Women.* Lincoln, Nebr.: iUniverse, Inc., 1998.

Eisler, Riane, David Loye, and Kari Norgaard. *Women, Men, and the Global Quality of Life.* Pacific Grove, Calif.: The Center for Partnership Studies, 1995.

Fausto-Sterling, Anne. *Myths of Gender.* New York: Pergamon Press, 1984.

Flexner, Eleanor. *Century of Struggle.* Cambridge, Mass.: Harvard University Press, 1959.

From *The Power of Partnership* by Riane Eisler (New World Library, 2002)

Gilligan, Carol. *In a Different Voice.* Cambridge, Mass.: Harvard University Press, 1982.

Hine, Darlene Clark, and David B. Barry. *More than Chattel: Black Women and Slavery in the Americas.* Bloomington, Ind.: Indiana University Press, 1996.

hooks, bell. *Feminist Theory from Margin to Center.* Boston: South End Press, 1984.

Hubbard, Ruth. *The Politics of Women's Biology.* New York: Rutgers University Press, 1990.

Kimmel, Martin S., and Thomas E. Mosmiller. *Against the Tide: Pro-Feminist Men in the United States 1776–1990.* Boston: Beacon Press, 1992.

Martin, Katherine. *Women of Courage.* Novato, Calif.: New World Library, 1999.

Mernissi, Fatima. *Beyond the Veil.* Bloomington, Ind.: Indiana University Press, 1987.

Miedzian, Myriam. *Boys Will Be Boys.* New York: Anchor Books, 1991.

Miller, Jean Baker. *Toward a New Psychology of Women.* Boston: Beacon Press, 1976.

Ogden, Gina. *Women Who Love Sex: An Inquiry into the Expanding Spirit of Women's Erotic Experience.* 2nd rev. ed. Cambridge, Mass.: Womanspirit Press, 1999.

Pietilä, Hilkka, and Jeanne Vickers. *Making Women Matter: The Role of the United Nations.* London: Zed Books, 1994.

Spender, Dale, ed. *Feminist Theorists.* New York: Pantheon, 1983.

Stoltenberg, John. *Refusing to Be a Man.* New York: Penguin Books, 1990.

PAPERS AND ARTICLES

Beneke, Tim. "Deep Masculinity as Social Control: Foucault, Bly, and Masculinity." *Masculinities,* vol. 1 (Summer 1993): 13–19.

"Closing the Gender Gap: Educating Girls." Washington, D.C.: Population Action International, 1993. Accessible at http://www.populationaction.org/programs/gendergap.htm.

Eisler, Riane. "A Time for Partnership." *UNESCO Courier* (2001). Accessible at http://www.partnershipway.org/html/subpages/articles/timefor.htm.

"Gender and Human Development," *United Nations Development Programme Report* (1995). Accessible at http://www.undp.org/hdro/1995/95.htm.

Koegel, Rob. "Healing the Wounds of Masculinity: A Crucial Role for Educators." *Holistic Education Review,* vol. 7 (March 1994): 42–49.

"Men, Masculinities, and Gender Relations in Development." Papers from the

From *The Power of Partnership* by Riane Eisler (New World Library, 2002)

annual conference held by the University of Bradford (UK). Accessible at
http://www.brad.ac.uk/acad/dppc/gender/mandmweb/contents.html.

"Progress of the World's Women 2000." United Nations, UNIFEM (2000).
Accessible at http://www.undp.org/unifem/progressww/2000/index.html.

"Promoting Equality: A Common Issue for Men and Women." Seminar documents, Palais de l'Europe, Strasbourg, France (17–18 June 1997).
Accessible at http://www.europrofem.org/02.info/22contri/2.04.en/
1en.gend/06en_gen.htm.

United Nations Convention on the Elimination of All Forms of
Discrimination Against Women, 1979. Accessible at http://www.un.org/
womenwatch/daw/cedaw/cedaw.htm.

VIDEOS

Katz, Jackson. *Tough Guise: Violence, Media & the Crisis in Masculinity.* Media
Education Foundation. Order online at http://www.mediaed.org/catalog/
media/guise.html.

Hadleigh-West, Maggie. *War Zone.* Media Education Foundation. Order
online at http://www.mediaed.org/catalog/media/warzone.html.

ORGANIZATIONS

American Association of University Women (AAUW)
1111 16th Street NW
Washington, DC 20036
Tel: (800) 326-AAUW
http://www.aauw.org/

Dads and Daughters
P.O. Box 3458
Duluth, MN 55803
Tel: (888) 824-3237
http://www.dadsanddaughters.org

The Feminist Majority
1600 Wilson Blvd., Suite 801
Arlington, VA 22209
Tel: (703) 522-2214
http://www.feminist.org

From *The Power of Partnership* by Riane Eisler (New World Library, 2002)

International Research and Training Institute
for the Advancement of Women (INSTRAW)
Calle César Nicolás Penson 102-A
Santo Domingo, Dominican Republic
Tel: (809) 685-2111; Fax: (809) 685-2117
http://www.un-instraw-gains.org/

Jean Baker Miller Training Institute
Stone Center, Wellesley College
Wellesley, MA 02481
Tel: (781) 283-3007
http://www.jbmti.org

National Organization for Women (NOW)
733 Fifteenth Street NW
Washington, DC 20004
Tel: (202) 268-8669
http://www.now.org

The Older Women's League (OWL)
666 11th Street NW, Suite 700
Washington, DC 20001
Tel: (202) 783-6686 (for DC Area) or (800) 825-3695; Fax: (202) 638-2356
http://www.owl-national.org/

United Nations Development Fund for Women (UNIFEM)
304 East 45th Street, 15th floor
New York, NY 10017
Tel: (212) 906-6400; Fax: (212) 906-6705
http://www.undp.org/unifem/

United Nations Men's Group for Gender Equality
Further information: <james.lang@undp.org>
http://www.undp.org/gender/programmes/men/men_ge.html

Women's Environment and Development Organization (WEDO)
355 Lexington Avenue, 3rd Floor
New York, NY 10017-6603
Tel: (212) 973-0325; Fax: (212) 973-0335
http://www.wedo.org/

From *The Power of Partnership* by Riane Eisler (New World Library, 2002)

HEALTH

BOOKS

Burmeister, Alice, and Tom Monte. *The Touch of Healing.* New York: Bantam, 1997.

Johnson, Don Hanlon. *Body: Recovering Our Sensual Wisdom.* Berkeley, Calif.: North Atlantic Books, 1983, 1992.

Lewis, Michael, Robert Wood, and Jeannette M. Haviland-Jones. *Handbook of Emotions.* 2d ed. New York: Guilford Publications, 2000.

Northrup, Christiane, M.D. *Women's Bodies, Women's Wisdom.* New York: Bantam, 1994.

Orbach, Susie. *Fat Is a Feminist Issue.* New York: Berkeley Books, 1978.

Ornish, Dean. *Reversing Heart Disease.* New York: Ballantine Books, 1990.

Robbins, John. *The Food Revolution: How Your Diet Can Help Save Your Life and Our World.* Berkeley, Calif.: Conari Press, 2001.

————. *Reclaiming Our Health.* Tiburon, Calif.: H.J. Kramer, 1996.

Sack, Fleur, with Anne Streeter. *Romance to Die For: The Startling Truth about Women, Sex, and AIDS.* Deerfield Beach, Fla.: Health Communications, 1992.

Shafarman, Steven. *Awareness Heals: The Feldenkrais Method of Dynamic Health.* Menlo Park, Calif.: Addison-Wesley Publishing, 1997.

Weil, Andrew, M.D. *8 Weeks to Optimum Health.* New York: Alfred A. Knopf, 1997.

PAPERS AND ARTICLES

Dyer, Gwynne. "Frankenstein Foods," *The Globe and Mail* (20 February 1999). Accessible at http://www.netlink.de/gen/Zeitung/1999/990220d.htm.

Consumer Reports Study: "Do You Know What You're Eating?" Press release: http://www.consumersunion.org/food/pestny899.htm; full text of study: http://www.consunion.org/food/do_you_know2.htm.

Frank, John W., and J. Fraser Mustard. "The Determinants of Health from a Historical Perspective," *Daedalus,* vol. 123, no. 4 (Fall 1994).

EDUCATION

BOOKS

American Association of University Women Educational Foundation. *How Schools Shortchange Girls: A Study of Major Findings on Girls and Education.* New York: Marlowe and Co., 1995.

From *The Power of Partnership* by Riane Eisler (New World Library, 2002)

Bigelow, Bill, Linda Christensen, et al. *Rethinking Our Classrooms: Teaching for Equity and Justice.* Milwaukee, Wisc.: Rethinking Schools, 1998. Order online at http://www.rethinkingschools.org/SpecPub/Clsrms.htm.

Bigelow, Bill and Bob Peterson. *Rethinking Columbus.* Monroe, Maine: Common Courage Press, 1998.

Brooks, Jacqueline G., and Martin G. Brooks. *In Search of Understanding.* Alexandria, Va.: Association for Supervision and Curriculum Development, 1993.

Bucciarelli, Deirdre, and Sarah Pirtle, eds. *Partnership Education in Action: A Companion to* Tomorrow's Children. Tucson, Ariz.: Center for Partnership Studies, 2001.

Clark, Edward T., Jr. *Designing and Implementing an Integrated Curriculum: A Student-Centered Approach.* Brandon, Vt.: Holistic Education Press, 1997.

Eisler, Riane. *Tomorrow's Children: A Blueprint for Partnership Education for the 21st Century.* Boulder, Colo.: Westview Press, 2000.

Eisler, Riane, and David Loye. *The Partnership Way: New Tools for Living & Learning.* Brandon, Vt.: Psychology Press, 1998.

Gardner, Howard. *Frames of Mind.* New York: Basic Books, 1983.

Gibbs, Jeanne. *Tribes: A New Way of Learning Together.* Santa Rosa, Calif.: Center Source Publications, 1994.

Goldstein, Lisa. *Teaching with Love.* New York: Peter Lang, 1997.

Johnson, David W. *Cooperative Learning in the Classroom.* Alexandria, Va.: Association for Supervision and Curriculum Development, 1994.

Kane, Jeffrey, ed. *Education, Information, and Transformation.* Upper Saddle River: N.J.: Prentice-Hall, 1999.

Martin, Jane Roland. *Schoolhome: Rethinking Schools for Changing Families.* Cambridge, Mass.: Harvard University Press, 1992.

Miller, Ron. *What Are Schools For?* Brandon, Vt.: Holistic Education Press, 1990.

Noddings, Nel. *The Challenge to Care in Schools.* New York: Teachers College Press, Columbia University, 1992.

Roberts, Monty. *The Man Who Listens to Horses.* New York: Random House, Inc., 1997.

Sadker, Myra and David Sadker. *Failing at Fairness: How Our Schools Cheat Girls.* New York: Touchstone Books, 1995.

Schniedewind, Nance, and Ellen Davidson. *Open Minds to Equality.* Needham Heights, Mass.: Allyn and Bacon, 1997.

Sleeter, Christine E., and Carl A. Grant. *Making Choices for Multicultural Education.* Columbus, Ohio: Merrill, 1994.

From *The Power of Partnership* by Riane Eisler (New World Library, 2002)

Teaching Tolerance. Available from Southern Poverty Law Center, 400 Washington Avenue, Montgomery, AL 36104; Tel: (334) 956-8200; http://www.splcenter.org/.

PAPERS AND ARTICLES

Bigelow, Bill, and Linda Christiansen. "Promoting Social Imagination through Interior Monologues." *Rethinking Schools,* vol. 8 (Winter 1993).

Noddings, Nel. "Learning to Engage in Moral Dialogue." *Holistic Education Review,* vol. 7 (Summer 1994).

Riggs, Rosemary. "The Rodriguez Files." Accessible at http://lonestar.utsa.edu/rriggs/contents.htm.

Watson, Marilyn, Victor Battistich, and Daniel Solomon. "Enhancing Students' Social and Ethical Development in Schools: An Intervention Program and Its Effects." *International Journal of Education Research,* vol. 2, no. 7 (1998): 571–586.

MAGAZINES

Education Week. 4301 Connecticut Ave. NW, Suite 432, Washington, DC 20008; Tel: (202) 364-4114.

Encounter. Order by phone at (800) 639-4122 or online at http://www.greatideas.org/encorder.htm.

Independent School Magazine. To order: NAIS, P.O. Box 91188, Washington, DC 20090-1188; Tel: (202) 973-9700; Fax: (202) 973-9790.

Paths of Learning. Order by phone at (800) 639-4122 or online at http://www.great-ideas.org/pathordr.htm.

Tomorrow's Child. Order by phone at (800) 655-5843 or online at http://www.montessori.org/TomorrowsChild/TableIndOrderForm.cfm.

VIDEOS

"Tomorrow's Children: Partnership Education in Action." Order online from the Media Education Foundation at http://www.mediaed.org or from the Center for Partnership Studies at http://www.partnershipway.org or phone (520) 546-0176.

ORGANIZATIONS

Association for Supervision and Curriculum Development (ASCD)
1703 North Beauregard Street
Alexandria, VA 22311-1714
Tel: (703) 578-9600 or (800) 933-ASCD; Fax: (703) 575-5400
http://www.ascd.org/

From *The Power of Partnership* by Riane Eisler (New World Library, 2002)

National Association of Independent Schools (NAIS)
1620 L Street NW
Washington, DC 20036-5695
Tel: (202) 973-9700; Fax: (202) 973-9790
http://www.nais.org

Montessori Foundation
17808 October Court
Rockville, MD 20855
Tel: (301) 840-9231; Fax: (301) 840-0021
http://www.montessori.org/index.htm

Partnership Education Institute
c/o The Center For Partnership Studies
P.O. Box 51936
Pacific Grove, CA 93950
Tel: (831) 626-1004; Fax: (831) 626-3734
http://www.partnershipway.org/pep/home.htm

MEDIA

BOOKS

Bagdikian, Benjamin H. *The Media Monopoly.* Boston: Beacon Press, 2000.

Chomsky, Noam, and Edward S. Herman. *Manufacturing Consent: The Political Economy of the Mass Media.* New York: Pantheon Books, 1988.

Gerbner, George. "The Politics of Media Violence: Some Reflections." In Cees J. Hamelink and Olga Linne, eds., *Mass Communication Research.* Norwood, N.J.: Ablex, 1994.

Griffin, Susan. *Pornography and Silence.* New York: Harper & Row, 1981.

Grossman, David, and Gloria Degaetano. *Stop Teaching Our Kids to Kill: A Call to Action Against TV, Movie and Video Game Violence.* New York: Crown Publishing Group, 1999.

Kilbourne, Jean. *Can't Buy My Love.* New York: Touchstone Books, 2000.

Lederer, Laura. *Take Back the Night.* New York: William Morrow, 1980.

Postman, Neil. *Amusing Ourselves to Death: Public Discourse in the Age of Show Business.* New York: Viking Penguin, 1986.

Rampton, Sheldon, and John Stauber. *Trust Us, We're Experts: How Industry Manipulates Science and Gambles with Your Future.* New York: Putnam Publishing Group, 2000.

From *The Power of Partnership* by Riane Eisler (New World Library, 2002)

235

Russell, Diana. *Against Pornography: The Evidence of Harm.* Berkeley, Calif.: Russell Publications, 1993.

VIDEOS

The Media Education Foundation is an excellent source for videos that offer a critical look at the media. They are accessible online at http://www.mediaed.org/enter.html.

"Advertising and the End of the World." Order by calling (800) 897-0089, or online at http://www.mediaed.org/catalog/commercialism/endof.html.

"The Myth of the Liberal Media." Media Education Foundation. Order by calling (800) 897-0089, or online at http://www.mediaed.org/catalog/commercialism/myth.html.

"Killing Us Softly 3." Order by calling (800) 897-0089, or online at http://www.mediaed.org/catalog/media/softly.html.

PAPERS AND ARTICLES

Gerbner, George. "Reclaiming our Cultural Mythology," *The Ecology of Justice,* Spring 1994. Accessible at http://www.context.org/ICLIB/IC38/Gerbner.htm.

"Kids' Petition Against Violent Video Games." American Medical Association, 2001. Accessible at http://www.ama-assn.org/ama/pub/article/2714-3108.html.

Jhally, Sut. "Advertising at the Edge of the Apocalypse." Department of Communication, University of Massachusetts, Amherst (2000). Accessible at http://www.sutjhally.com/onlinepubs/apocalypse.html.

MSNBC. "Today's Toy Test 2000: Top-rated video games for kids." Kids give nonviolent video games high ratings. Accessible at http://www.msnbc.com/news/490442.asp.

Varhola, Michael J. Interview with David Grossman on violent video games. Accessible at http://www.skirmisher.com/grossint.htm.

ORGANIZATIONS

Center for Media and Democracy
520 University Avenue, Suite 310
Madison, WI 53703
Tel: (608) 260-9713; Fax: (608) 260-9714
http://www.prwatch.org/

From *The Power of Partnership* by Riane Eisler (New World Library, 2002)

Cultural Environment Movement
P.O. Box 31847
Philadelphia, PA 19104
Tel: (888) 445-4526; Fax: (215) 204-5823
http://www.cemnet.org/

Fairness and Accuracy in Reporting (FAIR)
130 W. 25th Street
New York, NY 10001
Tel: (212) 633-6700; Fax: (212) 727-7668
http://www.fair.org/

Media Watch
P.O. Box 618
Santa Cruz, CA 95061-0618
Tel: (831) 423-6355 or (800) 631-6355
http://www.mediawatch.com/

National Coalition on Television Violence
5132 Newport Avenue
Bethesda, MD 20816
http://www.nctvv.org/

Project for Excellence in Journalism
1900 M Street NW, Suite 210
Washington, DC 20036
Tel: (202) 293-7394; Fax: (202) 293-6946
http://www.journalism.org/

WORK AND BUSINESS
BOOKS

Arrien, Angeles, ed. *Working Together: Producing Synergy by Honoring Diversity.* Pleasanton, Calif.: New Leaders Press, 1998.

Block, Peter. *The Empowered Manager.* San Francisco: Jossey-Bass, Inc., 1990.

Helgesen, Sally. *The Female Advantage: Women's Ways of Leadership.* New York: Doubleday, 1990. Reprint, May 1995.

Isen, Alice M. "Positive Affect and Decision Making." In J. M. Haviland and M. Lewis, eds., *Handbook of Emotions.* New York: Guilford, 1993.

From *The Power of Partnership* by Riane Eisler (New World Library, 2002)

237

Jaffe, Dennis T., and Cynthia D. Scott. *Take This Job and Love It: How to Change Your Work without Changing Your Job.* New York: Simon & Schuster, 1988.

Kanter, Rosabeth Moss. *When Giants Learn to Dance: Mastering the Challenge of Strategy, Management, and Careers in the 1990s.* New York: Simon & Schuster, 1990.

Korten, David. *When Corporations Rule the World.* San Francisco: Berrett-Koehler/Kumarian Press, 1996. Excerpts accessible at http://www.thirdworldtraveler.com/Korten/WhenCorpsRuleWorld_Korten.html.

Naisbitt, John, and Patricia Aburdene. *Reinventing the Corporation.* New York: Warner Books, Inc., 1986.

PAPERS AND ARTICLES

Butruille, Susan G. "Corporate Caretaking." *Training and Development Journal* (April 1990).

Eisler, Riane. "Changing the Rules of the Game: Work, Values, and Our Future." Accessible at http://www.partnershipway.org/html/subpages/articles/changingrules.htm.

———. "Women, Men, and Management: Redesigning our Future." *Futures* (January/February 1991). Excerpt available online at http://www.partnershipway.org/html/subpages/articles/management.htm.

Isen, Alice M. "The Asymmetry of Happiness and Sadness in Effects on Memory in Normal College Students." *Journal of Experimental Psychology,* General 114 (1985).

Krueger, Pam. "Three Myths about Partners: An Interview with Riane Eisler." *Fast Company* (November 1998). Accessible at http://www.partnershipway.org/html/subpages/articles/threemyths.htm.

Montuori, Alfonso and Isabella Conti. "The Meaning of Partnership." *Vision/Action,* vol. 14, no. 4 (Winter 1996): 7–10.

"Toward a Partnership Society: An Interview with Riane Eisler." *At Work* (January/February 1998). Accessible at http://www.partnershipway.org/html/subpages/articles/towardpart.htm.

MAGAZINES AND NEWSLETTERS

At Work, published by the World Business Network. Subscribe online at http://www.worldbusiness.org/services.cfm.

Business Ethics. Subscribe by calling (612) 879-0695, or online at http://www.business-ethics.com/newpage1.htm.

From *The Power of Partnership* by Riane Eisler (New World Library, 2002)

Network News, published by the Social Venture Network. Subscribe online at http://www.svn.org/membership/application.html.

Organizations

Businesses for Social Responsibility
609 Mission Street, 2nd Floor
San Francisco, CA 94105-3506
Tel: (415) 537-0888; Fax: (415) 537-0889
http://www.bsr.org/

Computer Professionals for Social Responsibility
P.O. Box 717
Palo Alto, CA 94302
Tel: (650) 322-3778; Fax: (650) 322-4748
http://www.cpsr.org/

Program on Corporations, Law, and Democracy
P.O. Box 246
S. Yarmouth, MA 02664-0246
Tel: (508) 398-1145; Fax: (508) 398-1552
http://www.poclad.org

Self-Employed Women's Association (SEWA)
Opp. Victoria Garden
Bhadra, Ahmedabad - 380 001, India
Tel: (91) 79-5506444, 5506477; Fax: (91) 79-5506446
http://www.sewa.org

Social Venture Network
P.O. Box 29221
San Francisco, CA 94129-0221
Tel: (415) 561-6501; Fax: (415) 561-6435
http://www.svn.org/

World Business Academy
428 Bryant Circle, Suite 109
Ojai, CA 93023
http://www.worldbusiness.org/main.cfm

From *The Power of Partnership* by Riane Eisler (New World Library, 2002)

Buying and Investing

To find products and services in accordance with partnership principles:

Co-op America
1612 K Street NW, Suite 600
Washington, DC 20006
Tel: (800) 58-GREEN; Fax: (202) 331-8166
http://www.coopamerica.org/

Green Marketplace (Social Venture Network)
5801 Beacon Street, Suite 2
Pittsburgh, PA 15217
Tel: (888) 59-EARTH
http://svn.greenmarketplace.com/

Realgoods.com
Call (800) 762-7325 for a free catalog of products.
http://www.realgoods.com/

Seventh Generation
212 Battery Street, Suite A
Burlington, VT 05401-5281
Tel: (802) 658-3773; Fax: (802) 658-1771
http://www.seventhgen.com/

Working Assets
Tel: (877) 255-9253
http://www.workingforchange.com/services/index.cfm

To find investments in accordance with partnership principles:

The Calvert Group
4550 Montgomery Avenue
Bethesda, MD 20814
Tel: (800) 368-2748
http://www.calvertgroup.org/

Domini Social Investments
Tel: (800) 762-6814
http://www.domini.com/

From *The Power of Partnership* by Riane Eisler (New World Library, 2002)

KLD Research and Analytics Inc.
Russia Wharf
530 Atlantic Avenue, 7th Floor
Boston, MA 02210
Tel: (617) 426-5270; Fax: (617) 426-5299
http://www.kld.com/

Social Investment Forum
1612 K Street NW, Suite 650
Washington, DC 20006
Tel: (202) 872-5310; Fax: (202) 822-8471
http://www.socialinvest.org/

SRI World Group, Inc.
74 Cotton Mill Hill, Suite A-255
Brattleboro, VT 05301
Tel: (802) 251-0500; Fax: (802) 251-0555
http://www.socialfunds.com/

To find independent booksellers:

Advanced Book Exchange (new, used, and hard-to-find books)
990 Hillside Ave, 2nd Floor
Victoria, BC, Canada V8T 2A1
http://www.abebooks.com

Book Sense (a network of independent bookseller websites)
http://www.booksense.com/

noamazon.com (lots of links to independent booksellers)
http://www.noamazon.com

ECONOMICS

BOOKS

Eisler, Riane, David Loye, and Kari Norgaard. *Women, Men, and the Global Quality of Life.* Pacific Grove, Calif.: The Center for Partnership Studies, 1995.
Folbre, Nancy, and James Heintz. *The Ultimate Field Guide to the U.S. Economy: A Compact and Irreverent Guide to Economic Life in America.* New York: New Press, 2000.

From *The Power of Partnership* by Riane Eisler (New World Library, 2002)

241

Gates, Jeff. *The Ownership Solution: Toward a Shared Capitalism for the Twenty-First Century.* Reading, Mass.: Perseus Books Group, 1999.

Henderson, Hazel. *Building a Win-Win World: Life beyond Global Economic Warfare.* San Francisco: Berrett-Koehler Publishers, 1997.

————. *Paradigms in Progress.* San Francisco: Berrett-Koehler Publishers, 1995.

Hock, Dee. *Birth of the Chaordic Age.* San Francisco: Berrett-Koehler Publishers, 1999.

Jain, Devaki, and Nirmala Banerjee, eds. *Tyranny of the Household: Women in Poverty.* New Delhi, India: Shakti Books, 1985.

Mander, Jerry, and Edward Goldsmith, eds. *The Case against the Global Economy: And for a Turn toward the Local.* San Francisco: Sierra Club Books, 1997.

Rose, Stephen J. *Social Stratification in the United States: The New American Profile with Poster.* New York: W. W. Norton & Company, Inc., 1999.

Waring, Marilyn. *If Women Counted.* San Francisco: Harper & Row, 1988.

PAPERS AND ARTICLES

Bernstein, Jared, Lawrence Mishel, and Chauna Brocht. "Any way you cut it: Income inequality on the rise regardless of how it's measured." *Economic Policy Institute,* September 2000. Accessible at http://www.epinet.org/briefingpapers/inequality/inequality.html.

Eisler, Riane. "Toward an Economics of Caring." Keynote lecture to the Boston Research Center for the 21st Century conference *From War Culture to Cultures of Peace: Challenges for Civil Society,* March 2001. Accessible at http://www.partnershipway.org/html/subpages/articles/brckeynote.htm

Krugman, Paul. "The Spiral of Inequality." *Mother Jones Magazine* (November/December 1996). Accessible at http://www.pkarchive.org/economy/spiral1.html.

Mantsios, Gregory. "Class in America: Myths and Realities." *Teaching Sociology,* vol. 22, no. 1 (January 1994): 131–43.

U.S. Bureau of the Census, Series P-60 Reports, "Consumer Income and Poverty." Accessible at http://www.census.gov/prod/www/abs/income.

Stallman, Richard. "Why Software Should Be Free." GNU Project. Accessible at http://www.gnu.org/philosophy/philosophy.html.

Woestman, Lois. "World Bank Structural Adjustment and Gender Policies: Strangers Passing in the Night — Fleeting Acquaintances or Best Friends." EURODAD and WIDE, Brussels, 1994.

From *The Power of Partnership* by Riane Eisler (New World Library, 2002)

ORGANIZATIONS

Center for Women Policy Studies
1211 Connecticut Avenue NW, Suite 312
Washington, DC 20036
Tel: (202) 872-1770; Fax: (202) 296-8962
http://www.centerwomenpolicy.org/

Economic Policy Institute
1660 L Street NW, Suite 1200
Washington, DC 20036
Tel: (202) 775-8810; Fax: (202) 775-0819
http://www.epinet.org

Friendly Favors
http://www.favors.org/

Responsible Wealth
37 Temple Place, 2nd Floor
Boston, MA 02111
Tel: (617) 423-2148; Fax: (617) 423-0191
http://www.responsiblewealth.org/

HUMAN RIGHTS

BOOKS

Ahmed, Durre S. *Masculinity, Rationality and Religion: A Feminist Perspective.* Lahore, Pakistan: ASR Publications, 1993.

Barry, Kathleen. *Female Sexual Slavery.* New York: Avon Books, 1979.

Bunch, Charlotte, and Nimh Reilly. *Demanding Accountability: The Global Campaign and Vienna Tribunal for Women's Human Rights.* New Jersey: Center for Women's Leadership, Rutgers University; New York: United National Development Fund for Women (UNIFEM), 1994.

Eisler, Riane. *The Equal Rights Handbook: What ERA Means to Your Life, Your Rights & the Future.* Lincoln, Nebr.: iUniverse, Inc., 1998.

Hosken, Fran. *The Hosken Report: Genital and Sexual Mutilation of Females.* 4th ed., Lexington, Mass.: Women's International Network News, 1994.

Kassindja, Fauziya, and Layli Miller Bashir. *Do They Hear You When You Cry.* New York: Delacorte Press, 1998.

From *The Power of Partnership* by Riane Eisler (New World Library, 2002)

Pollis, Adamantia, and Peter Schwab. *Human Rights: New Perspectives, New Realities.* Boulder, Colo.: Lynne Rienner Publishers, 2000.

Walker, Alice. *Possessing the Secret of Joy.* New York: Harcourt Brace Jovanovich, 1992.

PAPERS AND ARTICLES

Butegwa, Florence. "From Basic Needs to Basic Rights: Women's Claim to Human Rights." *Women, Law and Development International,* Margaret Schuler, ed. Accessible at http://www.cwgl.rutgers.edu/butegwa.html.

Butruille, Susan G. "An Ancient Truth: Women's Rights Are Human Rights" Accessible at http://www.aracnet.com/~sbvoices.

Eisler, Riane. "A Challenge for Human Rights: What We Can Do." *WIN NEWS,* vol. 19, no. 4 (Autumn 1993). Accessible at http://www.partnershipway.org/html/subpages/articles/humanrights.htm.

————. "Human Rights: Toward an Integrated Theory for Action." *Human Rights Quarterly,* vol. 9 (August 1987): 287–308.

Okin, Susan Moller. "Is Multiculturalism Bad for Women?" *Boston Review* (October/November 1997). Accessible at http://bostonreview.mit.edu/BR22.5/okin.html.

Osborn, Andrew. "Mass Rape Ruled a War Crime." *The Guardian* (23 February 2001). Accessible at http://www.guardianunlimited.co.uk/Print/0,3858,4140914,00.html.

DOCUMENTS

Bora Laskin Law Library. "Women's Human Rights Resources." Accessible at http://www.law-lib.utoronto.ca/diana/.

"Convention to Eliminate All Forms of Discrimination Against Women." United Nations. Accessible at http://www.unhchr.ch/html/menu3/b/e1cedaw.htm.

Human Rights Watch. "Corporations and Human Rights: Corporate Social Responsibility." Accessible at http://www.hrw.org/advocacy/corportions/index.htm.

Human Rights Web. Accessible at http://www.hrweb.org/resource.html.

International Covenant on Economic, Social, and Cultural Rights. Accessible at http://www.unhchr.ch/html/menu3/b/a_cescr.htm.

Peacenet. Accessible at http://www.igc.org/igc/gateway/pnindex.html.

United Nations. "Convention on the Rights of the Child." Accessible at http://www.unicef.org/crc/fulltext.htm.

United Nations. "State of the World's Women Report." 1985.

From *The Power of Partnership* by Riane Eisler (New World Library, 2002)

United Nations. "Universal Declaration of Human Rights." Accessible in over three hundred languages at http://www.unhchr.ch/udhr/index.htm. University of Minnesota Human Rights Library. Accessible at http://www11.umn.edu/humanrts/index.html.

ORGANIZATIONS

Amnesty International USA
322 Eighth Avenue
New York, NY 10001
Tel: (212) 807-8400; Fax: (212) 627-1451
http://www.amnesty-usa.org/

Global Exchange
2017 Mission Street #303
San Francisco, CA 94110
Tel: (415) 255-7296; Fax (415) 255-7498
http://www.globalexchange.org

Human Rights Watch
350 Fifth Avenue, 34th Floor
New York, NY 10118-3299
Tel: (212) 290-4700; Fax: (212) 736-1300
http://www.hrw.org/

International Women's Rights Action Watch
Hubert Humphrey Institute of Public Affairs
University of Minnesota
301 19th Avenue South
Minneapolis, MN 55455
Tel: (612) 625-5093; Fax: (612) 624-0068
http://www.igc.org/iwraw/

The Simon Wiesenthal Center
1399 South Roxbury Drive
Los Angeles, CA 90035
Tel: (310) 553-9036 or (800) 900-9036; Fax: (310) 553-4521
http://www.wiesenthal.com/

From *The Power of Partnership* by Riane Eisler (New World Library, 2002)

Southern Poverty Law Center
400 Washington Avenue
Montgomery, AL 36104
Tel: (334) 956-8200
http://www.splcenter.org/

Women's Rights: A division of Human Rights Watch
350 Fifth Avenue, 34th Floor
New York, NY 10118-3299
Tel: (212) 290-4700; Fax: (212) 736-1300
http://www.hrw.org/women/

POLITICS

BOOKS

Adorno, T. W., and Else Frenkel-Brunswick, et al. *The Authoritarian Personality.* New York: John Wiley & Sons, Inc., 1964.

Domhoff, G. William. *Who Rules America: Power and Politics in the Year 2000.* 3d ed. Mountain View, Calif.: Mayfield Publishing Company, 1998.

Hightower, Jim. *There's Nothing in the Middle of the Road but Yellow Stripes and Dead Armadillos.* New York: HarperCollins, 1998.

Keating, Daniel P., ed. *Developmental Health and Wealth of Nations: Social, Biological, and Educational Dynamics.* New York: Guilford Publications, Inc., 2000.

Loye, David. *The Leadership Passion.* Lincoln, Nebr.: iUniverse.com Inc., 1998.

Reich, Wilhelm. *The Mass Psychology of Fascism.* Salinas, Calif.: Masters of Perception Press, 1970.

Schneir, Miriam, ed. *Feminism.* New York: Vintage Books, 1972.

———. *Feminism in Our Time.* New York: Vintage Books, 1994.

Steinem, Gloria. *Outrageous Acts and Everyday Rebellions.* New York: Holt, Rinehart & Winston, 1983.

West, Cornel. *Race Matters.* Boston: Beacon Press, 1993.

PAPERS AND ARTICLES

Bovard, James. "Archer Daniels Midland: A Case Study in Corporate Welfare." The Cato Institute, Policy Analysis No. 241 (26 September 1995). Accessible at http://www.cato.org/pubs/pas/pa-241.html.

From *The Power of Partnership* by Riane Eisler (New World Library, 2002)

Knode, Helen. "The School for Violence: A Conversation with Riane
    Eisler." *LA Weekly*, vol. 23, no. 45 (28 September–4 October 2001): 33.
Sklar, Holly. "Imagine a Country." *Teaching Sociology*, vol. 22, no. 1 (January
    1994): 121–30. Accessible at http://www.zmag.org/zmag/articles/
    sklarjuly97.html.

Organizations

American Friends Service Committee
1501 Cherry Street
Philadelphia, PA 19102
Tel: (215) 241-7000; Fax: (215) 241-7275
http://www.afsc.org/

Center for Economic and Policy Research
1015 18th Street NW, Suite 200
Washington, DC 20036
Tel: (202) 293-5380; Fax: (202) 822-1199
http://www.cepr.net/

The Center for Responsive Politics
1101 14th Street NW, Suite 1030
Washington, DC 20005-5635
Tel: (202) 857-0044; Fax: (202) 857-7809
http://www.opensecrets.org/

Center for Strategic and International Studies
1800 K Street, NW
Washington, DC 20006
Tel: (202) 887-0200; Fax: (202) 775-3199
http://www.csis.org/

Common Cause
1250 Connecticut Avenue NW, #600
Washington, DC 20036
Tel: (202) 833-1200
http://www.commoncause.org/

From *The Power of Partnership* by Riane Eisler (New World Library, 2002)

League of Women Voters
1730 M Street NW, Suite 1000
Washington, DC 20036-4508
Tel: (202) 429-1965; Fax: (202) 429-0854
http://www.lwv.org/

National Center for Policy Research for Women and Families
1444 Eye Street NW, Suite 900
Washington, DC 20005
Tel: (202) 216-9507
http://www.cpr4womenandfamilies.org

National Women's Political Caucus
1630 Connecticut Avenue NW, Suite 201
Washington, DC 20009
Tel: (202) 785-1100; Fax: (202) 785-3605
http://www.nwpc.org

People for the American Way
2000 M Street NW, Suite 400
Washington, DC 20036
Tel: (202) 467-4999 or (800) 326-7329
http://www.pfaw.org/

ALTERNATIVE NEWS MEDIA RESOURCES

E Magazine. P.O. Box 2047, Marion, OH 43305-2047; Tel: (815) 734-1242; http://www.emagazine.com/.

Mother Jones. 731 Market Street, 6th Floor, San Francisco, CA 94103; Tel: (415) 665-6637; Fax: (415) 665-6696; http://www.motherjones.com/.

Ms. 20 Exchange Place, 22nd Floor, New York, NY 10005; Tel: (212) 509-2092; Fax: (212) 509-2407; http://www.msmagazine.com/.

The Nation. 33 Irving Place, New York, NY 10003; Tel: (212) 209-5400; Fax: (212) 982-9000; http://www.thenation.com/.

Too Much. The Apex Press, Suite 3C, 777 United Nations Plaza, New York, NY 10017; Tel: (800) 316-APEX; http://www.cipa-apex.org/cat08.htm.

The Utne Reader. Tel: (800) 880-UTNE; http://www.utne.com/.

Women's International Network (WIN) News. 187 Grant Street, Lexington, MA 02420-2126; Tel: (781) 862-9431; Fax: (781) 862-1734; http://www.feminist.com/win.htm.

From *The Power of Partnership* by Riane Eisler (New World Library, 2002)

ENVIRONMENT

BOOKS

Carson, Rachel. *The Silent Spring.* New York: Houghton Mifflin Company, 1962, 1994.

Griffin, Susan. *Women and Nature.* San Francisco: Sierra Club Books, 1979, 2000.

Hawken, Paul, Amory Lovins, and L. Hunter Lovins. *Natural Capitalism: Creating the Next Industrial Revolution.* New York: Little, Brown & Company, 2000.

Human Development Report 1995. United Nations Development Program (UNDP). New York: Oxford University Press, 1995.

Merchant, Carolyn. *Radical Ecology.* New York: Routledge, 1992.

Orr, David. *Earth in Mind: On Education, Environment, and the Human Prospect.* Washington, D.C.: Island Press, 1994.

Rifkin, Jeremy. *The Biotech Century: Harnessing the Gene and Remaking the World.* New York: Tarcher/Putnam, 1998.

Robbins, Ocean, and Sol Solomon. *Choices for Our Future: A Generation Rising for Life on Earth.* Summerton, Tenn.: Book Publishing Company, 1995.

Shiva, Vandana. *Staying Alive.* London: Zed Books, 1988.

PAPERS AND ARTICLES

Borenstein, Seth. "Global-Warming Picture Looks More Dire, Panel Says." *The Philadelphia Inquirer,* 19 February 2001. Accessible at http://inq.philly.com/content/inquirer/2001/02/19/national/WARM19.htm.

Kendall, Henry. "World Scientists Warning to Humanity." *The Union of Concerned Scientist* (November 1992). Accessible at http://www.ucsusa.org/resources/warning.html.

Mesarovic, M., and E. Pestel. "Multilevel Computer Model of World Development System: Summary of the Proceedings." *International Institute for Applied Systems Analysis* (29 April–3 May 1974).

Renner, Michael. "Small Arms, Big Impact: The Next Challenge of Disarmament." *Worldwatch Institute* (1997). Excerpt accessible at http://www.worldwatch.org/pubs/paper/137a.html.

From *The Power of Partnership* by Riane Eisler (New World Library, 2002)

ORGANIZATIONS

Campaign to Ban Genetically Engineered Foods
(online news archive)
http://www.netlink.de/gen/home.html

The Earth Charter Initiative
P.O. Box 319-6100
San José, Costa Rica
Tel: (506) 205-1600; Fax: (506) 249-3500
http://www.earthcharter.org/

Earth Island Institute
300 Broadway, Suite 28
San Francisco, CA 94133
Tel: (415) 788-3666; Fax: (415) 788-7324
http://www.earthisland.org/

Environmental Defense
257 Park Avenue South
New York, NY 10010
Tel: (800) 684-3322
http://www.environmentaldefense.org

Friends of the Earth
1025 Vermont Avenue NW
Washington, DC 20005
Tel: (877) 843-8687 or (202) 783-7400
Fax: (202) 783-0444
http://www.foe.org/

Intergovernmental Panel on Climate Change
c/o World Meteorological Organization
7bis Avenue de la Paix, C.P. 2300
CH-1211 Geneva 2, Switzerland
Tel: (41) 22-730-8208; Fax: (41) 22-730-8025
http://www.ipcc.ch/

From *The Power of Partnership* by Riane Eisler (New World Library, 2002)

Pathfinder International
9 Galen Street, Suite 217
Watertown, MA 02472-4501
Tel: (617) 924-7200; Fax: (617) 924-3833
information@pathfind.org

Population Action International
1300 19th Street NW, 2nd Floor
Washington, DC 20036
Tel: (202) 557-3400; Fax: (202) 728-4177
http://www.populationaction.org

The Population Institute
107 Second Street NE
Washington, DC 20002
Tel: (800) 787-0038; Fax: (202) 544-0068
http://www.populationinstitute.org/

Rainforest Action Network
221 Pine Street, Suite 500
San Francisco, CA 94104
Tel: (415) 398-4404; Fax: (415) 398-2732
http://www.ran.org

The Sierra Club
85 Second Street, 2nd Floor
San Francisco, CA 94105-3441
Tel: (415) 977-5500; Fax: (415) 977-5799
http://www.sierraclub.org/

Union of Concerned Scientists
2 Brattle Square
Cambridge, MA 02238
Tel: (617) 547-5552
http://www.ucsusa.org/index.html

From *The Power of Partnership* by Riane Eisler (New World Library, 2002)

Youth for Environmental Sanity (YES)
420 Bronco Road
Soquel, CA 95073-9510
Tel: (877) 293-7226; Fax: (831) 462-6970
http://www.yesworld.org/

Zero Population Growth
1400 Sixteenth Street NW, Suite 320
Washington, DC 20036
Tel: (800) POP-1956
http://www.zpg.org

PREHISTORY AND CULTURAL TRANSFORMATION

BOOKS

Austin, Hallie Inglehart. *Heart of the Goddess: Art, Myth & Meditations of the World's Sacred Feminine.* Oakland, Calif.: Wingbow Press, 1991.

Birnbaum, Lucia. *Black Madonnas.* Boston: Northeastern University Press, 1993.

Capra, Fritjof. *The Web of Life.* New York: Anchor/Doubleday, 1996.

Chaisson, Eric. *The Life Era.* New York: Atlantic Monthly Press, 1987.

Demeo, James. *Saharasia: The 4000 BCE Origins of Child Abuse, Warfare, and Social Violence.* Ashland, Ore.: Natural Energy Works, 1998.

Gadon, Elinor. *The Once and Future Goddess.* San Francisco: Harper & Row, 1989.

Gimbutas, Marija. *The Civilization of the Goddess.* San Francisco: HarperSanFrancisco, 1991.

———. *The Goddesses and Gods of Old Europe.* Berkeley, Calif.: University of California Press, 1982.

Goodison, Lucy. *Death, Women, and the Sun.* London: University of London, 1989.

Eisler, Riane. *The Chalice and the Blade.* San Francisco: Harper & Row, 1987.

Hawkes, Jaquetta. *Dawn of the Gods.* New York: Random House, 1968.

Inglehart, Ronald. *Modernization and Postmodernization: Cultural, Economic, and Political Change in 43 Societies.* Princeton, N.J.: Princeton University Press, 1997.

Jiayin, Min, ed. *The Chalice and the Blade in Chinese Culture.* Beijing: China Social Sciences Publishing House, 1995.

Johnson, Buffie. *Lady of the Beasts.* San Francisco: Harper & Row, 1988.

From *The Power of Partnership* by Riane Eisler (New World Library, 2002)

252

Kramer, Samuel Noah, and John Maier. *Myths of Enki, the Crafty God.* New York: Oxford University Press, 1989.

Laszlo, Ervin. *Evolution.* Boston: Shambhala, 1987.

Lerner, Gerda. *The Majority Finds Its Past.* New York: Oxford University Press, 1979.

Lewin, Kurt. *The Complete Social Scientist: A Kurt Lewin Reader,* Martin Gold, ed. American Psychological Association, 1999.

Loye, David. *Darwin's Lost Theory.* New York: Seven Stories Press, 2002.

Loye, David, ed. *The Evolutionary Outrider: The Impact of the Human Agent on Evolution.* Westport, Conn.: Praeger Books; Twickenham, England: Adamantine Press, 1998.

Mallory, J. P. *In Search of the Indo-Europeans: Language, Archaeology, and Myth.* London: Thames & Hudson, 1989.

Marshack, Alexander. *The Roots of Civilization.* Mount Kisco, N.Y.: Moyer Bell Ltd., 1991.

Mellaart, James. *Catal Huyuk.* New York: McGraw-Hill, 1967.

————. *The Neolithic of the Near East.* New York: Scribner's, 1975.

Morbeck, Mary Ellen, Adrienne L. Zihlman, and Alison Galloway, eds. *The Evolving Female.* Princeton, N.J.: Princeton University Press, 1997.

Platon, Nicolas. *Crete.* Geneva: Nagel Publishers, 1966.

Ray, Paul H. "What Might Be the Next Step in Cultural Evolution?" In David Loye, ed., *The Evolutionary Outrider.* Bridgeport, Conn.: Praeger Books; Twickenham, England: Adamantine Press, 1998.

Stengers, Isabel, and Ilya Prigogine. *Order Out of Chaos.* New York: Bantam, 1984.

Tanner, Nancy N. *On Becoming Human.* Cambridge, Mass.: Cambridge University Press, 1981.

Wolkstein, Diane, and Samuel Noah Kramer. *Inanna.* New York: Harper & Row, 1983.

Zihlman, Adrienne. "Common Ancestors and Uncommon Apes." In *Human Origins,* John R. Durant, ed. pp. 81–105. Oxford: Clarendon Press, 1989.

ARTICLE

Gimbutas, Marija. "The First Wave of Eurasian Steppe Pastoralists into Copper Age Europe," *Journal of Indo-European Studies,* vol. 5 (Winter 1977).

From *The Power of Partnership* by Riane Eisler (New World Library, 2002)

SPIRITUALITY AND MORALITY

BOOKS

Davidson, Julian N. "The Psychobiology of Sexual Experience." In *The Psychobiology of Consciousness*. Julian N. Davidson and Richard J. Davidson, eds. New York: Plenum Press, 1980.

Eisler, Riane. *Sacred Pleasure: Sex, Myth & the Politics of the Body*. New York: HarperSanFrancisco, 1996.

Fiorenza, Elizabeth Schussler. *In Memory of Her: A Feminist Theological Reconstruction of Christian Origins*. New York: Crossroad Publishing Company, 1984.

Fox, Matthew. *Original Blessing*. New York: Putnam Publishing Group, 2000.

Fox, Robin Lane. *Pagans and Christians*. San Francisco: Harper & Row, 1986.

Gray, Elizabeth Dodson, ed. *Sacred Dimensions of Women's Experience*. Wellesley, Mass.: Roundtable Press, 1988.

Hanh, Thich Nhat. *Present Moment Wonderful Moment: Mindfulness Verses for Daily Living*. Berkeley, Calif.: Parallax Press, 1990.

Heyward, Carter. *Touching Our Strength*. San Francisco: Harper & Row, 1989.

Lerner, Michael. *Spirit Matters*. Charlottesville, Va.: Hampton Roads Publishing Co., Inc., 2000.

Lorde, Audre. "Uses of the Erotic: The Erotic as Power." In Audre Lorde, *Sister Outsider: Essays and Speeches*. Freedom, Calif.: Crossing Press, 1984.

Maitland, Sara. "Passionate Prayer: Masochistic Images in Women's Experience." In Linda Hurcombe, ed., *Sex and God: Some Varieties of Women's Religious Experience*. New York: Routledge & Kegan Paul, 1987.

Mendel, Heather. *Towards Freedom: A Feminist Haggadah for Men and Women*. San Luis Obispo, Calif.: Words of Art, 1994. Available from www.wordartist.com

McFague, Sallie. *The Body of God*. Minneapolis, Minn.: Fortress Press, 1994.

Melville, Arthur. *With Eyes to See: A Journey from Religion to Spirituality*. Walpole, N.H.: Stillpoint Publishing, 1992.

Schlegel, Stuart A. *Wisdom from a Rainforest: The Spiritual Journey of an Anthropologist*. Athens, Ga.: University of Georgia Press, 1998.

Teish, Luisah. *Jambalaya*. San Francisco: Harper & Row, 1985.

Wink, Walter. *Engaging the Powers*. Minneapolis, Minn.: Fortress Press, 1992.

PAPERS AND ARTICLES

Eisler, Riane. "Spiritual Courage." *Tikkun* (January 1999). Accessible at http://www.partnershipway.org/html/subpages/articles/spirtitual.htm.

From *The Power of Partnership* by Riane Eisler (New World Library, 2002)

Harris, Mark. "Sex, Spirituality, and Evolution: Are We Victims to the Beast Within?" Interview with Riane Eisler. *Conscious Choice* (February 1999). Accessible at http://www.partnershipway.org/html/subpages/articles/sexspirtevol.htm.

Loye, David. "Moral Sensitivity and the Evolution of Higher Mind." *World Futures: The Journal of General Evolution,* vol. 30 (1990): 41–51.

———. "Charles Darwin, Paul MacLean, and the Lost Origins of 'The Moral Sense': Some Implications for General Evolution Theory." *World Futures: The Journal of General Evolution,* vol. 40 (1994): 187–96.

Snider, Jerry. "Sacred Pleasure: Sex, Myth and the Politics of the Body: An Interview with Riane Eisler." *Magical Blend* (January 1996). Accessible at http://www.partnershipway.org/html/subpages/articles/sacredpleasure.htm.

Sreenivasan, Jyotsna. "Making Sex a Sacred Pleasure: An Interview with Riane Eisler." *New Moon Network* (March/April 1996). Accessible at http://www.partnershipway.org/html/subpages/articles/sexsacred.htm.

From *The Power of Partnership* by Riane Eisler (New World Library, 2002)

INTRODUCTION

1. *Joining Up* is a video that shows how easily and naturally Monty Roberts's partnership with horses works. You can get it from Monty and Pat Roberts, P.O. Box 1700, Solvang, CA 93464, or you can read Monty's book *The Man Who Listens to Horses* (New York: Random House, 1997).

2. For example, in ancient Athens fathers had the legal right to decide whether a baby would live or be "exposed" (left outside to die) regardless of the child's mother's wishes, and still today in some world regions men who kill their wives can go scot-free.

3. Precisely because ours is a time of such rapid flux and disequilibrium, it is also a time when transformational change is possible. The chemists Ilya Prigogine and Isabel Stengers, for example, show that living systems can change from one state to a different one during such periods; see Ilya Prigogine and Isabel Stengers, *Order Out of Chaos* (New York: Bantam, 1984). The social psychologist Kurt Lewin described what he called unfreezing and refreezing as characteristic of such social periods; see Kurt Lewin, *Resolving Social Conflict: And Field Theory in the Social Sciences* (New York: American Psychological Association, 1997). My own work on cultural transformation further supports the possibility of foundational change in turbulent times; see, e.g., Riane Eisler, *The Chalice and the Blade* (San Francisco: Harper & Row, 1987); Riane Eisler, *Sacred Pleasure: Sex, Myth, and the Politics of the Body* (San Francisco: HarperSanFrancisco, 1995); and Riane Eisler, *Tomorrow's Children* (Boulder, Colo.: Westview Press, 2000).

4. The movement toward partnership is growing in all spheres of life — from the search by millions of people for better personal, business, and community relationships to the work of thousands of grassroots groups for peace, human rights, and the environment. Though it has not been given this name, the movement toward partnership is also being recognized by a number of social scientists and futurists. See, e.g., Ronald Inglehart, *Modernization and Postmodernization: Cultural, Economic, and Political Change in 43 Societies* (Princeton, N.J.: Princeton University Press, 1997); Paul H. Ray and Sherry Ruth Anderson, *The Cultural Creatives* (New York: Harmony Books, 2000); and Paul Ray, "What Might Be the Next Step in

Cultural Evolution?" in *The Evolutionary Outrider*, ed. David Loye (Bridgeport, Conn.: Praeger Books, 1998; Twickenham, England: Adamantine Press, 1998).

CHAPTER 1

1. There was a movie made about the tragic fate of the St. Louis called *Voyage of the Damned*. For more information, see www.cdn-friends-icej.ca/antiholo/voyage.html, http://aish.com/holocaust/issues/he86n63.htm, and www.eonline.com/Facts/Movies/0,60,18622,00.html.
2. See Eisler, *The Chalice and the Blade* and Chinese Academy of Social Sciences, *The Chalice and the Blade in Chinese Culture: Gender Relations and Social Models,* ed. Min Jiayin (Beijing: China Social Sciences Publishing House, 1995).
3. Don Hanlon Johnson, *Body: Recovering Our Sensual Wisdom* (Berkeley: North Atlantic Books, 1983, 1992), 81.
4. Steven Shafarman, *Awareness Heals: The Feldenkrais Method of Dynamic Health* (Menlo Park, Calif.: Addison-Wesley Publishing, 1997), 188–89.
5. Ibid., 189.
6. Johnson, 76–77. Johnson describes his own experiences as a Jesuit monk, how his vow of obedience not only enjoined him "to bend my mind into conformity with that of my superior, behaving like an old man's staff without a will of my own," but also how novices "were given instructions about how to carry our bodies erectly, where to place our eyes when dealing with superiors, and how to insure that our hands never drifted near our genitals." He also notes how the training of soldiers was modeled on monastic discipline, and how "throwing back the shoulders and stiffening the overall alignment constitute an effective model for inhibiting sensual impulses," and "a body thus shaped over years of training becomes an effective tool of national policies, unlikely to resist commands at inappropriate moments" (ibid., 96).
7. See Jean Kilbourne, *Can't Buy My Love* (New York: Touchstone Books, 2000).
8. Lisa Singer, "Do You Apologize Too Much?" *Glamour* (June 1998): 105.
9. Riane Eisler and David Loye, *The Partnership Way* (Brandon, Vt.: Holistic Education Press, 1998).
10. Alice Burmeister with Tom Monte, *The Touch of Healing* (New York: Bantam, 1997); Shakti Gawain, *Creative Visualization* (Novato, Calif.: Nataraj Publishing, 1998); Thich Nhat Hanh, *Present Moment, Wonderful Moment: Mindfulness Verses for Daily Living* (Berkeley: Parallax Press, 1990).
11. Chris McMullen, "Mortal Kombat — Main Review (Divine Thing)," www.gamesdomain.com/gdreview/zones/reviews/pc/oct97/mkt.html.
12. These issues as well as related ones are explored in depth in Riane Eisler, *Sacred Pleasure: Sex, Myth, and the Politics of the Body* (San Francisco: HarperCollins, 1995), particularly chapters 9–14.
13. John Robbins, *Reclaiming Our Health* (Tiburon, Calif.: H.J. Kramer, 1996), 179.
14. Andrew Weil, M.D., *Eight Weeks to Optimum Health* (New York: Alfred A. Knopf, 1997). See also Christiane Northrup, M.D., *Women's Bodies, Women's Wisdom* (New York: Bantam, 1994).
15. Riane Eisler and Dan Levine, "Nurture, Nature, and Caring: We Are Not Prisoners of Our Genes," *Brain and Mind 3* (2002).
16. Michael Liebowitz, *The Chemistry of Love* (New York: Berkeley, 1983).
17. For a more detailed discussion, see chapter 9 of Eisler, *Sacred Pleasure*.

CHAPTER 2

1. For a good summary, see David Loye, *Darwin's Lost Theory of Love* (New York: iUniverse, 2000). For educators, the section on evolution in Eisler, *Tomorrow's Children: A Blueprint for Partnership Education in the 21st Century* (Boulder, Colo.: Westview Press, 2000).

2. This is discussed in more depth in Eisler, *Sacred Pleasure;* Eisler, *Tomorrow's Children;* and Eisler and Levine, "Nurture, Nature, and Caring: We Are Not Prisoners of Our Genes"; and Riane Eisler and Daniel Levine, *The Caring Brain* (work in progress).

3. Dogs also have a great capacity for empathy and caring.

4. A resource for parents, teachers, and anyone interested in learning about these findings and their implications for childcare is the video *I Am Your Child: The First Years Last Forever,* hosted by Rob Reiner and produced by the Reiner Foundation. See www.iamyourchild.org.

5. See, e.g., Dennis D. Embry and Daniel J. Flannery, "Two Sides of the Coin: Multilevel Prevention and Intervention to Reduce Youth Violent Behavior," in *Youth Violence: Prevention, Intervention, and Social Policy,* ed. D.J. Flannery and C. Ronald Huff (Washington, D.C.: American Psychiatric Press, in press); B.D. Perry and J.E Marcellus, "The Impact of Abuse and Neglect on the Developing Brain," Colleagues for Children 7 (1997): 1–4, Missouri Chapter of the National Committee to Prevent Child Abuse. Accessible online at http://www.childtrauma.org/AbuseBrain.htm.

6. Eisler and Levine, *The Caring Brain.*

7. Rob Koegel, "Healing the Wounds of Masculinity," *Holistic Education Review* 7 (March 1994): 42–49.

8. Karen Taylor, "Blessing the House," *Journal of Psychohistory* 15 (Summer 1987): 431–54.

9. Raffael Scheck, "Childhood in German Autobiographical Writings, 1740–1820," *Journal of Psychohistory* 15 (Summer 1987): 391–422.

10. See, e.g., Hanna Rosin, "A Tough Plan for Raising Children Draws Fire: 'Babywise' Guides Worry Pediatricians and Others," *Washington Post* (February 27, 1999), p. A01, for a harrowing account of the damage done to children and parents by this approach. See also Hanna Rosin, "Critics Question Extreme Childrearing Method," *Washington Post* (reprinted in *The Monterey County Herald,* March 1, 1999, p. A10).

11. Hanna Rosin, "A Tough Plan for Raising Children Draws Fire: 'Babywise' Guides Worry Pediatricians and Others."

12. William and Martha Sears, *The Baby Book* (New York: Little Brown, 1993); Penelope Leach, *Your Baby and Child* (New York: Knopf, 1997); and Thomas Gordon, *Parent Effectiveness Training* (New York: Three Rivers Press, 2000).

13. Penelope Leach, "The New Thinking on . . . Violent Toys, Toilet Mastery, Positive Discipline, and More," *Child* (April 1998): 62.

14. Hyman quoted in Margery D. Rosen, "Is It Ever Okay to Spank Your Child?" *Child* (September 1997): 20.

15. Dave Grossman and Gloria Digaetano, *Stop Teaching Our Kids to Kill: A Call to Action against TV, Movie and Video Game Violence* (New York: Crown Publishers, 1999).

16. A good video on this point is *Tough Guise: Violence, Media & the Crisis in Masculinity,* featuring Jackson Katz, produced by the Media Education Foundation [phone: (800) 897-0089; www.mediaed.org].

17. Riane Eisler, *Dissolution: No-Fault Divorce, Marriage, and the Future of Women* (New York: McGraw-Hill, 1977) and Riane Eisler, *The Equal Rights Handbook: What ERA Means to Your Life, Your Rights, and the Future* (New York: Avon, 1978). Both books are now available from www.iUniverse.com.

18. William H. Masters and Virginia E. Johnson, *The Pleasure Bond* (New York: Bantam Books, 1976).

19. Julian N. Davidson, "The Psychobiology of Sexual Experience," in *The Psychobiology of Consciousness,* ed. Julian N. Davidson and Richard J. Davidson (New York: Plenum Press, 1980).

20. See Eisler, *Sacred Pleasure.*

21. Harvey Jackins, *The Human Side of Human Beings: The Theory of Re-Evaluation Counseling* (Seattle, Wash.: Rational Island Publishers, 1982).

CHAPTER 3

1. Alice M. Isen, "Positive Affect and Decision Making," in *Handbook of Emotions,* ed. M. Lewis and J.M. Haviland (New York: Guilford, 1993), 264.

2. Ibid., 261.

3. Ibid., 264.

4. Alice M. Isen, "The Asymmetry of Happiness and Sadness in Effects on Memory in Normal College Students," *Journal of Experimental Psychology General* 114 (1985): 388–91; K. Duncker, "On Problem Solving," *Psychology Monographs* 58 (No. 5, see entire issue) (1945).

    Showing that these kinds of results were actually due to positive emotions rather than merely emotional arousal was another experiment. In this case, a negative effect was induced by showing subjects segments of a documentary on Nazi death camps. Although their emotions were greatly aroused, the subjects of this experiment did not perform better than the control group. [Alice M. Isen, "Positive Affect, Cognitive Processes, and Social Behavior," in vol. 20 of *Advances in Experimental Social Psychology,* ed. L. Berkowitz (New York: Academic Press, 1987), 203–53.]

5. Rosabeth Moss Kanter, *When Giants Learn to Dance: Mastering the Challenge of Strategy, Management, and Careers in the 1990s* (New York: Simon and Schuster, 1990), 32.

6. Thomas Peters and Robert Waterman, *The Search for Excellence* (New York: Harper & Row, 1982), 86.

7. John Naisbitt and Patricia Aburdene, *Reinventing the Corporation* (New York: Warner Books, 1986).

8. Clement L. Russo, "Productivity Overview: Recognizing the Human Dimension," *ReVISION* 7.2 (Winter 1984/Spring 1985): 68–73.

9. Dennis T. Jaffe and Cynthia D. Scott, *Take This Job and Love It: How to Change Your Work without Changing Your Job* (New York: Simon & Schuster, 1988), 159.

10. Brian Dumaine, "Creating a New Company Culture," *Fortune* (January 15, 1990).

11. For the story of VISA, see Dee Hock, *Birth of the Chaordic Age* (San Francisco: Berrett-Koehler Publishers, 1999).

12. Jeff Gates, *The Ownership Solution* (New York: Penguin, 1998).

13. John W. Frank and J. Fraser Mustard, "The Determinants of Health from a Historical Perspective," *Daedalus* 123.4 (Fall 1994): 8–9.

14. Sally Helgesen, *The Female Advantage: Women's Ways of Leadership* (New York: Doubleday, 1990).

15. For instance, 43 percent of medical school students are women. On the AMA website, see the following link: www.ama-assn.org/ama/pub/article/171-196.html.

16. Susan G. Butruille, "Corporate Caretaking," *Training and Development Journal* (April 1990).

17. Riane Eisler, David Loye, and Kari Norgaard, *Women, Men, and the Global Quality of Life* (Pacific Grove, Calif.: Center for Partnership Studies, 1995), see particularly 50–52.

18. See Eisler, *Tomorrow's Children.*

19. An example of a community currency is the HOUR issued by the Bow Chinook Barter Community (BCBC) in Calgary, Alberta, Canada. The BCBC uses a bimonthly newspaper, monthly potlucks, and their web page (www.bcbc.ab.ca/) to connect businesses and individuals who want to get what they need without using money. To facilitate bartering, BCBC has printed a local currency called a Bow Chinook HOUR, which allows you to buy and sell goods or services. Each Bow Chinook HOUR is worth $10 or an hour of your time.

CHAPTER 4

1. See "Consumer Reports Finds Pesticide Residues Too High in Some Domestic and Imported Produce," Consumer Policy Institute (February 18, 1999). In this first-of-its-kind analysis of government data on 27,000 samples of domestic and imported produce, *Consumer Reports* found that even a single daily serving of some produce can deliver unsafe levels of toxic pesticide residues for young children. Some excerpts follow: "Though virtually all the foods tested were within legal limits, those limits are often at odds with what the government deems safe for young children.... The analysis found that seven popular fruits and vegetables (apples, grapes, green beans, peaches, pears, spinach, and winter squash) have toxicity scores up to hundreds of times higher than the rest of the foods analyzed.... Domestic produce had more, or more toxic, pesticides than imported produce in two-thirds of the cases where imports were tested.... The findings are especially pertinent to children, who eat far more produce per pound of body weight than adults and who are more sensitive to the effects of pesticides because their nervous systems are changing and developing so rapidly. Some pesticides are suspected of causing cancer and some may interfere with endocrine activity.

    "What parents can do: (1) Avoid giving children large amounts of the foods with the highest toxicity scores; (2) peel those foods with a high toxicity score, such as apples, peaches, and pears; (3) wash produce with a very diluted dishwashing detergent, an important step for green, leafy vegetables; and (4) buy organically grown produce (when *Consumer Reports* tested organic produce in 1998, it found little or no toxic pesticide residues)."

    For more information on this report, go to the Consumers Union website (www.consumersunion.org/food/pestny899.htm). For *Consumer Reports* comparison of organic produce to regular produce, see their article at www.consumerreports.com. Related articles can be found at www.pestlaw.com/article/.

2. See John Robbins, *The Food Revolution: How Our Diet Can Help Save Your Life and the World* (Berkeley: Conari Press, 2001).

3. I propose in *Tomorrow's Children* that, instead of teaching modern history as isolated dates and successions of rulers, we should teach young people to identify the underlying pattern of the movement toward partnership countered by dominator resistance and periodic regressions.

4. Some of the statistical increases are because this violence was formerly unreported. It was not prosecuted and was often blamed on the victims.

5. Organizations such as Responsible Wealth phone: 617-423-2148; www.responsible wealth.org/) provide solid information and work on the important policy issues this reconcentration of wealth raises for a democratic society.

6. United States Bureau of the Census Current Population Reports, Series P-60, Number 146, 1989; Steven Rose, *The American Profile Poster* (New York: Pantheon Books, 1986), 31; and Paul Krugman, "Disparity and Despair," *U.S. News and World Report* (March 23, 1992): 54.

7. U.S. Census figures reported in Randolph E. Schmid, "Income, But Not for the Poor," *The Associated Press* (September 30, 1997).

8. Reported in Louis Uchitelle, "As Class Struggle Subsides, Less Pie for the Workers," *New York Times* (December 5, 1999).

9. "The *Forbes* 400," *Forbes* (October 11, 1999). See also www.forbes.com.

10. United Nations Development Program, *Human Development Report* 1998 (New York: Oxford University Press, 1998), 29–30.

11. G. William Domhoff, *Who Rules America?* (New York: Prentice Hall, 1967). Hazel Henderson, *Building a Win-Win World* (San Francisco: Berrett-Koehler Publishers, 1996); David Korten, *When Corporations Rule the World* (San Francisco: Berrett-Koehler Publishers, 1995); Nancy Folbre, *The New Field Guide to the U.S. Economy* (New York: New Press, 1995); Jerry Mander and Edward Goldsmith, eds., *The Case against the Global Economy* (San Francisco: Sierra Books, 1996); and Jeff Gates, *The Ownership Solution* (Boulder, Colo.: Perseus Books, 1999). Bill Bigelow, ed., *Rethinking Our Classrooms: Teaching for Equity and Justice* (Milwaukee: Rethinking Schools, 1994), particularly the articles "Math, Equity, and Economics," page 94, and "Teaching for Social Justice: One Teacher's Journey" by Bob Peterson, page 30. Holly Sklar, "Imagine a Country," *Teaching Sociology* 22.1 (January 1994): 121–30. Gregory Mantsios, "Class in America: Myths and Realities," *Teaching Sociology* 22.1 (January 1994): 131–43. The quarterly *Too Much* is another good source that is easily accessible and includes cartoons that are amusing while at the same time providing important information. It is published by the Counsel on International and Public Affairs (CIPA), 777 United Nations Plaza, Suite 3C, New York, NY 10017; phone or fax: (800) 316-2739.

12. See www.cato.org/pubs/pas/pa-241.html.

13. Rather than reporting on how energy giants are effectively in control of federal regulatory agencies and presidential policies, the media coverage of these shocking connections has at best been spotty and fragmented. See, e.g., "Energy Chief Unfazed by Legal Threat," *Los Angeles Times* (reprinted in *The Monterey County Herald*, May 31, 2001, p. A10) with just a paragraph on how California officials estimated that the state had already been overcharged $6 billion for power yet the Federal Energy Regulation Commission had ordered only $124 million in refunds; Stella M. Hopkins and Peter Wallsten, "Price Spikes Revealed," *The Monterey County Herald* (June 2, 2001, p. A1) reporting an analysis of federal documents that "provide a rare public look at closely guarded pricing in California's convoluted energy market"; and Joseph Kahn, "Bush Advisers on Energy Report Tie to Industry," *New York Times News Service* (reprinted in *The Monterey County Herald*, June 3, 2001, p. A3) with just a paragraph reporting that Texas-based Enron is one of President Bush's largest campaign contributors.

14. Ben Bagdikian, *The Media Monopoly*, 6th ed. (Boston: Beacon Press, 2000). As Bagdikian points out, the media mergers authorized by the 1996 Telecommunications Act have resulted in the most radical consolidation of media control in U.S. history, reversing more than sixty years of communications law. Most of the media moguls are from the United States, but there are also powerful foreign players, such as the German-owned media giant Bertelsmann, which is one of the world's largest book

publishers (owning Random House and all its subsidiary publishing houses here in the United States), one of the largest music publishers (BMG and many others), and owns many magazines across Europe and the United States. Another foreign media mogul is Prince Alwaleed of Saudi Arabia, who is estimated to be worth $20 billion, and who has substantial interests in Murdoch's News Corp., Netscape Communications, Apple Computer, America Online, Paris Disneyland, and other media in his immense investment portfolio. For a new book on the media moguls, see Alma and Rod Holmgren, *Outrageous Fortunes* (Carmel, Calif.: Jackson Press, 2001).

15. George Gerbner, Personal communication with author, 1999.

16. This has been documented repeatedly by studies conducted by the Annenberg School of Communications Cultural Indicators Project.

17. George Gerbner, "The Turtles Live to Ooze Again," *Journal of the Center of Commercialism,* vol. 1, no. 3 (October 1991). A copy of Professor Gerbner's articles can be ordered from the Cultural Environment Movement, P.O. Box 31847, Philadelphia, PA 19104. Consider the increase of children killing children, such as the four-year-old boy in Georgia who stomped a fifteen-month-old baby to death and the twelve-year-old boy in Washington who killed his nineteen-month-old cousin by repeatedly slamming the toddler to the floor; these children had been in households where wrestling matches were "family entertainment" (Jacqueline Cutler, "Warning: TV Could Be Dangerous to Your Child's Health," *The Monterey County Herald TV Guide,* June 3, 2001, p. 3). Children imitate what they see, and the increase in such crimes is one of the most visible and shocking results of the constant diet of violence on the mass media.

18. There are great nonviolent video games, such as Myst. But games such as Doom, Time Crisis, and Postal literally teach children how to kill. For an excellent short interview with Lt. Col. David Grossman, who explains how these video games are like the simulators used by the military to teach soldiers to kill, with similar psychological effects, see www.skirmisher.com/grossint.htm. See also Grossman and Degaetano, *Stop Teaching Our Kids to Kill: A Call to Action against TV, Movie and Video Game Violence.*

19. A good video on this is *The Myth of the Liberal Media: The Propaganda Model of News,* produced and distributed by the Media Education Foundation, [phone: (800) 897-0089; mediaed.sitepassport.net/].

20. Jim Hightower, *There's Nothing in the Middle of the Road but Yellow Stripes and Dead Armadillos* (New York: Harper Perennial, 1997), 113.

21. See www.commoncause.org. Common Cause is an excellent source of information on campaign finance reform and corporate power — two interconnected issues. Common Cause can be reached at 1250 Connecticut Avenue, NW, Washington, DC 20036-2613; phone (202) 833-1200.

22. Jonathan D. Salant, "Tobacco Giants Gave Millions to Politicians," The Associated Press (reprinted in *The Monterey County Herald,* February 23, 1999, page A6). See also "...Just Follow the Money," *San Francisco Chronicle* (June 19, 1998): A22; David Tannenbaum, "Buying Votes, Buying Friends: Tobacco Industry Political Influence," *Multinational Monitor,* 19 (Jul/Aug 1998): 11–19; David Espo, " Senate Stubs Out Tobacco Measure," *The Monterey County Herald* (June 18, 1998): A1.

23. Figures are from Center for Responsible Politics, reported in Arthur L. Rowse, "A Lobby the Media Won't Touch," *Washington Monthly* (May 1998): 9. Columnist William Safire called this act a "ripoff on a scale vaster than dreamed by yesterday's robber barons." (Safire quoted in Alma and Rod Holmgren, *Outrageous Fortunes,* ix).

As Ben Bagdikian extensively documents in his book *The Media Monopoly,* ironically, while the 1996 Telecommunications Act was ostensibly passed to promote more competition and lower rates — none of which ever materialized — it opened the floodgates to the largest and greatest industrial mergers in U.S. history.

24. See http://emperors-clothes.com/docs/camps.htm and www.tenc.net [Emperor's Clothes] for a reprint of the article by Tim Weiner, "Afghan Taliban Camps Were Built by NATO," *The New York Times,* August 24, 1998. Mr. Weiner noted that "The Afghan resistance was backed by the intelligence services of the United States and Saudi Arabia with nearly $6 billion worth of weapons." As the editor of Emperor's Clothes noted, "This 'N.Y. Times' article appeared shortly after the U.S. bombed a pill factory in Sudan and facilities in Afghanistan." President Clinton went on TV and said the Afghan facilities the U.S. had bombed were "... terrorist facilities and infrastructure in Afghanistan. Our forces targeted one of the most active terrorist bases in the world ... a training camp for literally thousands of terrorists from around the globe." The most important part of Mr. Weiner's piece, sadly relevant today, is that the territory targeted was "a set of six encampments around Khost, where the Saudi exile Osama bin Laden has financed a kind of terrorist university," which was "well known to the Central Intelligence Agency." The reason it was well known, this now generally ignored *New York Times* article reported, is that "the C.I.A.'s military and financial support for the Afghan rebels indirectly helped build the camps. . . . And some of the same warriors who fought the Soviets with the C.I.A.'s help are now fighting under Mr. Bin Laden's banner." The *Times* coverage of these Clinton bombing attacks is also discussed in "Credible Deception" at www.emperors-clothes.com/articles/jared/sudan.html. See also Norman Markowitz, "Who is Osama Bin Laden?" *History News Service,* September 13, 2001.

25. See, e.g., Ben Bagdikian, *The Media Monopoly;* Robert McChesney, *Rich Media, Poor Democracy* (Champaign, Ill.: University of Illinois Press, 1999); and Dean Alger, *Megamedia: How Giant Corporations Dominate Mass Media, Distort Competition, and Endanger Democracy* (Lanham, Md.: Rowland & Littlefield, 1998).

26. Sheldon Rampton and John Stauber, *Trust Us, We're Experts* (New York: Tarcher/Putnam, 2001).

27. Ibid., 32.

28. "World Scientists Warning to Humanity," statement published by the Union of Concerned Scientists, April 1993. (The Union of Concerned Scientists is located at 26 Church Street, Cambridge, MA 02238.)

29. Reported in John Robbins, *The Food Revolution* (Berkeley, Calif.: Conari, 2001), 274.

30. Ibid., 47.

31. Elizabeth Schussler Fiorenza, *In Memory of Her* (New York: Crossroad, 1983).

32. See Eisler, *The Chalice and the Blade,* chapter 9.

33. Boris Johnson, "What Islamic Terrorists are Really Afraid of Is Women," *Daily Telegraph* (September 27, 2001): comment and opinion page, available at www.daily telegraph.com/opinion. See also Helen Knode, "The School for Violence: A Conversation with Riane Eisler," *LA Weekly* (September 28–October 4, 2001).

34. Charles Sykes, "The Ideology of Sensitivity," *Imprimis* 21.7 (July 1992).

35. A good source for the costs of military spending is the website of the War Resisters League (www.warresisters.org/). For example, while the official statistic for the 2002 military budget is 23 percent of the total budget, according to their calculations, military spending comes to 47 percent when you add 24 percent for veterans' benefits and 80 percent of the interest on the national debt stemming from earlier military spending.

The War Resisters League can be reached at 339 Lafayette Street, New York, NY 10012; phone: (212) 228-0450.

36. See Nomi S. Wronge, "Study Links High-Quality Child Care to Low Rates of Juvenile Delinquency," *San Jose Mercury News* (March 15, 2001), p. 15A.

37. See chapter 7 of this book for a brief summary; see also *The Chalice and the Blade, Sacred Pleasure, Tomorrow's Children,* and *The Partnership Way.*

38. Ken Kusmer, "Muslims Confront Domestic Abuse," *The Associated Press* (October 14, 2000).

39. Richard Grossman's Program on Corporations, Law, and Democracy (P.O. Box 246, South Yarmouth, MA 02664; phone: (508) 398-1145; www.poclad.org) has done extensive work in this area.

40. The workshops and consulting offered through the Center for Partnership Studies' Partnership Education Institute, and resources such as *Tomorrow's Children* and *Partnership Education in Action* (a CPS guidebook for teachers and other educators) can help you do this.

41. For a more detailed account of PODER, see Hightower, *There's Nothing in the Middle of the Road but Yellow Stripes and Dead Armadillos,* 177–81.

42. American Friends Service Committee, 1501 Cherry Street, Philadelphia, PA 19102; Co-op America, 1612 K Street NW, #600, Washington, DC 20006; The Children's Defense Fund, 25 E Street NW, Washington, DC 20001; Children Now, 1212 Broadway, 5th Floor, Oakland, CA 94612 (www.childrennow.org.); Committee on U.N. CEDAW (an organization working to obtain U.S. Senate ratification of the United Nations Convention on the Elimination of Discrimination Against Women, which has now been ratified by most of the world's nations), 320 N. Camden Drive, Beverly Hills, CA 90210-3202.

43. We need to liberate our mass media from centralized commercial control and, as Gerry Mander points out, take advantage of noncentralized technologies such as the Internet.

CHAPTER 5

1. See http://emperors-clothes.com/doc/camps.htm and www.tenc.net [Emperor's Clothes] for a reprint of the article by Tim Weiner, "Afghan Taliban Camps Were Built by NATO," *The New York Times,* August 24, 1998.

2. For information on the Earth Charter, which outlines basic principles to guide policies, including "gender equality and equity as prerequisites to sustainable development," contact the Earth Council, P.O. Box 319-6100, San José, Costa Rica; phone: (506) 205-1600; fax: (506) 249-3500; e-mail: info@earthcharter.org.

3. For details on military aid to Indonesia, see http://historylinks.freeservers.com/article11.html, which gives exact numbers going back to 1980. Look especially at the MAP column, which is actual grant aid — not sales or loans. Check out 1980! Also see www.fas.org, a web page from the Federation of American Scientists Arms Sales Monitoring Project. It documents how the United States has been a leading supporter of the Indonesian military: "The United States has sold $1.25 billion dollars worth of weaponry to Indonesia since 1975. The U.S. has also provided some form of security assistance virtually every year since 1950, including $388 million in grants and loans to pay for U.S. arms."

4. Robert Scheer, "Bush's Faustian Deal with the Taliban," *Los Angeles Times* (May 22, 2001). The gift was to obtain a promise from the Taliban to ban the growing of

opium. But as Scheer writes, even though some farmers may comply (since under the Taliban those who break minor rules are simply beaten on the spot by religious police or stoned to death), it was even then highly doubtful that the ban would be effective. He noted that most of the farmers who grew the poppies would have no other way to survive. In any case, as he also noted, "there's little doubt that the Taliban will turn once again to the easily taxed cash crop of opium in order to stay in power." See also www.mapinc.org/media/248.

5. Charlotte Bunch and Nimh Reilly, *Demanding Accountability: The Global Campaign and Vienna Tribunal for Women's Human Rights.* [New Brunswick, N.J.: Center for Women's Leadership, Rutgers University, and New York: United National Development Fund for Women (UNIFEM), 1994].

6. "A Landmark Ruling on Rape," *New York Times* (February 24, 2001).

7. Abita and I wrote a poem together which was read in English, Swahili, French, Spanish, German, Russian, and Urdu during the 1985 United Nations Conference on Women held in Nairobi, Kenya. It was called "Paean to Women," and honors women from every continent in their struggle against traditions of domination.

8. For an important work on this subject, see Fran Hosken, *The Hosken Report: Genital and Sexual Mutilation of Females,* 4th ed. (Lexington, Mass.: Women's International Network News, 1994). For the moving account of a young woman who, when threatened with genital mutilation, fled her homeland and finally, in a landmark case, obtained political asylum in the United States, see Fauziya Kassindja and Layli Miller Bashir, *Do They Hear You When You Cry* (New York: Delacorte Press, 1998). Even though this brutal practice, which is often done without anesthetic or even minimal hygiene, kills many children and causes lifelong damage to the survivors, including later toxic shock syndrome; when women began to ask human rights organizations for support, the response was that it was not possible to interfere with other people's cultural traditions.

9. Today, Amnesty International publishes a *Women's Rights Watch* newsletter, thanks to the efforts of women's rights advocates who for years fought against human rights violations that are condoned on the basis of noninterference with traditions. A key article was Riane Eisler, "Human Rights: Toward an Integrated Theory for Action," *Human Rights Quarterly* 9.1 (November 1987), which marked the first time a piece on this issue was published by this influential human rights journal. The issue is far from settled, as shown in Susan Moller Okin, "Is Multiculturalism Bad for Women?" *Boston Review* (October/November 1997), which addresses the use of multicultural diversity to justify human rights violations, particularly violations of the human rights of women. Another discussion of this problem is the insightful analysis in Ann Elizabeth Mayer, "Comment on Majid's 'The Politics of Feminism in Islam,'" *Signs* (Winter 1998): 369–76.

10. Amartya Sen, "More than 100 Million Women Are Missing," *New York Review* (December 20, 1990): 61–66.

11. United Nations Development Program, *1995 Human Development Report* (New York: Oxford University Press, 1995), 35. This report, published for the year of the United Nations Conference on Women in Beijing, is unfortunately unique in its wealth of statistical data focusing on gender discrimination.

12. Ibid., page 35.

13. Riane Eisler, David Loye, and Kari Norgaard, *Women, Men, and the Global Quality of Life* (Pacific Grove, Calif.: The Center for Partnership Studies, 1995), 6–7.

14. United Nations Development Program, *1990 Human Development Report* (New York: Oxford University Press, 1990), 130, 158.

15. Eisler, Loye, and Norgaard, *Women, Men, and the Global Quality of Life.*

16. Raffi, "The Loving Challenge: A Child-Honoring Society," on www.raffinews.com/about/institute.html.

17. Ruth Leger Sivard, *World Military and Social Expenditures 1991* (Washington, D.C.: World Priorities, 1991), 5.

18. Michael Renner, "Transforming Security," in *State of the World 1997*, ed. Lester R. Brown (New York: W.W. Norton, 1997), 131.

19. United Nations Development Program, *Human Development Report 1998* (New York: Oxford University Press, 1998), 29–30. This report also provides a chart of average wealth for the world's 225 richest people by region, ranging from an average of $2 billion in sub-Saharan Africa to $7.1 billion in the Arab states (see Box Table 1.3, page 30).

20. Lois Woestman, "Male Chauvinist SAPs: Structural Adjustment and Gender Policies," a EURODAD-wide briefing paper (December 1994–January 1995).

21. Hazel Henderson, "Accounting for the Love Economy," *Futures* (October 1998). Henderson is working with the Calvert Fund on Country Futures Indicators, the first version of which is the Calvert-Henderson Quality-of-Life Indicators for the USA (see www.calvertgroup.org).

22. See Helen Knode, "The School for Violence: A Conversation with Riane Eisler," *LA Weekly* (September 28–October 4, 2001).

23. Korten, *When Corporations Rule the World.*

24. Gates, *The Ownership Solution,* 74. This book provides both an excellent analysis of the inadequacies of present economic rules and proposals for effective alternatives.

25. A variation on community currency is the website for Friendly Favors, a virtual community started by Sergio Lub in 1999. Friendly Favors members offer to each other their products or services at a discount rate ranging from 10 percent to 100 percent (free). These discounts and/or gifts are acknowledged with Thankyous. When a person writes a Thankyou for saving on services or products received, she/he assumes a moral commitment to return Favors to others in the community. Friendly Favors allows communities to identify its most generous members, offering positive role models for its youth. It also acknowledges services and gifts that normally are not recognized by the monetary economy. Membership is by invitation from another member, and members can reside anywhere in the world.

26. A number of these groups are described in this book, as well as in *Sacred Pleasure* and *Tomorrow's Children.*

27. "Children Overcome Poverty," New Renaissance 10, 3 (2001) 38–9 (Source: Share International); YES can be reached at 1-877-2-YES-CAMP. Ocean Robbins and Sol Solomom are also the authors of the wonderful book: *Choices for Our Future: A Generation Rising for Life on Earth,* (Summerton, Tenn.: Book Publishing Company, 1994).

28. CAPACITAR is located at 23 East Beach St., Suite 206, Watsonville, CA 95076; phone: (831) 456-9426; fax: (831) 722-7703; e-mail: capacitar@igc.apc.org. CAPACI-TAR is also described in chapter 12 of *Sacred Pleasure.*

29. For more information on SEWA, see www.sewa.org; for information on the Green Belt movement, see www.rightlivelihood.se/ and go to the 1984 awards page.

30. This documentary premiered on June 11, 1998, on HBO, and was filmed in twenty-one countries where the filmmakers spoke directly to children.

31. Women's Environment & Development Organization (WEDO), 355 Lexington Avenue, 3rd Floor, New York, NY 10017-6603 (www.wedo.org); Women's International Network (WIN) News, 187 Grant Street, Lexington, MA 02173.

32. Grassroots organization packets and other information can be obtained from the

National Committee on UN/CEDAW, Billie Heller (chair), 520 North Camden Drive, Beverly Hills, CA 90210-3202; phone: (310) 271-8087.

33. As Marie Cocco writes in "Levi's Deserve a Teen's Support," *Newsday* (reprinted in *The Monterey County Herald,* March 3, 1999, p. 7A), Levi-Strauss was "the first company to write a code of conduct for its network of subcontractors around the globe" and one of the few companies to worry "whether a 10-year-old girl in Mexico is getting a warped spine and going blind because she is stitching jeans all day and into the night."

34. In the U.S., women are still less than 20 percent.

35. The Nobel Academy offers a Peace Prize and national conferences organized by men to bring attention to violence against women and work to end it. As two Scandinavian men, Jorgen Lorentzen and Per Are Lokke, wrote, "Many men have come to believe that violence against a woman, child, or another man is an acceptable way to control another person. By remaining silent about the violence, we allow other men to poison our environments. We also allow the picture of men as dangerous to stay alive. We are working to change this picture because we care about what happens in the lives of men.... Without interest from, and work by, men in this area, we think it will be very difficult to stop the violence. Domestic violence is a problem within existing masculinity and it is we, as men, who have to stop it." (Jorgen Lorentzen and Per Are Lokke, "Men's Violence against Women: The Need to Take Responsibility," presented at the international seminar *Promoting Equality: A Common Issue for Men and Women,* Palais de l'Europe, Strasbourg, France, June 17–18, 1997, p. 4).

CHAPTER 6

1. Union of Concerned Scientists, "World Scientists Warning to Humanity," April 1993. The Union of Concerned Scientists, 26 Church Street, Cambridge, MA 02238.

2. For a summary of this scientific meeting, see Seth Borenstein, "Effects of Global Warming May Be Worse than Expected," *The Monterey County Herald* (February 19, 2001): A6. The conclusion was again reached by a National Academy of Sciences study commissioned by the White House released on June 7, 2001, that global warming "is real and particularly strong within the past twenty years" and that a leading cause is emission of carbon dioxide from burning fossil fuels ("Scientists See Global Warming Rise," *The Associated Press,* June 7, 2001).

3. As Sheldon Rampton and John Stauber show in *Trust Us, We're Experts,* billions are spent on PR agencies that put the right "spin" on policies designed to push us back to times when those on top essentially had the freedom to do as they pleased: 7–30.

4. But just having an environmental agency is not enough. As Jane Anne Morris of the Program on Corporations, Law, and Democracy documents in "Sheep in Wolf's Clothing," government regulatory agencies are often pawns in the hands of the powerful corporate interests they were set up to regulate. Jane Anne Morris, "Sheep in Wolf's Clothing," www.poclad.org. The Program on Corporations, Law, and Democracy is an excellent source of information and action ideas to help move us toward an economics of partnership rather than domination. It offers many articles, including writings by Richard Grossman, one of the pioneers in the movement to change corporate charters to be socially and environmentally responsible. Their address is P.O. Box 296, South Yarmouth, MA 02664; phone: (508) 398-1145; e-mail: people@poclad.org. To order materials, call (800) 316-2729 or send e-mail to cipany@igc.apc.org.

5. Mihajlo Mesarovic and Eduard Pestel, *Mankind at the Turning Point: The Second Report to the Club of Rome* (New York: Dutton, 1974).

6. Perdita Huston, *Third World Women Speak Out* (New York: Praeger, 1979), 75.

7. For an analysis of this, see Riane Eisler, David Loye, and Kari Norgaard, *Women, Men, and the Global Quality of Life,* (Pacific Grove, Calif.: The Center for Partnership Studies, 1995), 43–47.

8. Kathleen Newland, "Choice Beyond Childbearing," *Worldwatch Paper No. 16* (Washington, D.C.: Worldwatch, 1977).

9. Report on Progress Toward World Population Stabilization, *Closing the Gender Gap: Educating Girls* (Washington, D.C.: Population Action International, 1993).

10. Jeremy Rifkin, *The Biotech Century: Harnessing the Gene and Remaking the World* (New York: Tarcher/Putnam, 1998).

11. Editorial in *The Economist* quoted in Jeremy Rifkin, "The Ultimate Therapy: Commercial Eugenics on the Eve of the Biotech Century," *Tikkun* (May/June 1998): 36.

12. Ray Moseley, "'Frankenstein Foods' Cause Public Health Scare in Great Britain," *Chicago Tribune* London Bureau (reprinted in *The Monterey County Herald,* February 18, 1999: A6).

13. Lauran Keergaard, "Biologic Terror Danger Real, Doctors Told," *The Associated Press* (reprinted in *The Monterey County Herald,* February 17, 1999: A3). The article quotes Dr. D. A. Henderson of Johns Hopkins University, who led the world's efforts against smallpox and is now mobilizing health workers and the government against bioterrorism, on the reality of the problem. It also quotes Col. Gerald Parker, the U.S. Army's chief of infectious disease, who said that the worst agents would be anthrax and smallpox, and Jessica Stern, former director for Russian, Ukrainian, and Eurasian affairs of the National Security Council, who pointed out that there is already precedent for these kinds of attacks in what happened in 1985 in Oregon, when a religious cult poisoned salad bars with salmonella, infecting 750 people. After a series of terrorist killings of physicians who provide abortion services (with their names posted on a website where each name was crossed out after the murder) and many clinic bombings by so-called pro-life terrorists, a spate of letters was sent out to clinics throughout the United States, containing powdery substances and notes saying they contained anthrax. While this action proved to be a scare tactic to disrupt operations and intimidate, it shows that some anti-abortion terrorists are contemplating using biological terror ("Clinic Gets Letter with Alleged Anthrax Inside," *The Monterey County Herald,* February 23, 1999: A2).

14. David Orr, *Earth in Mind* (Washington, D.C.: Island Press, 1994).

15. A brilliant video on this is *Advertising and the End of the World* available from the Media Education Foundation.

16. For a movie on the investigator who took on PG&E, see *Erin Brockovich,* starring Julia Roberts. For another exposé, on how giant oil companies kept denying their toxin-emitting storage plants were poisoning people living near them, see Hightower, *There's Nothing in the Middle of the Road but Yellow Stripes and Dead Armadillos,* 177–81.

17. See the website of the Natural Step, www.naturalstep.org.

18. Paul Hawken, Amory B. Lovins, and L. Hunter Lovins, *Natural Capitalism: Creating the Next Industrial Revolution* (Boston: Little Brown & Company, 1999).

19. For information on solar ovens, the Internet is a good source. Everything from country reports and articles on the advantages of solar cooking to recipe books and discussion boards can be found at www.accessone.com/~sbcn/. One website, www.sunoven.com,

not only provides information on the benefits and history of solar cooking, but actually sells solar ovens over the Internet. They claim when food is cooked in a solar oven, not only does it stay moister and taste better, but also more vitamins are retained.

20. Michael Renner, "Small Arms, Big Impact: The Next Challenge of Disarmament," *Worldwatch Institute* (1997).

21. Nicolas Platon, *Crete* (Geneva: Nagel Publishers, 1966), 148. I summarize the evidence of a massive shift in prehistory from an earlier, more partnership-oriented cultural direction to the dominator system in *The Chalice and the Blade* and *Sacred Pleasure.* See also James Mellaart, *Catal Huyuk* (New York: McGraw-Hill, 1967); Marija Gimbutas, *The Civilization of the Goddess* (San Francisco, HarperSanFrancisco, 1991); Nicolas Platon, *Zakros* (New York: Charles Scribner's Sons, 1971); Jacquetta Hawkes, *The Dawn of the Gods* (New York: Random House, 1968); Lucy Goodison, *Death, Women, and the Sun* (London: University of London, 1989). For example, Gimbutas describes the shift from what she calls the civilization of Old Europe (which goes back to about 7000 B.C.E.) to later war-like Indo-European-language-speaking cultures. Scholars such as Jacquetta Hawkes have described the shift from the Minoan civilization that flourished on the island of Crete until approximately 1400 B.C.E. to its later Indo-European-ruled Mycenaean period. In *The Chalice and the Blade in Chinese Culture,* a work that tests my cultural transformation theory in Asia, scholars at the Chinese Academy of Social Sciences in Beijing show that this shift also took place in China. See Min Jiayin, *The Chalice and the Blade: Gender Relations and Social Models* (Beijing: China Social Sciences Publishing House, 1995). Anthropologist June Nash's study of the Aztecs shows a similar shift in the Americas. On this continent too, there seems to have been a change from societies where women had higher status and warfare was not endemic to a violent way of life in which domination and conquest were idealized. See June Nash, "The Aztecs and the Ideology of Male Dominance," *Signs* 4 (Winter 1978).

22. For example, in 1968, a visionary businessman named Ed Bullard founded TechnoServe in the belief that with the proper tools, skills, and knowledge people can overcome even the harshest challenges, and since then, TechnoServe has enabled nearly 3 million people on three continents to launch thriving rural enterprises: farms, schools, and health clinics in twenty-one nations. For more information on the work TechnoServe is doing or how you can help, please contact them at 49 Day Street, Norwalk, CT 06854-3106; phone: (203) 852-0377 or toll free (800) 99-WORKS.

23. The 1994 Packaging and Packaging Waste Directive (94/62/EC) covers primary, secondary, and tertiary packaging for all products.

24. Co-op America is located at 1612 K Street NW #600, Washington, DC 20006; phone: (202) 872-5307; website: www.coopamerica.org.

25. Most of these organizations have websites. For example, Population Action International is at www.populationaction.org and the Population Institute is at www.populationinstitute.org.

26. These technologies are essential in our time when burgeoning populations threaten natural resources. Already eighty-two nations are unable to grow or buy enough food to provide for their people, forests are being cut down, cities are overcrowded and increasingly polluted — and within the next generation 3 billion young people will enter their reproductive years!

27. A good source for education and information on this issue is The Population Institute, 107 Second Street NE, Washington, DC 20002; phone: (800) 787-0038; www.populationinstitute.org.

CHAPTER 7

1. The story of Lot is in Genesis 19.
2. See, for example, Rev. 21:8, 1 Cor. 6:9, 2 Thess. 1:8–9, Ps. 9:17, and Mark 16:16.
3. Pope Gregory the Great quoted in Uta Ranke Heineman, *Eunuchs for the Kingdom of Heaven* (New York: Penguin Books, 1991), 137.
4. For an excellent book on the witch burnings, see Anne Lewellyn Barstow, *Witchcraze* (London and San Francisco: Pandora, 1994). *The Burning Times,* a documentary by the award-winning Canadian filmmaker Donna Read, is a dramatic account of the witch hunts. Far more sources exist with information about the Crusades and the Inquisition than about the witch hunts, which are still largely ignored by scholars. Even newspaper articles deal with the Crusades; for example, Karen Armstrong, writing for the *New York Times Magazine* in 1999, observed that "when the first Crusaders captured Jerusalem in July 1099, they slaughtered some 30,000 of the city's Jewish and Muslim inhabitants in two days. At the Haram al-Sharif, the third holiest place in the Islamic world, an exultant witness reported that the blood reached the horses' knees. The massacre shocked many Europeans, but within a few years scholarly monks began describing Muslims as a 'savage race...fit only for extermination'" (http://www.nytimes.com).
5. Michael Lerner speaks of two voices of God: the voice of the God of love and the voice projecting onto God the accumulated cruelty, violence, and pain that, as we have seen, is inherent in a domination model of relations. See Michael Lerner, *Jewish Renewal: A Path to Healing and Transformation* (New York: Harper Perennial, 1995), 87–95.
6. See James Mellaart, *Catal Huyuk* (New York: McGraw-Hill, 1967); Marija Gimbutas, *The Civilization of the Goddess* (San Francisco, HarperSanFrancisco, 1991); Nicolas Platon, *Zakros* (New York: Charles Scribner's Sons, 1971); Jacquetta Hawkes, *The Dawn of the Gods* (New York: Random House, 1968); Lucy Goodison, *Death, Women, and the Sun* (London: University of London, 1989). For a summary, see Eisler, *The Chalice and the Blade* and *Sacred Pleasure.*
7. For example, the archeologist Marija Gimbutas describes the shift from what she calls the civilization of Old Europe (which goes back to about 7000 B.C.E.) to later warlike Indo-European-language-speaking cultures. Scholars such as Jacquetta Hawkes have described the shift from the Minoan civilization that flourished on the island of Crete until approximately 1400 B.C.E. to its later Indo-European-ruled Mycenaean period.
8. Chinese Academy of Social Sciences (Min Jiayin, ed.), *The Chalice and the Blade in Chinese Culture: Gender Relations and Social Models.*
9. June Nash, "The Aztecs and the Ideology of Male Dominance," *Signs* 4 (Winter 1978): 349–62.
10. Sallie McFague, "God as Mother," in *Weaving the Visions: New Patterns in Feminist Spirituality* ed. by Judith Plaskow and Carol P. Christ (San Francisco: Harper & Row, 1989), 147.
11. We already find sexual imagery thirty thousand years ago in Paleolithic carvings of vulvas and phalluses — carvings that nineteenth-century archeologists sometimes called "indeterminate markings" because they could not or did not want to see what they were. And in the Neolithic period, sculptures of the sacred union of female and male appear. For example, this sacred union is depicted in a remarkable stone plaque with two "panels" excavated in Catal Huyuk, Turkey. The first panel shows a woman and man embracing. The second shows the product of their union: the woman with a baby in her

arms (Marija Gimbutas, *The Goddesses and Gods of Old Europe* [Berkeley: University of California Press, 1982]; James Mellaart, *Catal Huyuk* [New York: McGraw-Hill, 1967]).

12. These hymns were committed to writing about four thousand years ago, but as the Sumerologist Samuel Noah Kramer notes, they go back to much earlier oral traditions. What we find here is a joyously erotic poem, extolling the ecstasies of sexual pleasure but at the same time connecting sex with images of the Earth's fecund beauty and the growth of plants from the womb of the Goddess every spring. See Diane Wolkstein and Samuel Noah Kramer, *Inanna* (New York: Harper & Row, 1983). See also Eisler, *Sacred Pleasure,* chapter 3, which places the Hymns of Inanna in their historic context.

13. Wolkstein and Kramer, *Inanna,* 43.

14. In the King James Bible, this book is called the Song of Solomon — even though it does not mention King Solomon.

15. Song of Solomon 1:2, 13 and Song of Solomon 7, King James Bible. For a discussion, see chapter 1 of Eisler, *Sacred Pleasure.*

16. For a discussion of these mystical traditions from the perspective of the shift from a partnership to a dominator spirituality, see chapter 8 of Eisler, *Sacred Pleasure.*

17. This is described in detail in Eisler, *Sacred Pleasure,* chapter 8.

18. For an excellent treatise on the sexual sadomasochism of Christian women mystics, see Sara Maitland, "Passionate Prayer: Masochistic Images in Women's Experience," in *Sex and God: Some Varieties of Women's Religious Experience,* ed. Linda Hurcombe (New York: Routledge & Kegan Paul, 1987), 125–40.

19. In his book *The Glacier and the Flame* (work in progress), David Loye distinguishes between partnership moral sensitivity and dominator moral insensitivity. See also David Loye, "Can Science Help Construct a New Global Ethic? The Development and Implications of Moral Transformation Theory," *Zygon* 34, 2 (1999): 221–35 and David Loye, "Moral Sensitivity and the Evolution of the Higher Mind," *World Futures: The Journal of General Evolution* 30, 1–2 (1990): 42–52.

20. Loye, *The Glacier and the Flame.*

21. Eisler, *Tomorrow's Children.*

ACKNOWLEDGMENTS

SO MANY PEOPLE HAVE HELPED ME with this book that it is truly a partnership effort. I am grateful to you all.

I ESPECIALLY WANT TO THANK Bill Gladstone for his wise guidance in conceptualizing and organizing materials that needed a clear focus and a more direct tone. I could not have written this book without his help. I also especially want to thank Martin Eberhard, Leah Gowron, Rob Koegel, Hannah Liebmann, Barclay Palmer, Wendy Sinek, Gregg Stebben, and Rona Zollinger, all of whom read the entire manuscript and were enormously helpful. In addition, I want to express my gratitude to my wonderful friend H (who wishes to remain anonymous), whose help was invaluable. And I especially

273

want to thank my wonderful life-partner, David Loye, not only for his sage comments but for putting up with my immersion in this project for a seemingly endless period.

I ALSO WANT TO THANK Lance Baucher, Jan Black, Cathy Geenan, Mark Harris, Toshi Hoo, Marion Hunt-Badiner, Allan Hunt-Badiner, Sylvia Johnson, Charly Johnston, Del Jones, Judy Kahrl, Carol Massanari, Bruce Novak, Georgia O'Keefe, Parker Page, Heather Peet, John Robbins, Vicki Robins, Belvie Rooks, and Christine Sleeter, all of whom looked at parts of the manuscript in various stages and contributed to it in important respects.

IN ADDITION, I WANT TO THANK my friend and publisher, Marc Allen, and the others at New World Library, including Steve Anderson, Katie Blount, Mary Ann Casler, Katie Farnam Conolly, Marjorie Conte, Georgia Hughes, Barbara King, Munro Magruder, Tona Pearce Myers, and Mary Beth Salmon, for all the work and love they have invested in this book. I am also grateful to my agents Ellen Levine and Louise Quayle, and to Chris Van Buren and, last, but not least, to the reference librarians who have so generously helped me with my research for this book, including Victor Baush, Janet Bombard, Rosie Brewer, Jean Chapin, Lani Fremier, Tamara Hennessy, Doug Holtzman, Joe Johnson, Britget McConnell, Steve Parker, Denise Sallee, and Halina Szczeziak.

IF I HAVE FORGOTTEN SOMEONE, it was not by intention, but because this has been such a big project and has gone on for so many years.

©Author photo by Michael Collopy

RIANE EISLER is an internationally renowned scholar, futurist, and activist. She is the author of several groundbreaking books, including *The Chalice and the Blade, Tomorrow's Children,* and *Sacred Pleasure.* She is charismatic speaker who keynotes conferences worldwide, a consultant to business and government, and president of the Center for Partnership Studies in Tuscon, Arizona. She lives in Pacific Grove, California, with her husband, writer David Loye.

New World Library is dedicated to
publishing books and audio projects that inspire
and challenge us to improve the quality
of our lives and our world.

Our books and audios are available
at bookstores everywhere.
For a complete catalog, contact:

New World Library
14 Pamaron Way
Novato, California 94949

Phone: (415) 884-2100
Fax: (415) 884-2199
Or call toll-free: (800) 972-6657
Catalog requests: Ext. 50
Ordering: Ext. 52

E-mail: escort@nwlib.com
Website: www.newworldlibrary.com